DATE DUE		

REPORTING
THE
WAR

Freedom of the Press
from the American Revolution
to the War on Terrorism

John Byrne Cooke

palgrave
macmillan

First published in 2007 by
PALGRAVE MACMILLAN™
175 Fifth Avenue, New York, N.Y. 10010 and
Houndmills, Basingstoke, Hampshire, England RG21 6XS.
Companies and representatives throughout the world.

PALGRAVE MACMILLAN is the global academic imprint of the Palgrave Macmillan
division of St. Martin's Press, LLC and of Palgrave Macmillan Ltd. Macmillan® is a
registered trademark in the United States, United Kingdom and other countries.
Palgrave is a registered trademark in the European Union and other countries.

ISBN-13: 978–1–4039–7515–7
ISBN-10: 1–4039–7515–9

Cooke, John Byrne.
  Reporting the war : freedom of the press from the Revolution to the War on
terrorism / by John Byrne Cooke.
    p. cm.
  Includes bibliographical references and index.
  ISBN 1–4039–7515–9 (alk. paper)
  1. War—Press coverage—United States—History. I. Title.
  PN4888.W37C66 2007
  070.4'3330973—dc22

                                                                    2007012364

A catalogue record of the book is available from the British Library.

Design by Letra Libre   ·

First edition: November 2007

10 9 8 7 6 5 4 3 2 1

Printed in the United States of America.

For my father, Alistair Cooke

Journalist

1908–2004

All forms of human government, have, like men, their natural term, and those only are long-lived which possess in themselves the power of returning to the principles on which they were originally founded.

—Niccolò Machiavelli

CONTENTS

ACKNOWLEDGMENTS

A fortuitous conversation with Hugh McGraw made me aware of Isaiah Thomas, printer-editor of the Revolutionary-era *Massachusetts Spy*. Betsy Siggins kindly loaned me a rare biography and other materials about her celebrated ancestor. From this discovery the idea to focus on freedom of the press in wartime and to seek out exceptional voices in opposition—as a way to explore the vital importance of the free press in a democratic society—took hold. Betsy and Hugh provided hospitality that made possible my research in Boston and Cambridge, as did Eric Levenson, Martha Sweezy, Theo Sweezy and Rob Postel. Lodging and good company were also provided by Dave and Vera-Mae Fredrickson and Peter and Judy Mollica in Berkeley, my sister Susan Cooke Kittredge and her husband Charlie in Vermont, and Sylvia and Bob Gordon and my ever-supportive stepmother, Jane Cooke, in New York City.

Harvard University's Newspaper Microfilm Reading Room in Widener Library was my primary resource for newspaper research; I am grateful to the staff there, and particularly for the assistance of Elizabeth Do, Jean Lenville and Sean Crawford. I also made use of the microfilm archives at Harvard's Lamont Library, Boston Public Library, New York Public Library, the main library at the University of California at Berkeley, Berkeley Public Library, and the Library of Congress. I reviewed microfiches of Marguerite Higgins' *Newsday* columns loaned by the Newsday Library in Melville, New York. Carol Connors was unfailingly helpful in obtaining interlibrary loan materials through the Teton County Library in Jackson, Wyoming, and with other research requests. Beth Potier and Marvin Hightower of Harvard University provided helpful information by mail and email.

Access to the extraordinary historical and contemporary newspaper databases of ProQuest CSA was made possible by the generosity of

ProQuest CEO Alan Aldworth and the assistance and good offices of Elicia Wolowidnyk, Kevin Barkume, Kathleen T. Ross, and Linda Dupree.

Clif Garboden, senior managing editor of the *Boston Phoenix* graciously took time from his demanding schedule to give me a history of the paper and access to its archives. *Phoenix* publisher Stephen M. Mindich, editor Peter Kadzis, Mark Jurkowitz, Camille Dodero and Ian Sands were also helpful.

Joseph Albright and Marcia Kunstel offered memories of their experiences in reporting from the Middle East during the first Gulf War, reviewed the first draft of my chapter "Desert Storm," and made helpful suggestions that improved it. Former *San Francisco Chronicle* reporter Michael Harris welcomed me to his home and was generous with his memories.

My literary agent, Joëlle Delbourgo, labored diligently and successfully to find the right home for this book. Alessandra Bastagli, my editor at Palgrave Macmillan, encouraged me to remain focused on my topic and not to stray into the interesting but less relevant byways that I discovered in my research. Without their efforts, this project might have been only an intriguing idea denied the chance to reach fruition.

I owe an immeasurable debt to the men and women of the American press who have labored for more than two centuries to fulfill the trust placed in them by the founders of the republic. My choice of newspapers to represent the press in each war, and therefore of the reporters, editors and publishers whose work I have featured in this book, was sometimes based on which publications were available in the archives that were accessible to me. I tried to include in each war newspapers and journalists that were influential in their time, and I have included others, less well known, that offered exceptional examples of courage in opposing the American government in wartime.

To anyone whose contribution I have overlooked, I offer my apologies; I will do my best to make amends. For any errors of fact or interpretation that remain, despite the best efforts of myself and others to root them out, the responsibility is mine alone.

To Susan Brearey, incomparable artist, teacher, friend, companion and partner, who gave this project her unwavering support and encouragement from start to finish, I give my thanks and my love always.

Without my father's love of American jazz, and the movies, I might have been born in England instead of in New York City. Because he came as an immigrant to these shores, he saw the Declaration of Independence and the Constitution, the federal system—the whole of American history—as fascinating and fresh. He learned about these things as an adult. As a journalist, he had a need to set current events in their historical context. He saw today's news as tomorrow's history and he looked at historical events from the perspective of a newspaperman reporting on them as today's news. Without intending to emulate his experience, I successfully shunned an interest in history throughout my formal education. I then got the bug by borrowing books sent to my father by hopeful publishers seeking a "blurb" for the jacket. He was happy to let me take my pick— anything to reduce the stacks of unsolicited tomes that surrounded the sofa in his study. And so I learned American history as an adult, and then as a writer, and I slowly became aware of the patrimony I had absorbed along the way. I bless him for it.

John Byrne Cooke
Jackson, Wyoming
June 2007

INTRODUCTION

Civil liberties are rarely more endangered than in wartime, and none is more at risk than freedom of the press. The press is called on to rally patriotic fervor. It is expected to be the voice of the government and the voice of the people—the voice of the country at war. If instead it challenges the government, if it questions the rationale for war, it provokes the government's impulse, already strong in times of crisis, to repress liberties in the name of security, and too often the people acquiesce. This is the paradox that threatens the freedoms we take for granted in peacetime. In the shock of war we feel that our way of life is threatened; in response we are willing to abandon (temporarily, we think) the principles on which that way of life is founded, in the hope of regaining our security.

The Founding Fathers saw government's inclination to suppress the rights of the citizens not as occasional, or rare, but constant. They trusted in freedom of speech, and of the press, to encourage a free flow of opinions, to keep the people informed and to warn them whenever their liberties were threatened from any quarter, so they might give, or withhold, the consent that is government's only legitimate source of power. Above all, the Founders trusted in the free press. In the debate over ratifying the Constitution, no right was more often proclaimed inviolable. The federalists, who wrote the Constitution and advocated its adoption, and their opponents, the anti-federalists, vied to outdo each other in championing freedom of the press as the most essential safeguard of the liberties the Revolution had been fought to secure. The heart of the constitutional debate was not what freedoms Americans held sacred—they had proclaimed these rights "unalienable" in the Declaration of Independence—but whether the government proposed by the Constitution would protect or usurp them.

The federalists declared that the government could never threaten personal freedoms because it had no power to suppress them—it would have only those powers specifically bestowed by the Constitution. This didn't satisfy a Pennsylvania anti-federalist who protested that the framers of the Constitution "have made no provision for the *liberty of the press, that grand palladium of freedom,* and *scourge of tyrants.*"[1] Without exception, the constitutions of the states had declarations or "bills" of rights. The anti-federalists wanted such a bill in the federal Constitution. In the end they got their way, and some federalists as well agreed that affirming the most vital liberties in a bill of rights was a good thing. Even well after the Constitution was accepted as the foundation of the American government and the Bill of Rights enshrined the fundamental freedoms on which the republic was founded, James Madison felt it was important to emphasize that "among those sacred rights considered as forming the bulwark of their liberty, which the government contemplates with awful reverence and would approach only with the most cautious circumspection, there is no one of which the importance is more deeply impressed on the public mind than the liberty of the press."[2]

The First Amendment cares nothing for a fair and balanced press. It is freedom of the press as the bulwark of liberty and the scourge of tyrants that the Founders protected. To be sure, we ask more of the press than simply to oppose the government. We expect it to report the facts accurately. We expect events of the day to be set in a larger context. We expect opinion to be separated from news. We expect fairness. We expect the press to seek the truth in the welter of conflicting claims and opinions. But when government threatens the checks and balances the Founders crafted to protect the rights of the people, we expect the press to speak the truth in the face of governmental intimidation, secrecy, evasions and lies.

In the past sixty years, the integrity of the press has been threatened by the relentless commercialism of radio and television and the submersion of publishing and broadcasting enterprises into larger corporate entities who value profit over the obligations of a free press. More recently we have returned to something closer to what the Founding Fathers had in mind, since the development of the Internet has enabled anyone with access to a computer to publish his or her opinions online for the world to read. The lasting effects of these developments on the dissemination of news and opinion are not yet fully clear. It seems certain that the role of the electronic media will only increase, and equally certain that the primary goals of the broadcast media will continue to be entertainment and profit.

Newspapers, descended from the Revolutionary weeklies and unchallenged as the principle news medium until the middle of the twentieth century, continue to exert an influence that is disproportionate to their circulation. The print media influence policymakers. They form the core of the historical archive. In the first wars of the twenty-first century, newspapers and magazines still play a leading role in commenting on government policy and criticizing it.

My purpose is to examine the relationship of the press and the national government in wartime. In each of a dozen wars—those that threatened the nation's survival or transformed America's role in the world—I have looked for examples of how the press has fulfilled its constitutional responsibility by questioning and opposing the government. I have concentrated on how opposition arose within the swell of patriotic support that characterizes the start of a war, following the story until the press is focused on the contentious issues and public debate is assured. Sometimes one printer, one newspaper, one reporter or one publisher stood out from the rest; sometimes it was helpful to follow several newspapers that collectively represented shifting attitudes in wartime.

The attitudes of different administrations have been as varied as those of the press. Some have tried to suppress opposing opinions. Others have made no efforts at repression despite being subjected to vitriolic criticism. Some controversies revive in virtually every war—you would think by now we could agree that dissent is not disloyal—while other controversies are unique to one conflict. If there is a virtue in moving quickly from one war to the next, it is in discovering the patterns that emerge in the contests between wartime governments and the press. Like the stories of the wars themselves, these are journeys of discovery, with unexpected turns and outcomes. I hope my readers will find in them, as I do, frequent reminders of the wisdom of the Founders, who protected the ability of the press to inform the ongoing debates that are the lifeblood of democracy and to sound the alarm at the first glimpse of tyranny. These reminders come often from the press, but also from government officials, high and low, and sometimes from ordinary citizens in words as simple and eloquent as the best editorials, as demonstrated by a letter to the *New York Times* in

May 2004, from a woman who understood perfectly the role of the press in a free society: "The press has a responsibility to the public to be adversarial to any sitting administration. It is our only hope of keeping power in check and the government honest. . . . An adversarial press is doing its job. A timid, compliant press fails us all."[3]

1

CONCEIVED IN LIBERTY

The American Revolution (1775–1783)

Britain's victory in the French and Indian War (1754–1763) ended seventy years of contention over France's claim to the great Mississippi river basin and extended Britain's rule into the heart of the North American continent. To secure this domain, King George III and his ministers persuaded Parliament to increase the military garrison in America on the promise that the colonists would be made to pay a share of the cost. Over the next twelve years, the government in London imposed a series of duties and taxes on the American colonies to raise the promised funds. It was this "taxation without representation" that aroused the colonists' ire and brought them to the point of revolution.

Earlier trade and navigation taxes had only affected merchants and ship owners, but in 1765, Parliament passed a stamp act that imposed a tax on businesses throughout the colonies. The act required tax stamps on legal documents, licenses, writs, bills of sale, invoices, and each sheet of a newspaper. The tax enraged the colonists. They refused to use the stamps and boycotted British goods. The most radical colonists organized groups called the Sons of Liberty that spearheaded protests and harassed government officials. British merchants, already experiencing a post-war slump, felt the pinch, and protested to Parliament. Within a year of its passage, the Stamp

Act was repealed, but over the next three years Parliament levied new duties on several commodities, including tea.

In response to these new impositions, the colonists renewed their boycott of British goods and threatened royal officials. The king's ministry[1] ordered General Thomas Gage, the commander of the British army in America, to quarter several regiments in Boston. For the first time, Americans regarded the redcoats as an oppressive force. In March 1770, this resentment led to the first spilling of blood. When some young men taunted a British sentry, more soldiers came to his aid. Fighting broke out and resulted in a running skirmish through the streets. Five Bostonians received mortal wounds. The "Boston Massacre" provoked an outcry in the press, but there was no further violence, and soldiers and subjects resumed their wary standoff.

In the face of colonial opposition, many of the new trade duties were soon repealed, but Parliament left in place the duty on tea, whose importation into the American colonies was controlled by the East India Company, a British monopoly by charter of the Crown, as an object lesson to remind the colonists that the British government retained the right to tax them for revenue. Tea became the focus of new protests and boycotts. The colonists would not allow tea to come ashore and it sat on ships idled in colonial harbors. In December 1773, in Boston, the Sons of Liberty, haphazardly disguised as Indians and attended by some seven or eight thousand supporters, marched to the wharves, where they unloaded the cargo of three ships, more than three hundred crates of tea, into Boston harbor. As punishment for the Boston "tea party," Parliament closed the port of Boston, halting all shipping until such time as the upstart colonists should pay for the tea they had destroyed.

General Gage was appointed governor of the Massachusetts Bay colony. The colonists convened a "continental congress" in Philadelphia that voted a broad boycott of British goods. General Gage recommended a naval blockade of all the American ports and warned London that if he was forced to use the army to suppress the colonists, all of New England, and possibly the other colonies as well, would fight. King George and his ministry ignored this advice, and the fight, when it came, proved Gage prophetic.

⌒

After dark on April 16, 1775, Isaiah Thomas, printer and publisher of the *Massachusetts Spy*, a Boston newspaper, loaded his presses and types into a wagon with the help of two friends and "stole them out of town in the dead of night."[2] He put the wagon aboard the ferry to Charlestown, saw it unloaded on the other side and dispatched it to Worcester, forty miles inland, while he returned to Boston. Two nights later, Thomas was one of several messengers—Paul Revere was another—who spread the news that a brigade of British troops had crossed the Charles River and was marching to Concord to destroy a cache of the colonists' arms. Early on the morning of April 19, Thomas was at a public meeting in Charlestown, speaking in support of arming the people against the British. By dawn he was at Lexington, on the Concord road, where he witnessed the clash of arms between British troops and colonists that ignited the American Revolution.[3]

The next day, Thomas made his way to Worcester and arrived there late at night. Reunited with his press and types, he had no paper on which to resume printing the *Spy*. When the patriot leaders Samuel Adams and John Hancock stopped in Worcester on their way to Philadelphia to attend the second Continental Congress, Thomas appealed to them for help. Hancock had been an early investor in the *Spy*. While Thomas's press was in Boston, he had published the proceedings of the provincial congress, which was in effect the revolutionary government of the Massachusetts Bay colony. Hancock wrote a letter to the provincial committee of safety, which allocated supplies to the revolutionists, and the committee voted that "four reams of paper be immediately ordered to Worcester for the use of Mr. Thomas, printer."[4]

On May 3, two weeks after the battles at Lexington and Concord, Isaiah Thomas printed in the first Worcester edition of the *Massachusetts Spy* a banner across the front page, atop the masthead, that cried out: "AMERICANS!---Liberty or Death!---Join or Die!" On the second page, where the most current news was printed, Thomas published a clarion call that was reprinted throughout the colonies.

AMERICANS! forever bear in mind the BATTLE of LEXINGTON!— where British Troops, unmolested and unprovoked, wantonly, and in a most inhuman manner fired upon and killed a number of our countrymen, then robbed them of their provisions, plundered and burnt their homes! nor could the tears of defenceless women, some of whom were in the pain of child-birth, the cries of helpless babes, nor the prayers of old age, confined to beds of sickness, appease their thirst for blood!—or divert them from their DESIGN of MURDER and ROBBERY![5]

This was an extraordinary expression of editorial outrage. Unlike newspapers of our own time, or those published just fifty years after the Revolution, colonial papers did not gather and evaluate the news to present it in columns of text written by editors and reporters. The weekly newspapers of the 1770s (there were no daily papers until after the Revolution) had no editorial pages. They employed no reporters. The publisher, printer and editor were often the same man, who turned out the paper on a hand-operated press. Printers gathered news from friends and acquaintances in positions of influence, ships' captains, travelers, correspondence, and other newspapers. Essays from persons both prominent and unknown were the principal means by which newspapers offered divergent views on public issues. (It was this early custom of printing essays, usually received by letter, from correspondents not employed by the newspaper that gave rise to the term "correspondent" for a reporter working at a distance from a newspaper's home office.) Some printers of newspapers became adept at weaving their editorial perspective into the news, while others revealed their opinions more by what they chose to publish from other writers than by explicit statements of their own.

Alternately elevated and argumentative, calm and impassioned, the dialogues published in the pre-Revolutionary press were the Enlightenment made manifest in the civic life of the colonies. Fervent essays on natural law, the rights of man, the role of religion, and the powers and obligations of rulers and governments were offered up to be discussed, argued and pondered until the folio sheets were used to wrap the kitchen scraps and the next week's paper revived the ongoing debate.

What made Isaiah Thomas's appeal to his fellow "AMERICANS!" all the more notable was that it was written by a young man of twenty-six who in less than five years had made the *Massachusetts Spy* one of the most influential newspapers in Britain's American colonies.

Isaiah Thomas had been indentured to a Boston printer at the age of six. He ran away at fifteen and shipped out of Boston for Halifax, Nova Scotia, where he found employment with the province's only newspaper, the *Halifax Gazette*. The publisher was, by most accounts, plump, cheerful and lazy. Young Isaiah, by contrast, was lean, enterprising and ambitious.

Before long, he was editing and printing the newspaper. Fresh from Boston, his interests were shaped by the controversies of Massachusetts Bay, which already had a more contentious relationship with the ministry in London than any other colony, and where the foremost grievance of the year 1765 was the recently enacted Stamp Act. Isaiah amused himself by turning the pages of the *Halifax Gazette* in the press so the stamp appeared in an unusual, and therefore conspicuous, place, or snipping the stamps off the paper, and once printing a skull and crossbones in its place. On another occasion, he placed a small woodcut of his own creation next to the stamp, depicting the devil poking at the stamp with a pitchfork.[6] Eventually discharged for these insolences, Thomas returned to Boston and made peace with his former master, who could have prosecuted him under the terms of his indenture (newspapers of the period carried advertisements offering rewards for the return of escaped apprentices), but instead released him from his contract after a short period of further servitude.

Thomas spent the next few years traveling among the colonies, gaining more experience at printing and in the ways of the world. In 1770, at the age of twenty-one, he came back to Boston, and in the atmosphere of tension and distrust that prevailed in the wake of the Boston Massacre he founded the *Massachusetts Spy* to compete with the four weekly newspapers then publishing in the town.

At the outset, Thomas declared his intention to present the opinion of both Whigs and Tories[7] in the *Spy*, but that was not the same as promising to be impartial. No one who read the paper could mistake Thomas for a loyalist. From the *Spy*'s early days, it was far easier to find revolutionist agitations in the paper than Tory defenses. In the fifth issue, Thomas printed "A PARODY on SHAKESPEAR," which addressed the colonists' principal grievance against the Crown: "*Be taxt, or not be taxt, that is the question: / Whether 'tis nobler in our minds to suffer / The sleights and cunning of deceitful statesmen, / Or to petition 'gainst illegal taxes / And by opposing end them—*"[8]

According to Thomas's grandson, Benjamin Franklin Thomas, who wrote a biography of his by-then illustrious ancestor, "Overtures were made by friends of the government to induce the printer to enlist the *Spy* in its defence. They were of course rejected, and Mr. Thomas gave the paper without reserve to the cause of the people."[9] Thomas himself portrayed the conversion somewhat differently in describing the paper's beginnings: "For a few weeks some communications were furnished by those who were in favor of the royal prerogative, but they were exceeded by writers on the other side; and the authors and subscribers among the tories denounced and quitted the Spy. The publisher then devoted it to the cause of his country, supported by the whigs."[10]

These accounts overstate the ease with which Thomas made the transition to open support for the colonial, or patriot, cause. During his apprenticeship, maintaining a press that was open to all opinions was a point of principle among colonial printers. Thomas had developed a strong philosophical attachment to this principle, and he hoped to live by it when he established the *Massachusetts Spy*. But the climate in Boston was already so charged with partisanship in the early 1770s that he found it impossible to present balanced opinion in the pages of the *Spy*. Although his own leanings were on the side of resistance to the British—as he had demonstrated in Halifax, where there was no "patriotic" pressure to incite his displays of rebellion against the Stamp Act—being forced to take sides openly in his own newspaper went against his grain. In a letter to an acquaintance, Thomas wrote, "to incur the censure and displeasure of any party or persons, though carressed and encouraged by others, is very disagreeable to me."[11] (As late as 1772, Thomas considered moving to the West Indies, to remove himself from the turbulent passions of Massachusetts Bay, but he remained in Boston. By then, he found himself inseparably bound to the cause of his country.)

In the spring of 1771, a letter in the *Spy* addressed the royal governor of Massachusetts Bay as "the treasonable USURPER of an absolute DESPOTISM over the good people of the MASSACHUSETTS-BAY."[12] The writer, who signed himself "Leonidas," was one of the *Spy*'s most vitriolic correspondents and one of the few whose letters were brief. A month later, Leonidas lashed out at Governor Tryon of North Carolina for the conduct of that province's militia in an armed clash with colonists there. (The militia had violated what was to be an hour-long truce by opening fire without warning after fifteen minutes.) Leonidas branded Tryon a traitor and a villain and accused him of "avarice, ambition, injustice, perjury, perfidy and murder."[13] The letter caused both the writer and Isaiah Thomas to be burned in effigy in North Carolina. This violent response vividly demonstrated that the voice of the *Massachusetts Spy*, then less than a year old, was already being heard well beyond Massachusetts and New

England. (The paper's widening influence was made possible by a system of "exchanges" among colonial papers, under which each reprinted items from other papers freely.)

In the paper's second year, Thomas added a line from Joseph Addison's tragedy *Cato* to the masthead: "Do thou Great LIBERTY inspire our Souls.—And make our LIVES IN THY Possession happy.—or our Deaths glorious in thy JUST Defence!!"

Neither Isaiah Thomas nor any other printer in Britain's American colonies had a protected right to publish whatever he pleased. The government did not attempt to censor newspapers in advance, but if an essay or a letter sufficiently offended the colonial administration, retribution might follow. In November 1771, Thomas printed an essay, signed "Mucius Scævola," that attacked Parliament's taxes and the royal governor of Massachusetts Bay: "An Englishman should never part with a penny but by his consent, or the consent of his agent, or representative, especially as the money thus forced from us is to hire a man to TYRANNIZE over us, whom his *Master* calls our *Governor* . . . therefore I cannot but view him as a usurper, and absolutely deny his jurisdiction over this people."[14] In response to this attack, the governor, Thomas Hutchinson, convened the governor's council, which sent a messenger to summon the publisher of the *Massachusetts Spy.* Thomas demanded to know if the messenger had the council's order in writing. Told he did not, Thomas replied, "Then, sir, with all due respect to the Governor and Council, I am engaged in my own concerns and shall not attend."[15]

Governor Hutchinson was a lawyer and a former chief justice of the provincial superior court. He reluctantly concluded that the council lacked the authority to charge Thomas with contempt. He ordered the attorney general to prosecute Thomas for libel, but the colonial grand jury refused to indict Thomas, finding the evidence insufficient, whereupon Hutchinson turned his displeasure on the *Spy*'s correspondent, Mucius Scævola.[16]

The use of pen names to shield writers from official retaliation was a long-standing journalistic tradition. In pre-Revolutionary America, and for much of the following century, the names of prominent Romans from the time of the Republic were much in favor, along with Roman gods and the occasional Greek. Unfortunately, the *Massachusetts Spy*'s Mucius Scævola was known to be Joseph Greenleaf, justice of the peace for Plymouth

County. Greenleaf had not been particularly concerned to keep his *nom de plume* confidential, nor his business partnership with Thomas as co-publisher of the *Spy.* Having failed to punish Thomas, Governor Hutchinson and his council voted to fire Greenleaf from his position, but it is hard to imagine that Hutchinson saw this small revenge as anything more than a Pyrrhic victory.

In its third summer, the *Massachusetts Spy* had more subscribers than any other newspaper in Boston.[17] That fall, Thomas aroused the governor's ire again when he printed in the *Spy* a letter from one "Akolax" in the form of an address to King George that did not show proper respect for the sovereign. Governor Hutchinson ordered the provincial attorney to prosecute Thomas, who responded by reprinting, in the October 10, 1772, issue, an equally insolent address to the king that had been first published in an English newspaper, the *Middlesex Journal,* and was subsequently reprinted in America, in what Thomas identified only as "a neighboring province," without inciting official action against the printer in either case. Thomas appended to this address a bold editorial declaration: *"It seems as though* I. Thomas, *the printer of this paper, is the only person of his profession, marked out by a tool of the ministerial power for a SACRIFICE. For what reason is not known, unless it be for printing a FREE paper. . . . Should the liberty of the press be once destroyed, farewel the remainder of our invaluable rights and privileges! We may next expect padlocks on our lips, fetters on our legs, and only our hands left at liberty to slave for our* worse than Egyptian task-masters, *or—or—FIGHT OUR WAY TO CONSTITUTIONAL FREEDOM!"*[18]

In little more than two years of printing the *Massachusetts Spy,* Isaiah Thomas had progressed, not without some misgivings, from a satirical suggestion that the colonists *"petition 'gainst illegal taxes"* to a personal exhortation that they prepare to fight for freedom. (Once again Governor Hutchinson and his council found themselves powerless to make Thomas pay for his insolence, but he was marked as an enemy of the government.)

Following the "tea party" in December 1773, the Boston papers carried rumors in the winter and spring of 1774 of proceedings in Parliament under which the town was to be punished. The May 5 issue of the *Massachusetts Spy* reported the arrival of the ship *Minerva,* which brought news that men of war were sailing for America: "Some say it is to reduce the mutinous spirit of the Americans." The news of Parliament's "Boston Port

Bill," under which the port was to be closed to shipping on June 1, did not arrive until the second week of May. In the *Massachusetts Spy* of May 12, which printed the full text of the Port Bill, an unattributed item, probably written by Thomas himself, pointed out that the East India Company was not complaining about the cost of the tea destroyed in December. This complaint against the rude Bostonians, the item charged, "is solely taken up by the British parliament, and the friends of the British ministry, which plainly evinces, that the introducing said Tea into America upon that plan, was a scheme of the present Administration."

The *Boston Gazette,* a journal of fierce patriot sympathies published by Benjamin Edes and John Gill, printed in its May 16 issue a short article reprinted from the London *Public Advertiser,* which told of the Boston Port Bill being moved through Parliament while "every Hearer" was excluded, "and every door barred with uncommon Anxiety," in order that those who accused the town of Boston, and the evidence they offered, would not be known: "Even this would have been a Mode of Proceeding unknown to the Court of Star Chamber, and of which no Example could be found, but in the Courts of Inquisition abroad."[19]

On the first of June, the Port Bill took effect, Governor Hutchinson sailed for London, and Governor Gage officially assumed the duties of administering the Massachusetts Bay colony. On the 6th, the *Boston Gazette* announced, "The Corporation of Harvard College, considering the present dark Aspect of publick Affairs, have voted that there shall be no Commencement this year." The *Gazette* also reported that four regiments of troops earlier reported destined for America "are ordered to be encamped at Boston."

In the summer of 1774, the printers of the most inflammatory journals were at increasing risk. In addition to publishing the *Spy,* Isaiah Thomas printed handbills for the Sons of Liberty, who often met in his shop at night. According to his grandson, Thomas was "one of the most active" members of the clandestine organization.[20] Since the Port Bill had taken effect and General Gage had brought most of his army into Boston, Thomas's life had been publicly threatened, and a British officer of his acquaintance warned him that he was marked for assassination.

In September, a circular addressed to "the officers and soldiers of His Majesty's troops in Boston," and distributed among them, named John Hancock, Samuel Adams and other prominent agitators, and exhorted the

troops to seek out these men when—not if—the treasonous "patriots" of
Massachusetts Bay should launch an open rebellion against the Crown:
"The friends of your King and Country and of America hope and expect
from you soldiers, the instant the rebellion happens, that you will put the
above persons to the sword, destroy their houses and plunder their effects.
N.B. Don't forget those trumpeters of sedition, the printers Edes and Gill,
and Thomas."[21] The threat became public knowledge when the circular
was reprinted in the *Boston Evening Post.*

When General Gage cancelled the fall elections for the colonial legislature, the towns outside of Boston organized elections of their own and
formed a provincial congress. This marked the end of royal rule in Massachusetts, except in areas directly under the control of British troops. By
the spring of 1775, the situation of well-known patriots in Boston was
precarious. After printing the April 6 issue of the *Massachusetts Spy,* Isaiah
Thomas made his way to Concord, where he consulted with John Hancock and other leaders of the provincial congress. According to Benjamin
Franklin Thomas, "Mr. Hancock and his other friends advised and urged
him to remove from Boston immediately ; in a few days, they said, it
would be too late."[22] Before the British troops started for Concord, it appears, Hancock and the rest knew that events were coming to a head.

Earlier in the year, Thomas had been approached by Timothy Bigelow
of Worcester, who invited him to establish a press there. Worcester was
predominantly loyalist and Bigelow wanted a strong patriot voice to sway
the sentiments of the town. On the night of April 16, it was Bigelow,
along with Dr. Joseph Warren, a highly respected physician and the chairman of the provincial committee of safety, who helped Thomas remove
his press from Boston, and it was very likely Bigelow who drove the press
and types to Worcester.

From the day after the battles of Lexington and Concord, the British
Army in America was shut up in Boston, soon laid siege by colonial troops
from Massachusetts and the neighboring colonies, while the residents
sought passes from General Gage to leave the town.

When Isaiah Thomas took his print shop from Boston to Worcester,
he removed himself and his newspaper from the effective jurisdiction of
the Crown. If the rebellion were to fail, he knew he would face the hang-
man in short order, but this did not inhibit his support for the nascent insurrection. The masthead of the first Worcester edition carried the title,

"The Massachusetts Spy, or *American Oracle of Liberty."* Thomas's rallying cry to his fellow "AMERICANS!" to remember the Battle of Lexington, which appeared in this issue, was followed by a lengthy account of the fighting there and at Concord, and of the British retreat back to Lexington, where they rested for an hour, until the colonists drove them on to Charlestown "with great precipitation." In the same issue, Thomas reported the news, received from two ships recently arrived from England, that "eleven regiments of foot, and two of light horse, on board ninety five transports, with seventeen sail of men of war, all victualled for twelve months" were on their way to America. Thomas acknowledged that some accounts put the numbers at about half these figures, but, he wrote, "All accounts, however, agree, that the design of their coming, is to dragoon the British colonies into a surrender of their liberty and property, and to destroy the English constitution. *They who refuse to fight for their liberty, deserve to be slaves."*[23]

Two weeks later, in the *Spy* of May 17, Thomas reported, "The last ships brought over two more acts of Parliament, for restraining the colonies from the fisheries on their coasts, and from trading with one another, or any other part of the world, except Great-Britain, Ireland, and the West-Indies. They will doubtless next make an act to restrain us from rain and sunshine, which they have an equal right to do, and we shall equally regard." He printed a letter from an unnamed correspondent in London that contained ominous tidings about the safety of the patriot leaders. The writer had learned "from unquestionable authority," he wrote, that General Gage had been sent a royal proclamation "declaring the inhabitants of Massachusetts-Bay, and some others in the different colonies, actual rebels ; with a blank commission to try and execute such of them as he can get hold of. . . . I do not know them all, but Messrs. Samuel Adams, John Adams, Robert-Treat Payne, and John Hancock, of Massachusetts-Bay . . . are particularly named."[24]

This royal warrant for the heads of the patriot leaders no doubt firmed the resolve of the colonists. It was springtime in New England, a heartening time of year, the countryside verdant and, with the British bottled up in Boston, tranquil for the present. The colonists rejoiced in the knowledge that they had sent two thousand British regulars scampering back to Boston with their tails between their legs. The patriot newspapers printed vivid accounts that claimed the regular troops fired first, and accused the

British of setting fire to houses in which civilians, including women and children, were burned alive. Demonizing the enemy, a response as natural in warfare, even between peoples of the same lineage, as a quickening of the heart at the sound of fife and drum, had begun almost before the smoke from the shots heard 'round the world had cleared from Concord's village green.

Also in the May 17 issue, Thomas printed extracts of letters from British soldiers in Boston, intercepted by the colonists (the *Spy* provided no details about the circumstances), that gave accounts from their side of the battle. Several soldiers admitted burning the colonists' houses, but put the blame on the colonists—whom they called "peasants," "country people" and "rebels"—for not fighting fairly: "they did not fight like a regular army, only like Savages, behind trees and stone walls, and out of the woods and houses," one said, "where in the latter we killed numbers of them, as well as in the woods and fields." Another soldier wrote, "when we found they fired from houses, we set them on fire, and they ran to the woods like Devils." And another, "The rebels were monstrous numerous, and surrounded us on every side, when they came up we gave them a smart fire, but they never would engage us properly.—We killed some hundreds and burnt some houses. I received a wound in my head."[25]

One of the letters gave a vivid picture of conditions in Boston, cut off from the supplies on which the port city depended: "There is no market in Boston, the inhabitants all starving, the soldiers live on salt provisions, and the officers are supplied by the *Men of war cutters, who goes up the creeks and takes live cattle and sheep wherever they find them,*" one soldier wrote. Another was looking forward to exacting revenge on the rebels: "We have been busy in fortifying the town ever since we engaged, and in a few days we expect a good many more troops from England, and then we shall surely *burn the whole country before us if they do not submit,* which I do not imagine they will do, for they are an obstinate set of people."[26]

Few were more obstinate and resolved on their course than the patriot printers. Even as the *Massachusetts Spy* and other newspapers rallied support to the revolution, they continued to serve as journals of record, publishing proceedings of the provincial congresses, official documents and proclamations, and the communications of colonial and royal officials. In an exchange documented by the *Spy,* Jonathan Trumbull, governor of Connecticut, wrote to General Gage, "in behalf of the General Assembly of said Colony," expressing Connecticut's concern for their neighbors in Massachusetts and asking why Gage had attacked them at Lexington and Concord. In reply, General Gage explained that his actions were defensive; he claimed that the colonists fired first and did his best to portray the redcoats as the wronged parties: "Thus this unfortunate affair has happened through the rashness and impudence of a few people, who began firing on the Troops at Lexington."[27]

The colonial papers reprinted items from English journals as well. Parliamentary debates on colonial questions were covered at length. Many Englishmen saw threats to their own freedom in the government's actions toward the colonies, and the colonists had supporters in Parliament, among them William Pitt the Elder, earl of Chatham, and Edmund Burke. Burke did not favor the independence of the American colonies, but he abhorred the colonial policies of the ministry and the king, and he denounced them eloquently.

On June 12, General Gage issued a proclamation declaring Massachusetts Bay under martial law. When it was printed in the *Spy*, the document was introduced by a short notice calling it "an *infamous thing*" that the *Spy* printed "to satisfy the curiosity of the public." The notice said Gage's order was "replete with consummate impudence, the most abominable lies, and stuffed with daring expressions of tyranny," and it branded Gage a "perfidious, petty tyrant."

Unable to engage his enemies in the field, Gage was eager to attack them in print, giving full rein to the vocabulary of a classically educated gentleman: "WHEREAS, the infatuated multitudes, who have long suffered themselves to be conducted by certain well known incendiaries and traitors, in a fatal progression of crimes, against the constitutional authority of the state, have at length proceeded to avowed rebellion. . . . The infringements which have been committed upon the most sacred rights of the crown and people of Great-Britain, are too many to enumerate on one side, and are all too atrocious to be palliated on the other." Gage enumerated the offenses all the same, among them that "The press, that distinguished appendage of public liberty, and when fairly and impartially employed it's [*sic*] best support, has been invariably prostituted to the most contrary purposes." Gage reviewed at considerable length the causes for the current state of affairs and the events of April 19, and then proffered an olive branch: "I avail myself of the last effort within the bounds of my duty, to spare the effusion of blood," he wrote. He offered, in the king's name, "his most gracious pardon to all persons who shall forthwith lay down their arms and return to the duties of peaceable subjects, excepting only from the benefit of such pardons, *Samuel Adams,* and *John Hancock,* whose offenses are of too flagitious a nature to admit of any other consideration than that of condign punishment." It is easy to imagine the general, quill in hand, reviewing his text with satisfaction and some pleasure before sending it off to be printed and posted about the town.

A few days after issuing the proclamation, General Gage had chance to strike at the infatuated multitudes in a battle worthy of the name. When the colonial militia fortified a low hill on the Charlestown peninsula from which artillery could shell Boston and the harbor, Gage sent his second in command, General William Howe, to drive the rebels from the vantage point. British troops won the day, but at such cost—more than a thousand dead, to the colonists' four hundred or so—that Gage put off attempting to occupy the Dorchester Heights, the other high point that overlooked Boston. This result, and the spirit of the rebels' resistance, turned the battle of Bunker Hill into a moral, and eventually a tactical, victory for the colonists.

George Washington of Virginia, newly appointed by the Continental Congress as commander in chief of the army of the "United Colonies," arrived at Cambridge to take command on July 3, 1775. Washington tightened the siege of Boston while he trained his troops. In the city, General Gage's situation was becoming more dire. At first willing to let the American residents leave Boston with their belongings, Gage put an abrupt halt to the exodus after just one day and instituted a tortuous system of issuing permits that allowed a trickle of colonists to depart with only the clothes on their backs. In the *Spy*'s account of this sudden reversal, Isaiah Thomas speculated, "His intention no doubt is to divert our army until the arrival of more troops."[28] In late July, the *Spy* reported that 5,500 inhabitants remained in the town, where sickness was rampant among the British troops, killing fifteen to thirty a day.[29]

Elsewhere in the colonies the royal administration was collapsing wherever officials of the Crown had insufficient troops to enforce their authority. Beginning in 1774, the colonists had created a system of "constitutional" post offices and riders independent of the royal post. On July 26, 1775, the Second Continental Congress took control of the system and appointed Benjamin Franklin postmaster general. One impetus for the new network was to assure the distribution of patriot newspapers, which had sometimes been impeded by royal officials. The *New-York Journal* and the *Pennsylvania Journal* had been barred from the mails, and both Thomas's *Massachusetts Spy* and Edes and Gill's *Boston Gazette* had been delayed or otherwise interfered with.[30]

Postmaster General Franklin created a post office at Worcester, Massachusetts, for the first time, with Isaiah Thomas as postmaster. The position was invaluable for a newspaper editor, as the postmaster was the first to see out-of-town newspapers and hear interesting news from the recipients of letters. In addition to carrying out this new responsibility and printing the weekly *Spy,* Thomas published the official account of the battles of Concord and Lexington, which was compiled by a special committee of the provincial congress. The report bore the cumbersome title, "A NARRATIVE of the EXCURSIONS and RAVAGES of the KING'S TROOPS Under the Command of General Gage, On the nineteenth of April, 1775, Together With The DEPOSITIONS Taken by ORDER of CONGRESS, To support the Truth of it." Below the title Thomas added: "Published by AUTHORITY." As he was well aware, this imprimatur was usually reserved for publications authorized by the Crown. John Campbell's *Boston News-Letter,* one of the earliest colonial newspapers, had been printed "by Authority" for its first fifteen years. By placing this phrase on the official account of the Battles of Lexington and Concord, Thomas was recognizing the provincial congress as the legitimate government of Massachusetts Bay. This would have put yet another nail in his coffin if British authorities had regained control of the colony.

John Gill, co-publisher of the *Boston Gazette,* may have believed that giving up his role in printing that newspaper would be enough to protect him from royal retribution under the military occupation of Boston. The *Gazette,* like the *Spy,* had stopped publishing in the town shortly before the battles of Lexington and Concord. Benjamin Edes resumed publication on June 5, 1775, in Watertown, but it appeared that Gill remained in Boston, for the *Spy* reported in its August 23 edition that "Mr. John Gill, late one of the publishers of the Boston Gazette, was seized by order of Gen. Gage, in Boston, and cruelly committed to gaol."

As late as the autumn of 1775, some patriots still considered reconciliation with Britain possible, if the rights of the colonists were respected.

Many felt a deep connection with their English roots and allegiance to English institutions, but further actions by the British government doomed any hope for maintaining ties with the mother country. In November, Parliament withdrew royal protection from the American provinces and imposed a naval blockade. When word of the act reached America, the provincial congresses, one after another, declared independence from England. In March 1776, General Washington occupied the Dorchester Heights, which General Gage had declined to take. General Howe, who had succeeded General Gage as commander in chief of the British forces in America, evacuated his army from Boston and sailed to Halifax, freeing the rebellious colonists, temporarily, from the threat of British arms.

With the signing of the Declaration of Independence on July 4, 1776, the United Colonies became the United States of America, at least on paper. The document was published in the *Massachusetts Spy* on July 17. A week later, Isaiah Thomas read the declaration in Worcester to what his grandson described as "almost the entire population of that and adjoining towns,"[31] but this was Thomas's only contribution to spreading the news of the colonies' final break with King George. Before the celebratory day, beset by financial difficulties that had plagued him since his removal from Boston to Worcester, Thomas had leased some of his printing equipment, and the *Spy* itself, to two young men of Worcester, Harvard graduates and "gentlemen of the Bar of Worcester."[32]

In Boston, Thomas had more than three thousand subscribers, but with the onset of hostilities and the city under siege the mails were disrupted, and it became all but impossible for him to collect from his debtors. He placed notices in the early Worcester editions of the *Spy*, while he built a new list of subscribers from scratch, requesting his former customers to pay what they owed him, but he was not able to meet his debts. Responsibility for covering the proceedings of the provincial congress had passed to the *Boston Gazette* in Watertown soon after Benjamin Edes had set up shop there, denying Thomas that former source of support as well.

After he leased the *Spy*, Thomas went to Salem to set up a printing shop on a smaller scale, but his creditors followed him. As his grandson relates, when "three writs of attachment were served upon his press and types in a single evening . . . he was compelled to sell them to pay his debts." Of his grandfather's life over the next two years, Benjamin

Franklin Thomas says only, "How he was employed I have not been able to learn. I only know that he was always industrious."[33] The truth of this is evident in the fact that Isaiah Thomas returned to Worcester in 1778, after two years' absence, and resumed printing the *Spy*. His fortunes may still have been precarious for a time, but he never again left his press and types in other hands, except those of his own employees. In November of 1781, Thomas celebrated the news of Lord Cornwallis's surrender to George Washington at Yorktown, Virginia, heralding it as "an event that must affect every patriotick American with joy and pleasing sensibility. In consequence of this glorious intelligence, yesterday morning was ushered in with ringing of bells, discharging of cannon, displaying of colours, attended with the shouts of a grateful populace."[34]

Thomas and his fellow patriot printers had mobilized widespread support for independence by contributing to a vital public debate, by propagandizing for the revolution and by making villains of Governor Hutchinson, General Gage, King George III and the ministry of his government to provide the colonists with identifiable enemies. With the success of the Revolution, they were honored for their efforts.

Isaiah Thomas was thirty-three years old when the Treaty of Paris was signed, formally ending the war and recognizing American independence. In the years following the Revolution, he built a paper mill; he printed, bound and sold books; he established partnerships and presses in Worcester, Boston and elsewhere; and he prospered. In 1785, when the legislature, sometimes as obstinate as Parliament in its determination to raise revenue from Massachusetts, imposed a duty on advertisements in newspapers, Thomas attacked the duty in the pages of the *Massachusetts Spy* as "A shackle which no legislature but ours, in British or United America, have laid upon the press, which when free is the great bulwark of liberty."[35] Like many of the acts of Parliament that had incited similar protests, the duty was repealed.

When the Constitution was proposed to the states in 1787, Thomas editorialized for its ratification. In October 1789, six months into his term as the first president of the United States, George Washington visited Worcester, where Isaiah Thomas was among the notables to greet him. Thomas took the opportunity to introduce to President Washington his nephew, E. Smith Thomas, then fourteen years old and apprenticed to his uncle. The younger Thomas later wrote, "I was presented to Washington by my distinguished kinsman, Isaiah Thomas. I can never forget his words, or my feelings on the occasion. 'Young man, your uncle has set you a bright example of patriotism, and never forget that next to our God we owe our highest duty to our country.'"[36]

If the Revolution had failed, Isaiah Thomas and George Washington would certainly have been executed for treason. As it was, they were honored as patriots and lived to enjoy old age in a free nation they helped to create. At the time of their meeting in Worcester, there was as yet no protection, under the federal Constitution, for freedom of speech, of the press, or any of the other unalienable rights the Revolution had been fought to secure. Congress, in its first session, had submitted to the states just three weeks before President Washington's visit to Worcester twelve amendments to the Constitution, in response to requests by the ratifying conventions of several states for clarification of certain rights retained by the people and by the states. Among these, the third proposed amendment, later renumbered as the first (when the first and second were not ratified by the required number of states), protected individual rights that Americans identified, virtually unanimously, as among the most essential safeguards of liberty:

> Congress shall make no law respecting an establishment of religion, or prohibiting the free exercise thereof; or abridging the freedom of speech, or of the press; or the right of the people peaceably to assemble, and to petition the Government for a redress of grievances.

2

THE HALLS OF MONTEZUMA

The Mexican War (1846–1848)

In 1821, the American government reached two agreements that were intended to prevent future conflicts. Missouri was admitted to the Union as a slave state, and the first state west of the Mississippi River, in lands acquired by President Thomas Jefferson in the Louisiana Purchase. Missouri's admission was achieved by a congressional compromise that excluded slavery from the rest of the Louisiana Purchase above 36 degrees 30' north latitude. That same year, a treaty with Spain fixed the long-disputed southern boundary of the Purchase along the Red River and the Arkansas, which formed the northern border of Texas. Before the end of the year, Mexico won independence from Spain, and three hundred American families settled in Texas on Mexican land grants. More emigrants followed, until the Anglos outnumbered Hispanic tejanos by four to one. Anglo Texans rebelled against Mexican rule in 1835. In March 1836, they proclaimed independence as the Republic of Texas, suffered defeats at the Alamo and at Goliad, and won the war by defeating the Mexican dictator, General Antonio López de Santa Anna, at San Jacinto, on April 21.

Texans voted overwhelmingly in favor of immediate annexation by the United States, but they were rebuffed by the Congress because of Northern resistance to admitting Texas as a slave state, and for fear of provoking war with Mexico. The expanse then known as Texas included, in addition to the present, reduced, state, half of present-day New Mexico, the panhandle of Oklahoma, a small corner of Kansas, and a dog-leg of land that kicked up along the crests of the Rocky Mountains into what would become Colorado and Wyoming. Lying outside the Louisiana Purchase and thus not governed by the Missouri Compromise, if Texas were admitted as slave territory it might be divided into three or four states, each entitled to two members in the U. S. Senate, which would upset the precarious political balance between Northern and Southern interests that the Missouri Compromise was intended to preserve.

By 1845, other considerations argued strongly enough for the annexation of Texas to overcome the opposition of antislavery forces. Britain had strong economic ties with the Spanish-American republics that had become independent of Spain. There were rumors that England and France might use force to prevent American annexation of Texas. Britain and the United States jointly administered a vast area called the Oregon country that stretched from the Rocky Mountains to the Pacific shore, and from the northern border of California to 54 degrees 40' north latitude, beyond which was Russian Alaska. Since the early 1840s, American emigrants had been trekking overland to Oregon and California, drawn by the promise of fertile land and mild climates. In Oregon, the American settlers could not secure dependable title to the land so long as it was jointly held by England. In California, American immigrants were obtaining land grants and intermarrying with the Californios, as the Spanish inhabitants were called. As in Texas before the republic, the Hispanic population was sparse, and Mexico administered the province it called Alta California lightly. Britain was eyeing Mexican California as well, where by 1845 the American population was drawing even with the Californios.

In 1844, James K. Polk had campaigned for the presidency on a platform that favored immediate annexation of Texas and a strong stand on the Oregon country. These positions contributed to his decisive victory in November. Congress approved the annexation of Texas on March 2, 1845, two days before Polk's inauguration. Mexico broke diplomatic relations and withdrew its ambassador from Washington. Once in office, President Polk secretly sent an envoy to Mexico to negotiate the peaceful annexation of Texas and proposed a division of the Oregon country with Britain. When Polk's envoy to Mexico was rebuffed, Polk ordered General Zachary Taylor, who was at Corpus Christi with a small army, to occupy the disputed territory between the Nueces River, which Mexico regarded as her northern frontier, and the Rio Grande, farther south, which Anglo Texans claimed as the southern boundary of Texas.

∽

News from the Rio Grande was carried to New Orleans by coastwise steamer, up the Mississippi River and its tributaries by steamboat, and overland by express riders and railroad. Word reached Washington, D.C., on May 9, 1846, that a force of Mexicans reported to be two thousand strong had crossed the Rio Grande and ambushed two companies of General Taylor's cavalry on April 24, killing some and capturing the rest. Following this action, the Mexicans moved more troops north of the river and surrounded Taylor's camp.

Taylor had arrived on the Rio Grande in late March and camped opposite Matamoros. The Mexicans quickly gathered a force almost half again as large as Taylor's four thousand men to oppose him, but until the recent clash there had been no hostilities.

On May 10, the New York newspapers published rumors of war. On the 11th all the eastern papers were full of news from the distant field of battle. They printed reports from the *New Orleans Picayune* and the *Galveston News,* letters from American army officers and other correspondents, and accounts of the reactions in Congress. The *New York Tribune* pounced on the news, certain it was proof of a long-simmering plot: "The fruit of the Texas iniquity begins to ripen! Our army of occupation—insanely and wickedly pushed across the well-known boundary into the heart of a province of Mexico of unshaken loyalty . . . is cooped up in its quarters by a sudden advance of the Mexican forces, cut off from its stores and munitions, two companies of its cavalry annihilated, and its very existence endangered!"

In the heat of his condemnation, the *Tribune's* founder and editor, Horace Greeley, slipped into hyperbole. Taylor's cavalry companies were far from annihilated, although the newspapers were in disagreement about the number killed and captured. The "well-known boundary" Taylor had crossed was the Nueces River, but Greeley's description of the wedge of land between the Nueces and the Rio Grande as "a province of Mexico of unshaken loyalty" was stretching the truth. Greeley was a New England Whig[1] with a viewpoint that was humanitarian, idealistic, and staunchly patriotic. He was deeply suspicious of President Polk, a Jacksonian Democrat, and he brought to his editorials a moral passion that was evident from the first in his writing on the Mexican War. Greeley had founded the *Tribune* as a Whig paper in 1841, under the first Whig president, William Henry Harrison. At the start of the war, the *Tribune* was the most influential paper—Whig, Democratic or independent—in New York. The weekly edition enjoyed a large rural readership and carried Greeley's opinions across the Northeast.

Greeley's chief antagonist was James Gordon Bennett, an immigrant Scot who had founded the *New York Herald* in 1835. On May 11, the *Herald* offered its readers, atop the front page, a ship's-eye-view illustration of Galveston, three hundred miles from the fighting, and, on the editorial page, a map of the Rio Grande and Matamoros, showing the position of Taylor's army. The *Herald* reported that President Polk and his cabinet had met several times to discuss the situation. The president was expected to send a message to Congress soon. "Probably it will be a war message—if not a positive declaration of war," Bennett wrote. "We must now take possession of California. Go ahead—who's afraid?" he demanded. In an editorial, Bennett took President Polk to task for vacillating: "He has now positively got a war with Mexico upon his hands, at the very moment when his administration is recommending a reduction of the army and navy! . . . Such imbecility, incoherence, and inconsistency, have never been visible in any administration, as now appears to mark the conduct of the present one, with relation to foreign affairs."

President Polk, an austere Tennessean of uncompromising integrity and inflexible personal habits, had decided on war soon after the first reports reached Washington on May 9. The 10th was a Sunday and Congress was not in session, so the president's message went to Congress on Monday, the day of Bennett's agitated editorial. Polk asked for a declaration of war and the enlistment of "a large and overpowering force" to carry it to a swift conclusion. He declared that he desired "to bring all matters in dispute between this government and Mexico to an early and amicable adjustment," and stood ready to resume negotiations whenever the Mexican government might be willing.[2]

On May 12, Horace Greeley opened with an attack on his colleagues in the press, where war fever was evident in many of the news reports. In an editorial titled "Our Country, Right or Wrong!" Greeley wrote, "Such is the spirit in which a portion of the Press which admits that our treatment of Mexico has been ruffianly and piratical, and that the invasion of her territory by Gen. Taylor is a flagrant outrage, now exhorts our People to rally in all their strength, to lavish their blood and treasure in the vindictive prosecution of war on Mexico. We protest against such counsel as alike immoral and unwise. . . . Our government has been utterly wrong in this whole matter, and ought first of all to desist from wrong-doing. No true Honor, no National benefit, can possibly accrue from an Unjust War."

The next day, Greeley reacted with biblical severity to the news from Washington that the House of Representatives had passed the president's war bill by a three-to-one margin. In Greeley's view, the declaration of war meant that "the laws of Heaven are suspended and those of Hell established in their stead. It means that the Commandments are to be read and obeyed by our People thus—Thou *shalt* kill Mexicans ; Thou *shalt* steal from them, hate them, burn their houses, ravage their fields, and fire red-hot cannon balls into towns swarming with their wives and children. . . . It means security, quiet, and gladness are to be driven from Earth and Ocean, and their places usurped by Butchery, Rape, Devastation and Horror. It means that Improvement is to be arrested, the blessed arts of Peace neglected, and the world recede toward the midnight of Barbarism." Greeley called President Polk "the Father of Lies," and dared Americans to "believe that the Annexation of Texas was not planned in Washington and approved by Jackson before a single prominent actor in the drama had even pretended to emigrate to Mexican territory." The whole world, Greeley said, "knows that it is Mexico which has been robbed and imposed upon, and that our People are the robbers. . . . We are the wolf drinking from the stream above and complaining that the lamb below is troubling the water. The wolf lies, of course, but his excuse for this is his appetite for mutton."[3] Greeley had long crusaded against the vices of gambling, liquor, tobacco and prostitution, and he understood all too well the baser impulses of his countrymen. For Greeley, the free press, by providing a forum for open debate, was the best weapon against the dark side of the human spirit.

If the position of the *New York Tribune* was clear from the start, Bennett's *Herald* responded less certainly in the first days. After criticizing President Polk's inconsistency on May 11, Bennett offered no editorial viewpoint on May 12, but he printed letters that covered a range of opinions. A correspondent calling himself "Pacificator" declared that President Polk had sent General Taylor to the Rio Grande to provoke a war "for the purpose of taking possession of California, the purchase of which President Polk was foiled in by the government of Mexico standing upon their dignity and refusing to receive the Hon. Mr. Slidell except as a commissioner to settle the question of Texas." Pacificator was referring to the fact, which had become known shortly before the news arrived in Washington of fighting on the Rio Grande, that President Polk had sent his envoy, John Slidell, to Mexico with authorization to settle not only the annexation of Texas and to establish its southern border at the Rio Grande, but also to buy California and New Mexico for the best price possible. Slidell was authorized to go as high as $30,000,000.

Another *Herald* correspondent, "Ariel," agreed that Polk intended all along to start a war, but Ariel saw an English threat behind Mexico's strategy. "Some of our friends won't credit the idea that England has anything to do in this affair," he said. "They thought so too when Texas annexation was pending. My belief is that she has a finger in the pie." A third correspondent, "The Doctor," opened with a burst of patriotic fireworks in Gallic colors: "*Mexico—To Arms! To Arms—Vive la Republique—Vive Taylor—Vive le Grande Armée de la Occupacion—Vive le Administration—Vive Congress.*" War was just what the Doctor prescribed, and the more vigorously waged, the better. He thought it possible that within two months the American "Army of Occupation" could be encamped in the Grand Plaza of Mexico's capital city. "Up, guards, and at them!" he urged, but he cautioned, "The work may be done in a single demonstration ; if delayed, France and England, and perhaps Old Spain, may protract the termination of the carnival, and lead into a quartette which will shake the foundations of Christendom."

On May 13, Bennett decided on the course that the *Herald* would take for the duration of the war. He could not refrain from taking a few last cracks at President Polk, "by whose folly and imbecility this state of things has been so suddenly precipitated," but in the same breath Bennett declared that the time for criticizing the president was past: "We must support the Executive and the government as a united people, determined to do or die." Like his correspondent the Doctor, James Gordon Bennett saw the start of the war as a momentous turning point in the history of the republic: "This may be looked upon as the commencement of a vast, a terrible, a magnificent future. It may lay the foundation of a new age, a new destiny, affecting both this continent and the old continent of Europe. . . . The American army on the Rio Grande, reinforced as it will be, must go ahead . . . to take possession of the northern departments of Mexico, and particularly of California, and to retain them, if not to march to [the City of] Mexico[4] itself, until a full and ample settlement of all difficulties is accomplished."

Bennett had studied for the priesthood before emigrating from Scotland to America in his twenties, and he brought a true believer's zeal to the enterprise at hand. He had "no doubt that the British capitalists, merchants, and traders, in Mexico have fomented the spirit and furnished the usurpers in that republic with the means" to oppose Taylor's army at Matamoros, but in Bennett's view "the British and French governments will carefully abstain from any direct interference in the present movements between Mexico and the United States." He believed "that the invasion of Mexico will now take place, planned on the most gigantic scale." In Bennett's imagination the invading army included American citizens as well as soldiers; he foresaw "every probability that an armed voluntary emigration, of one hundred thousand persons, will follow in the rear of the invading army—an emigration which will mix and blend in turn with the Mexican people, and teach them the true principles of civil liberty and commercial enterprise. The emigration to Oregon and California may pause for the present—and that to Mexico begin with the progress of the invading army."[5]

Bennett was a publishing pioneer. He had posted correspondents to European capitals, he had introduced the use of illustrations and interviews, he printed stock reports from Wall Street, and he was not above catering to his readers' baser interests to expand his circulation. The *Herald* offered lurid reports on murders and other sensations. It was a scandal sheet before the phrase was coined. By the start of the war with Mexico Bennett had built the *Herald* into the most profitable paper in New York, with a daily circulation of 40,000. Echoing the founding declarations of Revolutionary newspapers, Bennett had proclaimed in his first issue, "We shall support no party—be the agent of no faction or coterie, and care nothing for any election, or any candidate from president down to constable." Although eschewing partisanship, he had not, however, promised never to support a war, and in the Mexican War he got his chance:

"California must be ours ; Monterey must be ours . . . we trust that the 70,000 American troops[6] that are about to be precipitated upon the halls of Montezuma . . . with the 100,000 military emigrants that will follow in the rear, will teach that divided, insulted, and plundered race, the way to reorganize a firm government, and to command the respect of the world."[7]

With this imperial vision, Bennett proposed the implementation of an objective first named in December 1845 by John L. O'Sullivan, the editor of the *New York Morning News,* who wrote that it was America's "manifest destiny to overspread and possess the whole of the continent which Providence has given us for the . . . great experiment of liberty and federated self-government." Sullivan's phrase seized the popular imagination and it became the rallying cry for expansionism. With the annexation of Texas, fifteen more states had been added to the original thirteen. The momentum of America's expansion across the continent seemed inexorable. Once the westward movement was christened Manifest Destiny, it took on, for many, the aspect of a holy crusade.

Horace Greeley was no less inspired than most Americans by the urge to expand the United States, but he was convinced that President Polk was using the border clashes with Mexico as an excuse not only to secure for America the land to the Rio Grande, but also to act on more far-reaching ambitions. His caution about Polk's motives was provoked by a concern that underlay the issues of Texas annexation, Manifest Destiny, or empire building by any other name. This was the question of whether the lands acquired by annexation or conquest would become slave territory or free soil. Greeley suspected that the president's unstated aim in acquiring Texas and the war with Mexico was to extend Southern slavery beyond Texas, into New Mexico and perhaps to California as well.

The lines between the *Herald* and the *Tribune* were drawn. (The notion that the two newspapers might one day merge would have been greeted with appalled disbelief by both founders.) Bennett and Greeley were already locked in a battle for circulation. In the Mexican War their editorial positions came to epitomize the opposing arguments in a national debate that continued throughout the conflict.

While the newspapers were drawing their battle lines, Zachary Taylor was practicing the arts of war. Affectionately dubbed "Old Rough-and-Ready" by his troops, because he slept with them in the field and was careless in his personal appearance, Taylor had thrown off the encircling Mexicans and defeated them in two small battles before his situation was known in Washington and war was declared.[8] He captured Matamoros on the day that James Gordon Bennett published his grandiose vision of subduing Mexico by force of American arms and an infusion of good Yankee bloodlines. With the Mexican army in retreat to the south, Taylor encamped his troops at Matamoros to await supplies and reinforcements, and the war settled into the rhythm of a time when armies moved by horse and foot and boat, with months separating the battles.

In Washington, the question of what to do about the Oregon country was coming to a head. President Polk had been elected with the strong support of Democrats who asserted the American claim to all of the Oregon country with the rallying cry "fifty-four forty or fight!" Polk himself would have been glad to see the northern border of the America's western territory established at that latitude, but he was a far more astute politician than his critics believed. When he asked Congress, in December 1845, to approve terminating the joint administration agreement with Britain, the request was calculated to appear bellicose, but Polk believed that London would never negotiate seriously about dividing the Oregon country so long as the joint agreement continued. He proposed that the northern border of the Louisiana Purchase, at 49 degrees latitude, be extended to the Pacific. The British minister at Washington rejected the offer without consulting his government. On April 23, 1846, Congress voted to approve Polk's request to terminate the Oregon agreement. When news of the congressional action reached London, Sir Robert Peel's ministry was tottering, the government was coping with a famine in Ireland, and Peel must have been daunted by the thought of fighting a war in Oregon, which would involve landing an army somewhere along the Columbia River gorge and keeping it supplied by the sea lanes that circled the globe or overland across the whole of Canada. Peel proposed a formal treaty on Polk's terms, the border between British and American territory to be at 49 degrees north latitude, with Britain keeping the whole of Vancouver Island. Polk sent the proposed treaty to the Senate on June 10 with a message in which he stated that if the Senate accepted the treaty, he would sign it.[9]

The Senate met in secret session to debate the treaty, leaving the newspapers to speculate on the probable result. James Gordon Bennett decided that the settlement with Britain was a good thing. "The friends of 54 40, in the Senate will undoubtedly oppose this mode of procedure, and throw obstacles in the way of a settlement," he said in the *Herald,* but he thought they would accept it in the end because of "the probability that, in the present crisis in our affairs with Mexico, we shall obtain California, and all the fine harbors of that territory. We think there can be no doubt of this result, and the possession of such a country, and such harbors on the Pacific, will amply balance the giving up of any territory north of 49 . . . in order to preserve peace with England."[10]

When the result of the Senate vote was announced, the *New York Tribune* celebrated the news with five headlines atop the column that reported it: "Peace with England Secured!" / "THE OREGON QUESTION SETTLED!" / "THE 50 40s EXTINGUISHED!" / "The Senate in favor of the Treaty—38 to 12" / "THE COUNTRY SAVED FROM WAR!"

"It is a triumph of true Patriotism over selfish and brutal Passion of which both Great Britain and the United States may well be proud," Greeley exulted. "The laurels won in this contest are unstained by human blood, and shall bloom in undying beauty when those achieved by War and Carnage are trampled in the dust!"[11] Some of Greeley's joy in the settlement may have derived from the prospect that Oregon would become a free-soil territory, and that this northwestern expanse could be divided into several states when the population in those remote regions justified statehood.

In the summer of 1846, during a long lull in which there was no news to report from Mexico, David Wilmot, a Democrat of Pennsylvania, introduced in the House of Representatives an amendment to an appropriations bill, which stipulated that "neither slavery nor involuntary servitude shall ever exist" in any territory that might be acquired by treaty with Mexico. The following week, Horace Greeley exhorted the *Tribune*'s readers, "Remember that we are involved in a most expensive and disgraceful War, which had its origin in the Annexation of Texas. . . . Remember that it is the purpose of the Annexationists to carve three or four more States out of Texas and make them all Slave States. . . . In short, remember that the whole drama of Annexation has been one of unparalleled rapacity, deceit and gigantic iniquity, against which every honest man and lover of Freedom should sternly and indignantly protest and struggle to the end."[12] Wilmot's proviso was approved by the House but was deleted from the bill in the Senate.

On September 3, the *Tribune* published the first fragmentary reports from California, the most distant theater of war, the news two months in transit: "It appears that Commodore Sloat entered the harbor of Monterey, on the Pacific, early in July, and on 7th issued his proclamation to the inhabitants of California, calling upon them to remain peaceful, assuring them that he did not come as the enemy of California, but as their friend." The report included word that "Colonel Fremont's advanced posts had reached Sonora, to the north of San Francisco." The appearance of this information in a New York newspaper in less than sixty days was exceptional.[13] More typical was a letter published in the *Tribune* of January 1, 1847, that had been written in Monterey on September 19, three and a half months earlier, in which Walter Colton, the chaplain of the U.S. frigate *Congress,* wrote that the Californios were pleased that California was now under American rule. "California must never be surrendered to Mexico," Colton wrote, as if the conquest were an accomplished fact. Many months would elapse before further dispatches from the American forces in California would provide a more complete picture of events on the distant coast, and correct the *Tribune*'s "Sonora" to Sonoma.

Soon after taking office, President Polk had instructed the commander of the U.S. Navy's Pacific squadron to seize the California ports the instant war with Mexico was declared. When Polk received word of the fighting on the Rio Grande, he sent orders to Colonel Stephen Kearny at Fort Leavenworth, on the Missouri River, instructing him to march an army to Santa Fe, take control of New Mexico, leave enough of his force at Santa Fe to hold it, and go on to California with the rest. Polk had decided it was vital that California should be in the hands of United States forces whenever peace might be negotiated with Mexico.[14]

The Californios acquiesced so graciously in the first phase of the American conquest that one participant later described it almost as a lark: "We simply marched all over California, from Sonoma to San Diego, and raised the American flag without opposition or protest," he wrote. "We tried to find an enemy, but could not."[15] The second phase, which began in December, involved real fighting, on a limited scale, between the Californios and American forces under the General Stephen Kearny (Polk had promoted him en route), Colonel John C. Frémont, and Commodore Robert Stockton, who had replaced Sloat as commander of the Pacific Squadron. The final treaty was signed at Los Angeles on January 13, 1847. In six and a half months, at a minimal cost in blood, considering the stakes, the United States gained dominion over Alta California.

Lulled by the early American success in California and lacking regular dispatches from that quarter, the eastern newspapers devoted more attention to the campaign in Mexico, which produced outbursts of dramatic news separated by months of inactivity. Zachary Taylor captured Monterrey[16], a hundred and seventy-five miles west of Matamoros, on September 21 after a hard-fought battle. In the chivalrous spirit that sometimes still surfaced in nineteenth century warfare, Taylor granted the Mexicans an armistice and allowed their troops to evacuate the city. These decisions found disfavor in Washington and brought criticism on Taylor, who seemed to have little relish for the role of empire builder in which James Gordon Bennett had cast him.

President Polk evidently concluded that Taylor lacked the aggressiveness to achieve the decisive victory Polk wanted in Mexico, for he gave General Winfield Scott command of an army that Polk had decided to land at Vera Cruz, on Mexico's east coast, just two hundred miles from the City of Mexico. To reinforce Scott's army, Polk approved the transfer of many of the most experienced troops from Taylor's command and ordered Taylor to keep his reduced force in defensive positions at Monterrey.[17] But Taylor had political as well as military ambition, and he did not intend to cool his heels while Scott grabbed the glory. The contrasting styles of the two generals was perfectly captured by Scott's nickname, "Old Fuss and Feathers," for his love of pomp and ceremony and his impeccable dress, even on the battlefield. Rough-and-Ready Zack Taylor marched his men fifty miles southwest of Monterrey, where he met General Antonio López de Santa Anna—the victor at the Alamo in 1836, but the loser at San Jacinto—who had recently fomented a revolution that restored him to the Mexican presidency and command of her armies. Taylor engaged Santa Anna's army of more than 15,000 men near the village of Buena Vista on February 22, 1847. Despite being outnumbered by three or four to one, Taylor fought the Mexicans to a standstill in two days of punishing battle, forcing Santa Anna to retreat to the south under cover of night, leaving his dead and wounded on the field, his army reduced by almost 2,000 casualties. The *New Orleans Delta* reported Taylor's casualties at about seven hundred.[18]

The *New York Tribune* reported General Taylor's victory at Buena Vista on March 22. On the 25th, apparently prompted by an errant rumor that Taylor had been killed our wounded, Horace Greeley lashed out at the Polk administration for weakening Taylor's army: "If Taylor has fallen, he has fallen a victim to the culpable imbecility, or the fiend-like malevolence of the Administration : If he has defeated the Mexicans, or escaped their battle-array, he has done so, without the concurrence of the Administration, and it may be, *in spite of its exertions to the contrary.* Either positive, or negative, has been the crime of this Administration against the bravest, the best tried, and most victorious of our Generals."[19]

In this report, as in all the *Tribune's* coverage of the war, Greeley was as steadfast in his support for the American commanders and soldiers in the field as Bennett's *Herald* or any other newspaper. Greeley celebrated the triumphs of American arms, praised the bravery of the officers and men, and defended them against perceived political meddling. He mourned American losses, but he also lamented with equal eloquence the usually much greater losses on the Mexican side and customarily included some broader comments in which he deplored the carnage of war.

On April 5, 1847, the *Tribune* reprinted a report from the *New Orleans Picayune,* based on letters from California by way of Mexico, that carried the news, "Upper California is now in our undisputed possession."

General Scott's army landed near Vera Cruz on March 9, 1847, surrounded the city by the 13th, and received its surrender on the 29th.[20] The *Tribune* applauded Scott for keeping American casualties to sixty-five dead and wounded.[21] "Of the Mexicans," the *Tribune* said, "the slaughter is said to have been immense." Greeley foresaw difficulties in invading the heart of Mexico, and he seized the opportunity to urge President Polk to offer terms for peace: "We can now push our arms to the City of Mexico, if we will, and, after a fashion, conquer the whole country ; but what end is thereby attained? Thirty Thousand troops can overrun such a country more easily than One Hundred Thousand can hold it in subjugation. . . . Do we want Mexicans as fellow citizens? Can we decently hold them as subjects? Peace! Peace! We implore an immediate and public proffer by our Government of favorable terms of Peace!"[22] (Greeley's comment on the need for a much larger force to hold a country than to conquer it could have applied equally well to Iraq in 2003.)

Soon after Scott's victory at Vera Cruz, President Polk dispatched a special envoy, Nicholas Trist, the chief clerk at the State Department, to join Scott's army. Trist was empowered to enter into negotiations with the Mexicans as soon as they would entertain Polk's terms. Landed at Vera Cruz, Trist had no difficulty overtaking General Scott's slow-moving column. On April 18, Scott fought Santa Anna, who would be his adversary for the rest of the campaign, at Cerro Gordo, near Jalapa. Since his defeat by Taylor at Buena Vista, Santa Anna had mustered a new army of more than 10,000 men. Scott's smaller force fought the Mexicans for a day and a night and sent them packing, taking 3,000 prisoners into the bargain.

It took Scott four months to trek the hundred and fifty miles, as the buzzard flies, to the City of Mexico, but he arrived with his army in fighting trim and won back-to-back battles on August 19 and 20. In the breathing space after these contests, Polk's peace envoy, Nicholas Trist, reached an agreement with the Mexicans to declare a cease-fire and convene peace talks.

Before reports of the most recent battles and the subsequent armistice reached New York, Horace Greeley was growing pessimistic: "Before we can believe in the probability of a permanent peace between our country and Mexico," he wrote in the *Tribune* on September 6, "we must first witness the expulsion from the positions they disgrace of both Santa Anna and his friend, Mr. President Polk, neither of whom has ability or popularity enough to arrange a satisfactory peace."

Bennett's *Herald* hailed the news of the victories and the cease-fire with a cascade of fourteen headlines—"Immense Loss of the Enemy," / "GEN. SCOTT WOUNDED," / "Negotiations with Mr. Trist for a Peace Commenced," etc.—but took a cautious view in an editorial: "We have very little faith in the Mexicans, and have no doubt they will avail themselves of the first opportunity to pitch into us. . . . If the negotiations going on at the last accounts fail, there will be no alternative left but to keep an armed possession of the whole country."[23]

The *Tribune* recalled that "It was the commercial interest of England that extorted from a reluctant monarch the recognition" of American independence, and ventured to hope that "the great monetary interest of present England will compel the obstinate Mexican to negotiation and peace."[24] From the early reports of the negotiations, Greeley gathered that Mexico would, at last, "surrender all claim to Texas," but only to the Nueces boundary, while the United States was demanding a cession to the Rio Grande, and all of New Mexico and California as well. "What *right* have Santa Anna & Co. to sell the free natives of Northern and Eastern Mexico to a nation their very souls abhor?" Greeley demanded to know. "What right have we to govern the New Mexicans and Californians by virtue of any such transfer?"[25]

After twelve days of negotiations, the Mexican commissioners rejected the American terms for peace. Fighting resumed the following day. On September 14, General Scott's troops occupied the City of Mexico while Santa Anna and the remnants of his force retreated to Guadalupe. As after San Jacinto, Santa Anna was forced to resign the Mexican presidency for having been defeated on the battlefield.

James Gordon Bennett never for a moment questioned the right of the United States to govern New Mexico, California or any other lands seized from Mexico by force of arms. Undeterred by the fact that his imagined legions of "armed voluntary emigration" had never materialized, and outraged that Mexico would reject the offer to absorb almost half of her territory, Bennett felt compelled to extend American governance to the whole of the conquered nation: "The doom of Mexico is at length sealed, and by her own hand. She cannot make war. She will not make peace. She must be subdued. . . . There is but one course to pursue. . . . In view of the impossibility of bringing Mexico to terms, we must now anticipate the necessity that must at some future period arise of occupying the whole country in perpetuity." It would have been impossible, Bennett pointed out, to suggest such a course while peace negotiations were pending. But if the Mexicans would not accept reasonable terms with an American army at the gates of their capital city, Bennett could not imagine what else might induce them to make peace: "Our terms will never again be so moderate, and there is no reason to believe that their tenacity to their own will ever be less."[26]

Bennett could see only one solution: "There is no middle course between a disgraceful surrender of claims, in support of which the best blood of the country has flowed, and a universal and permanent occupation of Mexico. . . . A force must be poured into the country, sufficiently powerful to overawe resistance. Every state government must be over-thrown, and new governments, half military, half territorial, must be erected. . . . The guerrillas must be swept from the roads; and under the protection of our eagles, commerce and industry must be encouraged where they already exist, and given birth to where they do not." He ended the editorial with a sentence that remains one of the most unabashed ex-pressions of Manifest Destiny ever put to paper: "It is a gorgeous prospect, this annexation of all Mexico. It were more desirable that she should have come to us voluntarily ; but as we shall have no peace until she be an-nexed, let it come, even though force be necessary, at first, to bring her. Like the Sabine virgin, she will soon learn to love her ravisher."[27]

The next day, the *Tribune* reprinted Bennett's editorial in full and Greeley rebutted it in a single, heartfelt paragraph. "Five years ago, such avowals as the above, such prospects as here opened, would have excited the intense abhorrence of the American people. And now, with the exam-ples of Russia in Circassia, France in Algiers, and England in Afghanistan before us, we are seriously incited to attempt the absolute subjugation of a Nation of Seven Millions of People, inhabiting a country nearly as large as all Europe except Russia." Greeley described the rugged geography of Mexico, "utterly destitute of navigable waters or railroads" and ventured that the effort to subdue such a country would cost "One Hundred Mil-lions addition of National Debt," thousands of lives, "and, worse than all, must engulf the Morals and Liberties of our country in the unfathomable abyss of bloodshed, desolation and National guilt. Where sleeps the judg-ment, what has stupefied the conscience of the American People?"[28]

Bennett's rapacious vision reckoned without the persistence of Nicholas Trist. When news of the failed negotiations reached Washington, President Polk sent orders recalling Trist. Learning that General Scott had taken the Mexican capital did nothing to change his mind. Trist had pre-sented Polk's peace terms and the Mexicans had rejected them. The presi-dent would not have Mexico believe that the United States stood ready to conclude a peace at any cost.

Trist received Polk's recall well after the final victory of arms, but he postponed his departure for weeks, then months. Perhaps something in the words or the manner of the Mexican commissioners had given him hope. On his own responsibility, with General Scott's support, Trist re-solved to conduct further negotiations. They began on December 4. On

February 2, 1848, in the town of Guadalupe Hidalgo, near Mexico City, Trist concluded a treaty with his Mexican counterparts that was couched substantially in President Polk's terms.

News of the treaty reached Washington and New York in the third week of February and brought to a head five months of rumor and speculation about the fate of Mexico. The proposed terms gave California and New Mexico to the United States, as well as Texas to the Rio Grande. The *New York Herald*'s first response was to express hope that "The great issue of the ultimate annexation of all Mexico—of the gradual absorption of the whole of that country—is just as open as it ever was."[29]

Horace Greeley criticized the treaty for demanding too much land rather than too little: "The acquisition of territory stipulated by this treaty we deem anything but desirable, and could we have peace without New Mexico, or any part of the Rio Grand valley, we should esteem it far preferable." Greeley conceded that "Upper California had but few Mexican inhabitants, has been measurably Yankeeized, and could never revert to Mexico, whatever the treaty might propose : but New Mexico is essentially Mexican, and to maintain our authority there will cost us millions to no good purpose whatever. . . . But sufficient to the day is its own evil; let us rejoice that we have Peace!"[30]

President Polk was under no obligation to accept the treaty that Trist had negotiated without authority. Polk's own preference was to demand more territory of Mexico, down to the Sierra Madre mountains, but he put aside his own feelings, rejected the similar position of his secretary of state, James Buchanan, and accepted the majority will of his cabinet that the treaty should be submitted to the Senate.[31] The Senate debated for two weeks in closed session before voting 38 to 14 for ratification.

Under the Treaty of Guadalupe Hidalgo, Mexico ceded to the United States the present states of Texas, New Mexico, Arizona, California, Nevada, Utah, and portions of Wyoming, Colorado, Kansas and Oklahoma, in exchange for $15,000,000 and the assumption by the United States of all claims by American citizens against Mexico. Taken together with the Oregon settlement, the United States gained, by annexation and treaty, in the years 1845–48, over a million square miles of land, an area greater than the Louisiana Purchase. After a further small adjustment of the border with Mexico in 1853, these acquisitions filled in the familiar boundaries of what became the forty-eight contiguous states.

With no reference to the evaporation of his imperial dream, James Gordon Bennett ventured in the *Herald,* "There may be a few persons hostile to peace with Mexico, as we have some singular voices opposed to it in the Senate; but we believe that the general feeling of the community, in this region, is gratified, not only at the events of the recent war, the glory which it has shed on the American name, but now, at its termination, by the ratification of a treaty of peace with Mexico."[32]

Horace Greeley also gave his grudging approval: "To pay Millions for land we do not need is bad; but to kill thousands for offences they never committed is much worse. . . . It is the insatiable, relentless appetite of Mr. Polk for Conquest that obliges us to pay Fifteen Millions for Peace."[33] Greeley would have preferred the Mexican counteroffer, proposed to Nicholas Trist in the first negotiations and subsequently supported by some American newspapers, which would have ceded to the United States only Mexican territory north of 37 degrees latitude (which would have included San Francisco, but not Monterey), and thus no land that would lie south of 36 degrees 30', the Missouri Compromise line, where slavery might be established. That solution, as Horace Greeley saw it, might have offered the hope that "the fearful convulsion which the question of Slave Extension is certain to create on the acquirement of a single foot of soil south of 36.30 would have been avoided—perhaps forever."[34] For the South, though, such an outcome would have been worse than a pact with the devil, for it would have guaranteed the eventual creation of enough new free-soil states north of the exclusion line to give the North a permanent majority in the Senate and thus assure the South's political subjugation.

⌒

Horace Greeley misjudged the motives and the character of James Polk, whose exceptional sense of duty moved him, both in the case of Oregon and in the final treaty with Mexico, to put aside his own inclinations and accept a compromise that lay between two extremes, rather than risk subjecting his countrymen to the hardships of a conflict that might, in the end, produce the same result or one less favorable to the United States. But Greeley's opposition to the extension of slavery and the overreaching impulses of Manifest Destiny represented a substantial body of public opinion that was opposed to the unrestrained imperialistic policy supported by much of the Democratic party—Polk's party—and advocated so enthusiastically by James Gordon Bennett and the *New York Herald*. Bennett wanted all of Mexico and Greeley wanted none of it—except California. In the end, neither editor, neither newspaper, and neither extreme got its way. Neither the *Tribune* nor the *Herald* wholly supported or wholly opposed President Polk's war policies, and both served the public interest by debating whether the United States should go to war with Mexico over the Rio Grande— or with Britain over the Oregon country—the conduct of the war, what we should demand in victory, and the ongoing question of slave territory versus free soil.

What lesson can we draw from the fact that America's colonial printers, at risk of life and limb from English officials and royal soldiers, so successfully galvanized an epochal revolution, while the free American press of the 1840s, unhindered by its own government, could not significantly alter the divisions over the questions of slavery and empire that emerged in the early days of the Mexican War? Perhaps only that the unimpeded exercise of a free press does not necessarily guarantee timely solutions to the nation's problems. The continuing debate in the newspapers in the years after the Mexican War, given added import by the enlargement of the United States that the war produced, could not compel America's political leaders to devise a solution to the problem of slavery. Congressman David Wilmot's amendment to prohibit slavery in annexed Mexican territory—popularly known as the Wilmot Proviso—passed again in the House in 1847, and again the Senate struck it out. It was introduced for a third time in 1848, but once more it failed to win the support of both houses.

The discovery of gold in California, which took place a few days before Nicholas Trist and his Mexican counterparts signed the Treaty of Guadalupe Hidalgo, was the catalyst that forced the issue. The massive westward migration that the news triggered accelerated the settlement of the western territories. Maintaining the political balance between the slave and free states became more difficult, then impossible. New compromises held only briefly, and a dozen years after the end of the Mexican War newspapers north and south faced new and difficult choices between loyalty and opposition when the "fearful convulsion" that Horace Greeley had feared produced a new contest of arms, this one fratricidal, that threatened the survival of the American Union.

3

A HOUSE DIVIDED

The Civil War (1861–1865)

In 1850, Congress approved a compromise that admitted California to the Union as a free-soil state, formed territorial governments for Utah and New Mexico—leaving the question of slavery to "popular sovereignty" in those places—and enacted a fugitive slave law that obliged the federal government, and all citizens, to aid in returning escaped slaves to their Southern owners. By opening the door to slavery in territory north of the Missouri Compromise line, the California Compromise delivered a mortal wound to the earlier compact. The death knell came four years later, in an act of Congress that organized Kansas and Nebraska territories—again leaving it to the inhabitants in those places to decide for slavery or free soil. In Kansas, free-soilers and pro-slavery groups fought so fiercely for control that Horace Greeley bestowed a dark sobriquet, "Bleeding Kansas," on the territory. At issue there and in all the territories was how each would vote when it gained statehood and sent two members to the U.S. Senate. The South feared the greater population and the free-labor economy of the North, whose increasingly industrialized economy outpaced the slave-labor cotton economy of the South. If popular sovereignty in the new states rejected slavery, the North would dominate the Senate and the South would become a vassal region.

Northern resistance to the Kansas-Nebraska Act of 1854 led to the founding of a new political party in the same year. The Whigs, irrevocably split between the anti-slavery "Conscience" north and the property-rights "Cotton" South, had evaporated as a political force after losing the presidency in the 1852 election. Northern Whigs and the other antislavery elements that coalesced into the new party called themselves Republicans to revive Jeffersonian ideals, and dedicated themselves to preventing the spread of slavery into the West.

These political and economic issues were at the roots of the rising tension between North and South, but it was slavery that incited the emotions and the violence that raised the threat of sectional war. The murder of several proslavery men in Kansas by the abolitionist firebrand John Brown in 1856 and his attack on the federal arsenal at Harpers Ferry, Virginia, three years later, aroused Southern fears that the North would seek to accomplish the abolition of slavery by armed might. The election of Abraham Lincoln, a Republican, to the presidency in 1860 increased the South's apprehension. Lincoln favored restricting slavery to the Southern states where it already existed and he opposed outright abolition, but in his 1858 debates with Stephen Douglas, when the two men were vying to represent Illinois in the U.S. Senate, Lincoln had uttered sentiments that made the South wary of the lean country lawyer: "A house divided against itself cannot stand," Lincoln had said. And, "I believe this government cannot endure permanently half slave and half free." As president, it was not his intention to force the issue, but others forced it for him. Kansas petitioned to join the Union as a free-soil state, further alarming the South. Between Lincoln's election in November 1860 and his inauguration in March 1861, seven Southern states seceded from the Union and formed the Confederate States of America. In his inaugural address, Lincoln hoped the separation could be mended. "We are not enemies but friends," he said. "Though passion may have strained, it must not break the bonds of affection."

⌒

The *New York Daily News* conceded that Lincoln's inaugural speech was "an able and statesmanlike document . . . courteous, considerate and even conciliatory," but cautioned that it was couched in "honeyed phrases" that might fool the casual reader. The danger, as the *Daily News* saw it, was in Lincoln's assertion that he would use the power of his office "to hold, occupy and possess the property and places belonging to the Government." Taken as a whole, the *News* concluded "The Inaugural is not satisfactory; it is ambiguous; and we *fear* the Republicans, even while professing the most peaceful intentions. Coercion could not have been put in a more agreeable form; it reads like a challenge under the code, in which an invitation to the field is vailed under the most satisfactory syllables."[1]

Among the property and places Lincoln intended to hold was Fort Sumter, which guarded the entrance to the harbor at Charleston, South Carolina. Since it became the first state to secede from the Union, in December 1860, South Carolina had demanded that Union troops manning the fort hand it over to state authorities. When state officials learned President Lincoln intended to send a relief expedition overland with provisions, but no military supplies, to prevent the Union force at Sumter from being starved into submission, South Carolina gave the Union commander, Major Anderson, one last chance to evacuate the fort. Anderson refused. On April 12, before sunrise, the state forces opened fire on Sumter.

Horace Greeley's *New York Tribune* had taken an equivocal view of Southern secession, but Greeley's resolve became more confident on hearing of the event the nation had anticipated for so long. "The Jeff. Davis rebellion, claiming to be the Confederate Government of the seven States which profess to have seceded from the Federal Union, commenced formal war upon the United States by opening fire on Fort Sumter at 4 o'-clock yesterday morning," the lead editorial announced on April 13. "Thus the great Cotton Rebellion inaugurates in blood its more direct and manly efforts to subvert the Federal Constitution and Government, and build up a Slaveholding Oligarchy on their ruins. Having chosen its ground and its time, it may of course count with reason on a temporary advantage. But the end is not yet. Let none doubt the ultimate triumph of the Right."[2]

The *New York Daily News* opened its editorial with a statement of fact: "Our telegraphic dispatches from Charleston announce the commencement of civil war." Opinion followed, couched in temperate language. "The course of the Administration, in determining to throw supplies into Fort Sumter . . . has hastened the crisis and prompted the authorities of the Confederate States to attempt its reduction when it could do so with the least loss of life and the best prospect of success." Now that war had begun, the *Daily News* said, how it might end "is known only to that Higher Power 'that shapes our ends, rough hew them how we may.'" The paper offered its own prediction just the same: "the South can never be subjugated by the North, nor can any marked successes be achieved against them. They have us at every advantage. They fight against us on their own soil, in behalf of their dearest rights—for their public institutions, their homes and their property."[3]

The *Daily News* had been founded in 1855 as the organ of Tammany Hall, the Democratic organization in the city of New York. In 1860, the paper was bought by Benjamin Wood, a first-term Democratic congressman, from his brother, Fernando, the mayor of New York. In January 1861, when only South Carolina had seceded, Mayor Wood proposed that the city secede from the state and the Union, should further secessions of the Southern states lead to war, to protect it from the machinations of the state legislature in Albany, which was controlled by Republicans, and to preserve the city's substantial trade with the South. The proposal had aroused Horace Greeley's wrath, moving him to charge in the *Tribune* that "Mr. Fernando Wood evidently wants to be a traitor; it is lack of courage only that makes him content with being a blackguard."[4]

Major Anderson surrendered Fort Sumter on April 13. On the 15th, President Lincoln called for enlisting 75,000 volunteers "to suppress combinations in the seceded States, and to cause the laws to be duly executed." The *Daily News* greeted the president's announcement gloomily: "Thus we have the first authoritative statement from Old Abe that coercion, on a scale of enormous magnitude, is to be forthwith inaugurated by this peace-professing Administration. We are at the beginning of the end."[5] Benjamin Wood saw the news as calamitous: "United, we might have defied the world in arms, but now the hand of brother is raised against brother, and the land is convulsed by intestine feuds. . . . Let not this perfidious Administration invoke the sacred names of the Union and the Constitution in the hope of cheating fools into the support of the unholy war which it has begun."[6]

When the opposing armies drew near each other in Virginia, not far from Washington, in the first days of summer, the *Daily News* contemplated what the gathering foreboded. Four more states, including Virginia, had joined the Confederacy since Lincoln's inauguration. "The two armies stand on the soil of Virginia to-day, invaders and defenders, almost within sight of each other," Wood wrote. "A mighty struggle is imminent, and the future of all those upon this continent who call themselves Americans, may depend upon its issue." Wood asked, "Why should so terrible a battle be fought at all? Why should two hundred thousand men, the bravest and the most intelligent soldiers in the world, led by educated generals and armed with the most devilishly ingenious inventions for the mutual destruction of life, be precipitated upon each other? Cannot this awful fratricide be averted?"[7]

It could not. The armies contemplated each other for several weeks before finally clashing at Bull Run on July 21. The *Daily News* relayed a barrage of early dispatches under fifteen column-headlines that included "GALLANT CONDUCT OF N.Y. TROOPS" and "SUCCESS OF THE FEDERAL TROOPS." The lead dispatch reported that Washington was "wild with joy" at the news that in the fighting, "Our troops engaged the enemy with a large force, silenced their batteries, and drove the Secessionists to the Junction." There was no indication in these first-day reports that the South had gained the victory.[8]

The next day, as the picture became clearer, the *Daily News's* headlines told of the "Defeat of McDowell's Column," "A COMPLETE PANIC," and "A FALL BACK UPON WASHINGTON." The reports contradicted each other, one saying that Union forces had retreated "in good order," another that they were "driven in disorder from the ground," which was closer to the truth. In an editorial, Wood despaired over the futility of war: "The prologue is over, and the first great act of the tragedy has commenced. . . . What we have from the first predicted is about to be verified, and already the bodies of the slain begin to be numbered by thousands. . . . If the defeat be ours, the same terrible scene will be resumed on the same spot ; if the victory be ours, it will be reenacted a little farther South. The shuttlecock of fortune, feathered with shafts of death, will go and come, and at the end, when thousands living shall be weeping for thousands dead, we shall be where we now are—no step nearer the object for which all this hellish work is being done."[9]

This was how the *Daily News* would report the war. "We" were the North and "they" were the South. Confederate forces were "the enemy," "Secessionists," "disunionists" or "rebels." From the outset, Wood bemoaned equally the deaths on both sides, as Abraham Lincoln would do, to immortal effect, on a battlefield at Gettysburg, Pennsylvania, in 1863.

Benjamin Wood's motives were never as noble as the president's. He opposed war as much, perhaps more, for practical and political reasons as for reasons of morality. Woods and his brother Fernando are often characterized too simplistically as "proslavery." Rather the Northern "peace" Democrats, later called Copperheads, were willing—far too willing, in the view of Republicans and "war" Democrats—to tolerate slavery and even secession rather than court the cataclysm of civil war. They opposed the Republican party as a sectional party in league with radical abolitionists. When secession came, they supported reconstituting, or "reconstructing" the Union by peaceful means, if possible, or letting the North and South coexist as sister republics if reconciliation was not possible. The peace Democrats were sympathetic with the South, but at no time did the *Daily News* or the other Democratic papers of New York advocate the victory of Southern arms.

The issues that prompted Benjamin Wood to launch his most forceful attacks on the Lincoln administration concerned whether, in this war, the people would be free to speak, and the press to publish, opinions hostile to the government. In the first summer of the war, Union supporters attacked anti-administration newspapers from Maine to Ohio. The mobs ransacked newspaper offices, destroyed presses and types, and sometimes tarred and feathered unfortunate editors.[10] In the pages of the *Daily News,* Wood laid the blame for the violence squarely on President Lincoln: "When the Chief Magistrate of a nation tramples upon the Constitution he has sworn to protect, and from his exalted position gives a conspicuous example of insubordination to the laws," the *News* warned, such an example could only encourage those who would silence contrary opinions by force. The attacks on the antiwar newspapers, Wood said, were "but a phase of that utter anarchy and rule of violence which walks in the footsteps of fanaticism and hangs on the skirts of despotism."[11]

Free speech was in jeopardy as well. On August 16, 1861, the *Daily News* reported, "Arrests are now made of individuals for uttering opinions hostile to the government. Several persons have been hurried from the city for fear of arrest, and the Conspiracy law may be considered in full force."[12] Some of those arrested for sedition in New York were imprisoned in Fort Lafayette, in New York harbor. "That fortress was erected to defend your liberties," Wood wrote, "and yet without the shadow of law it has been made to hide within its stony bosom men whose liberties have been stricken down at a blow by the mailed hand of despotic power."[13]

By the summer of 1861, the *Daily News* was the object of threats and criticism for its opposition to Lincoln's war policy. In August, a federal grand jury "presented" the *Daily News* and four other antiwar papers for giving "aid and comfort to the enemy." (A presentment was short of an indictment but suggested that the offenses were worthy of prosecutorial attention.) Wood responded to the presentment in an editorial that listed nine positions the *News* had consistently taken since the outbreak of war. The briefest of these asserted simply "That civil war is to be avoided, and that amity between the several States is to be cultivated." Others declared that "every drop of blood that has been shed in the present contest is a calamity," that the expenditure of money on the war "without permission of Congress" and many other actions by the government were unconstitutional, and that it would be better "to permit the disenchanted portion of the United States to depart in peace" than to allow the "internecine strife" to continue. If these opinions "render our paper worthy of indictment, we have only to say that we covet no better fate," Wood wrote.[14]

No indictment was forthcoming, but the Lincoln administration now turned the power of the federal government on the Democratic press. On August 22, 1861, the postmaster general denied the use of the mails to the *Daily News* and the other New York newspapers the grand jury had presented. On the same day, three thousand copies of the *News* were seized in Philadelphia by the U.S. marshal. The August 23 issue of the *News* told of the seizure and reported that the paper's "sale in Philadelphia and throughout the Southwest has been, by order of the Administration, suppressed." As for what led the government to "this arbitrary act," the *News* continued, "we have as yet no definite intelligence." Wood declared that the *News* had committed no crime. "It has abused no privilege as a free press. It has violated no courtesy to the Government or any of its officers by the publication of military facts." The paper's only offense, Wood wrote, "if offense it be—is, that we have fearlessly asserted and exercised the right which the Constitution has guaranteed to us, in war as well as in peace, to oppose, not the Government, but the policy of the national Administration. . . . While we feel that the most sacred of the private and public rights which an American citizen may enjoy have been violated in pure wantonness, we record the fact and our protest against it more in sor-

row than surprise . . . and until the pen is wrenched from our hand, one
press, at least, in New York shall dare to be free, and to speak without a
permit from the hand of arbitrary power."[15]

The *Daily News* found no sympathy from members of the press that
opposed its political views. Greeley's *Tribune* saw the Democratic press as
a threat to the Union: "While the very existence of the Republic is trem-
bling in the balance, while even the hold of the nation upon its Capital is
precarious, these intestine feuds cannot but tend to give aid and comfort
to the common enemy."[16] The *Tribune* predicted, "There *will* be hanging
for treason on this side of the Potomac ere long, and it will very likely be
wholesale. We warn those who are affording 'aid and comfort' to the
enemy to desist utterly and at once. Their own safety imperatively demands it."[17] The *Tribune* congratulated the marshal in Philadelphia for
preventing distribution of the *New York Daily News* in that city and it encouraged the wider suppression of anti-administration opinions: "What is
now at issue is the Constitution of the Union and the existence of Democratic Institutions," the *Tribune* declared. "Nor is this any longer a matter
of discussion. . . . The only principle that now controls the case is this:
that a Government at war cannot tolerate friends and advocates of the
enemy among the journals published in its territory."[18]

The Lincoln government showed no inclination to tolerate the *Daily
News*. On August 26, the U.S. marshal for New York seized from the
American Express Company copies that were intended for the paper's subscribers outside the city limits.[19] Protesting the latest seizure Wood wrote:
"If the Administration will persist in gathering information only from the
columns of the War Press, it will never be awakened to a sense of the danger it is provoking until it is too late. . . . Such wanton outrages upon right
and liberty as have been witnessed lately in our midst would have been
sufficient to 'stir the stones of Rome to rise and mutiny.' The wrongs that
precipitated the French Revolution were innocent in comparison."[20]

The *Tribune* believed that the administration had not gone far enough
in suppressing dissent. The constitution of the state of New York, a *Tribune* editorial pointed out, provided that although citizens were free to
"speak, write, and publish" their opinions, they were "responsible for the
abuse of that right." The *Tribune* stepped nimbly to the conclusion that
any abuse "will subject the offenders to punishment." Among those deserving punishment, the paper listed "Certain journals, whose value to the

communities where they are published, and to the country at large, was never clearly appreciable," that were "just now loud in their eulogies of the freedom of the press," but "equally loud in their sympathy for the Rebels with whom the country is at war." Continuing its redrafting of the First Amendment, the *Tribune* declared that the opposition journals, "are abusing the sacred right guaranteed to all men by the Constitution. Some of them have been mildly punished for their crimes. Others yet go unwhipt of Justice. Due retribution, we trust, is in store for the whole of them."[21]

Denied the mails and unable to guarantee the distribution of the *Daily News* outside the city under the threat of peremptory seizures by United States marshals, Wood struck back at his enemies in the press. He accused "a portion of the Republican journals of this city" with "dropping fresh fuel upon the raging fire that their incendiarism first kindled, and which now threatens to make one blazing funeral pyre of the magnificent fabric which our fathers founded."[22] Wood named his leading opponents "the transcendental *Tribune*," "the vindictive *Times*" and "the vituperative *Herald*." He charged that "The war organs are selling their birthright for a mess of pottage. Not for the sake of the Union do they stir up this crusade against a portion of the Press, but simply to cripple or destroy the rivals that they hate and fear."[23] In one editorial after another, Wood condemned the attempts by the Republican press and the Lincoln administration to silence the opposition. "All evils which afflict the country are imputed to opposition," he wrote. "It is the constant theme of every weak and wicked Administration." He quoted Daniel Webster, the great orator of the Northern Whigs—"It is the ancient and constitutional right of this people to canvass public measures, and the merits of public men"—and demanded to know, "Was this treasonable in his day?"[24]

Wood did not argue only for the redress of his own grievances. He extolled written constitutions as "the greatest of all safeguards to self-government" and cited the U.S. Constitution as "a mutual recognition of rights among equals, standing on a common platform as immortal and accountable free agents, and co-operating and consulting together in the great work of self-government." If the citizenry as a whole had any power, Wood believed, "it results from the separate manhood of each constituent of the mass, and liberty dies when a single individual is deprived of a constitutional right."[25] He pointed again to the men imprisoned in Fort Lafayette in New York harbor, who were charged with no crimes and denied the right to challenge their detention: "in each of their persons, a blow seems to have been struck at one of the inalienable rights guaranteed by that Constitution,"[26] Wood saw the deprivation of one man's rights as a step in a pattern of repression: "One thing is certain: if the people submit to have their natural rights of liberty of person, of speech, and of the Press taken away from them one by one, they will soon be in a condition in which they can make no resistance, let their views be what they may."[27]

As if worn out by his editorial efforts, Wood finally submitted. In the *Daily News* of September 14, 1861, he announced that he was forced to bid his readers "a temporary, but, we trust, a short farewell," and was suspending publication of the newspaper. Among the causes that forced the suspension, in addition to the denial of the mails and express transportation, Wood listed further intimidations: "Our advertising patrons have been threatened through anonymous communications, and some of those who have been in the habit of contributing to our editorial columns, for no other known cause, have been arrested and consigned to the dungeons of a fortress. Policemen, in their official capacity, have interfered with our circulation by practicing intimidation upon news vendors. Our readers have been subjected to insult and indignity, and it had absolutely become dangerous for a citizen to be seen perusing a copy of The Daily News in public places."[28]

If the administration believed that silencing a few newspapers would reduce the criticism of Abe Lincoln's war policy, it was soon disillusioned. With supporters like the abolitionists and radical Republicans, the government needed no enemies. The abolitionists pestered Lincoln with constant demands to emancipate the slaves. The radical Republican newspapers campaigned for new military offensives. Union generals bore the brunt of the criticism for not prosecuting the war more aggressively, but Lincoln himself was not exempted. The *New York Evening Post,* in the second summer of the war, charged that Lincoln "has trusted too much in his subordinates . . . and his whole Administration has been marked by a certain tone of languor and want of earnestness, which has not corresponded with the wishes of the people."[29]

General George McClellan became a lightning rod for criticism by failing to follow up when he gained the advantage, particularly after the Peninsular Campaign in the summer of 1862, when he dislodged the

Rebels from Yorktown and moved up the finger of land between the James and York rivers of Virginia, coming close enough to the Confederate capital, Richmond, to see its smoke, but failing to capture it. After this debacle, but before McClellan resumed command of the Union army following the second battle of Bull Run (August 29–30, 1862, another loss for the Union), Horace Greeley vilified McClellan so strongly that it was rumored the administration had ordered the *Tribune* closed down. Seizing on the rumor, the *New York World* took the opportunity to taunt Greeley by repeating it, and to inveigh against the administration for threatening constitutional liberties. Anyone walking the streets of New York, the *World* wrote, "could not have failed to notice the universal credence given to the rumor which flew through the city that the government had suppressed the publication of the *Tribune* and ordered the arrest of Mr. GREELEY." The rumor flew to Philadelphia by telegraph, the *World* reported, where it caused great excitement, "mixed with indignation at that journal for having accused Gen. McClellan of cowardice, indolence, or treachery." The fact that such a rumor could become so widely believed, the *World* suggested, sidling up to its real purpose, "may show us how the public sense has been bedeviled in the past twelvemonth—may show us what change has been worked in our habits of thought toward the government, in the general sense of personal rights and liberties, in public pride and of concern for the freedom of speech and of the press." Two years earlier, the *World* wrote, such a rumor could never have been believed. How this transformation might have been wrought "without our special wonder" gave the paper cause for deep concern. It could see only one reason for the change: "Fighting for the Constitution, we have almost been ready to abandon what of personal rights and liberties the Constitution secures. Compelling rebels to return to their allegiance, we have almost forgotten what more sacred things there were than the Union and the Constitution to which our allegiance was due—namely that precious inheritance of rights and liberties which the Union was framed to guard and keep, and which the Constitution enumerates as the very Decalogue of our National Faith."[30]

New York was the nexus of newspaper publishing in the Union and home to the most powerful Republican papers, but New Yorkers were predominantly Democratic, and the journal with the greatest circulation—the *Herald*—was implacably hostile to the most vocal of the Republican dailies. Benjamin Wood had lumped "the vituperative *Herald*" together with the Republican *Times* and *Tribune* among the "war organs" that had it in for him, but never since the Mexican War had James Gordon Bennett's *New York Herald* fallen even accidentally into step with Greeley's *Tribune* on any issue. There was a natural alliance between the *Tribune* and the *New York Times,* which had been founded in 1851 by Henry J. Raymond. Like Greeley, and William Cullen Bryant of the *Evening Post,* Raymond had been among the prominent men who created the Republican party. Bennett's *Herald,* in contrast, conducted a rivalry with the *Tribune* during the Civil War that was, if anything, more virulent than that of the war with Mexico.

Before the war began, the *Herald* had sided with the peace Democrats, willing to let the departing Southern states go their way in peace. After the cannons fired on Fort Sumter, the *Herald* put on a war Democrat's clothing. Thereafter, Bennett and his editorial staff supported the war to restore the Southern states to the Union but absolutely opposed making the abolition of slavery another of its aims. When President Lincoln announced in September 1862 that he would emancipate by proclamation "persons held as slaves" in areas still in rebellion against the United States on January 1, 1863, the *Herald* wrote that the proclamation "has been forced upon the nation by the abolitionists of the North and the secessionists of the South."[31]

The *New York World* had changed sides in the opposite direction. Before the war the *World* had stood shoulder-to-shoulder with the *Times* and the *Evening Post* in demanding that the seceding Southern states should be forced back into the Union, but the paper had since changed ownership and was now Democratic. In its own reaction to the Emancipation Proclamation, the *World* asked "to be informed whence the President derives his power to issue any such proclamation as he has now published? Not from the Constitution surely, for it is in plain violation of some of its leading provisions."[32]

The radical Republicans and abolitionists complained that the proclamation should have come sooner, and they criticized it for freeing only those slaves within the states in rebellion against the United States, where it would not be obeyed, and not those in areas under Union control. The *New York Tribune,* however, was not inclined to look a gift horse in the mouth. It reviewed the genesis of the proclamation and pronounced its judgment: "GOD BLESS ABRAHAM LINCOLN!"[33]

Behind the Emancipation Proclamation, the *Herald* saw the perfidy of the abolitionists and radical Republicans: "The radical abolition policy is unconstitutional," the *Herald* charged a week before the federal elections in the fall of 1862, "and the radical abolition leaders have repeatedly acknowledged its unconstitutionality. Therefore, before this war began, they deliberately and avowedly aimed to destroy the constitution in order to destroy slavery." If the Republicans, which the *Herald* called "the abolition party," could fool the voters into supporting it at the polls, "the radical abolitionists will triumphantly interpret this victory into a cordial endorsement of their dangerous policy."[34] The *Herald* advised voters to choose candidates on their merits rather than by party. It saw the election as a contest not between Democrats and Republicans, but between conservatives in both parties and fire-breathing radicals, between a "Union policy" and an "abolition policy," which it described in these terms: "The Union policy is to maintain the constitution; to prosecute the war constitutionally and vigorously; to bring back the seceded states by force of arms and force of justice; to put down the rebellion by might and right combined. The abolition policy is to supersede the constitution; to rely upon might alone; to annihilate the South instead of restoring the Union; to abrogate the government in order to institute a despotism; to inaugurate anarchy in order to reconstruct the nation; to return to chaos in order to be recreated."[35]

Of all the villains scheming to corrupt the Union, the *Herald* branded James Gordon Bennett's old adversary, Horace Greeley, the worst of the lot: "The Jacobins of France were not more insanely fanatical than our radical abolitionists. Jeff. Davis and his most guilty accomplices in treason are not more thorough haters of the constitution and more sincere and hearty disunionists than Horace Greeley. Jeff. Davis used abolitionism as a pretext to seduce the Southern people to trample upon the constitution. Horace Greeley and his accomplices use secessionism as a pretext to induce Northern men to supersede the constitution. . . . Horace Greeley and his aids desire to abolish the old Union in order to obtain power in a new, non-slaveholding nation."[36] (Since the Mexican War, Greeley had continued to oppose the extension of slavery into the lands west of the

Mississippi, but he was not an abolitionist, and it was not until the Civil War was under way that he supported emancipation for the slaves.)

Even as it heaped vituperation on Republicans and abolitionists in ever more vehement terms, the *Herald* continued to support the war to restore the Union and Abe Lincoln as the chief architect of that effort. Lincoln, meanwhile, employed some of the heavy guns in his arsenal of executive authority to control the news from the battlefields and to repress secessionist and anti-administration passions when he believed they threatened public order.

For the first time, reporters working for American newspapers were covering a war on and near the front lines in significant numbers. The *New York Herald* employed more than sixty correspondents. In the summer of 1861, General McClellan, as commander of the Union Army, had drawn up voluntary censorship guidelines as an aid to editors. In the field, censorship was often applied more forcefully, and arbitrarily, from one military district to another (the *Chicago Times* was shut down twice by military authorities in Illinois). The government controlled the telegraph wires as well as the mail. Even when the news was good for the Union cause, the impulse was to censor first and relax the restriction later, as the *New York Tribune*'s first reports, on July 3, 1863, of the battle at Gettysburg, Pennsylvania, reflected: "Such accounts of the engagement at Gettysburg as the Government has permitted to pass the wires, although on the whole not unfavorable, are too meager to support any decided opinion, or to require much comment."

The administration had suspended habeas corpus, the right to demand legal justification for detaining or imprisoning someone, in Maryland and in other parts of the Union where it judged that secessionist sentiments posed a danger. (The Constitution provides that habeas corpus may be suspended "when in Cases of Rebellion or Invasion the public Safety may require it.") And the government had imposed martial law, not only in areas of the Confederacy that were conquered by Union forces, but also in Union territory—in Baltimore and St. Louis, the District of Columbia, and Missouri, among other places, rather than risk riots and demonstrations that might result in wider disorder.

The worst civil disturbances to take place in the Union states during the war were the draft riots in New York city in July 1863. No longer able to depend solely on enlistments to fill the Union's need for men, Congress had enacted a draft law in the spring. Enrollments began in New York on July 13. Riots against conscription erupted the same day and continued for four days, leading to pitched battles in the streets as police backed by volunteer regiments tried to restore order. In addition to lashing out at figures of authority—firemen, policemen, soldiers—the rioters, many of them foreign-born laborers, viciously attacked blacks, who competed with them for unskilled jobs, and went after anyone who represented support for the war—rich men, abolitionists, and Republican newspapers. They attacked the *Tribune* building and were only prevented from setting it afire by the timely arrival of police. Benjamin Wood, of the *Daily News,* which had resumed publication in May after a suspension of twenty months, helped to protect the building of his rival, the *New York Times,* by warding off rioters with a pistol and lecturing them on the sanctity of property rights, while the *Times*'s publisher, Henry J. Raymond, manned a Gatling gun in one of the windows.[37]

In response to the first day of rioting, the *Tribune* declared: "The plain obvious duty of the Government is to declare at once Martial Law in this city, and to place some officer in command who will enforce it." The only sure means of restoring order, in Greeley's view, was "by declaring that promptly, exercising it mercilessly, and maintaining it till the last vestige of treason is annihilated."[38] Greeley was not the only one to call for martial law, but martial law was never imposed in New York, although some regiments of militia and regular troops from the Army of the Potomac were dispatched to the city to quell the riots.

The *Daily News* argued strenuously for an end to the violence while expressing sympathy for the rioters' opposition to the draft. When William Cullen Bryant's *Evening Post* blamed the Democratic papers for inciting the riots, the *Daily News* declared these charges to be "the antipodes of truth," and threw the blame back on the *Post,* which, it claimed, "has been the avowed champion of the doctrine of augmenting Federal authority" and, when the conscription act was introduced in Congress, "was its zealous supporter, and has been indefatigable in its attempts to bring about its enforcement."[39] The *News* took the position that the draft was unconstitutional because the Constitution had created the federal government, "and it now performs its functions under that instrument alone. Hence if the power of conscripting the citizens of the several states is not found to be created by that document it does not exist at all." The government had the power to call up the militia, the *News* acknowledged, but it maintained that the power to create it was vested in the states.[40]

The Lincoln war government was not disposed to admit any such limitation. Several of Lincoln's actions as president—issuing the Emancipation Proclamation, making arrests under the suspensions of habeas corpus, imposing martial law and replacing civil courts with military tribunals in parts of the Union not threatened by the rebellion, and suppressing the opposition press—all represented expansions of executive power. A week before the draft riots began in New York, Lincoln sent a letter to an Ohio committee that had written him on behalf of Clement Vallandigham, a peace Democrat and former Congressman from that state who had been sentenced to life imprisonment by a military commission in Ohio for violating an order by the commanding general of the district not to counsel obstruction to the draft. Lincoln's reply to the committee was open to the interpretation that he believed he had the authority to suspend other constitutional liberties, in addition to habeas corpus, in cases of rebellion or invasion. In response to Lincoln's letter, the *New York Daily News* charged, "Mr. Lincoln now proclaims that there is no law, no requirement of the Constitution, no guaranteed right of citizens, which is not set aside by his higher prerogatives as Commander-in-Chief of the Army and Navy, and that his own will and pleasure—what he may think 'the public safety requires'—is the only rule and guide by which the country is to be piloted until the civil war shall end. He claims, in fact, the same despotic power of life, death and liberty, over every individual in the country, which the 'Committees of Public Safety' exercised under Robespierre's Reign of Terror, during the French Revolution."[41]

In his letter to the Ohio committee, Lincoln offered justification for the imprisonments under suspensions of habeas corpus: "The military arrests and detentions which have been made . . . have been for *prevention,* and not for *punishment,* as injunctions to stay injury—as proceedings to keep the peace—and hence, like proceedings in such cases, and for like reasons, they have not been accompanied with indictments, or trials by jury, nor, in a single case, by any punishment whatever beyond what is purely incidental to the prevention."[42] From our perspective, with indeterminate detentions, trial by military commission, and denial of habeas corpus for detainees once more contentious issues, Lincoln's reasoning is not entirely convincing. In his own time, Lincoln's suspension of habeas corpus in the early days of the war was ruled unconstitutional, absent the concurrence of Congress, in a circuit court opinion written by Chief Justice Roger Taney.[43] Lincoln ignored Taney's ruling but subsequently obtained congressional approval, given after the fact, and with misgivings, for all such suspensions, for the duration of the war, when in his opinion the public safety required them.

In November of 1864, Lincoln was resoundingly reelected. The *New York Daily News* accepted the result and offered this hope for the president's second term: "From this day forward let there be an end to arbitrary arrests, to military dictatorship, to the policy of menace and intimidation that has long prevailed. The new term cannot be more conspicuously inaugurated than by a full restoration to all the States under the Federal authority of all the rights and privileges guaranteed to them by the Constitution. Habeas corpus, trial by jury, a free press, free speech, full enjoyment of liberty of conscience—let these never again be ignored or violated by the President re-elect or his subordinates."[44]

Benjamin Wood's articulate editorials stand as resilient examples of the free press insisting on its own rights, and the rights of others, during a war in which the federal government resorted to unprecedented means to suppress opposition in speech and in the press. Abraham Lincoln abolished slavery and preserved the Union. His government permitted many attacks on its conduct of the war and on the measures it took in the interests of "public safety" to be printed without hindrance. Repressive measures against the press were relaxed as Union victory became more certain. But in the early days of the war, Lincoln extended the reach of executive power and sought congressional approval only later, almost as an afterthought. Under his administration, opposition newspapers were denied the use of the mails, seized by federal marshals, intimidated and shut down (the *New York Day Book,* suppressed at the same time as the *Daily News,* never resumed publication). Citizens who spoke against the administration were arrested by the thousands and imprisoned without charge, with no recourse to the courts. Encroachments on liberties enumerated in the Bill of Rights were more widespread during Lincoln's administration than at any time since the Alien and Sedition Acts were in force at the turn of the nineteenth century. The Lincoln government was supported in these efforts by leading members of the press, including Horace Greeley's *New York Tribune,* which advocated martial law in northern cities, the "wholesale" hanging of traitors and the suppression of opposition newspapers.

Benjamin Wood's tolerance for Southern slavery makes it difficult for us to appreciate his achievement in opposing these abuses. We consider slavery an abomination. In the mid-nineteenth century, while many nations had outlawed the trade in slaves, human slavery was still widely practiced. Even then many Americans viewed it as an abomination, but to many others the idea that the institution could be abolished by war, by legislation, or by a stroke of the presidential pen was dangerously radical, even revolutionary. By branding Benjamin Wood a proslavery Copperhead, the victors' history of the Civil War has diminished him and his important efforts to defend freedom of the press and other civil liberties in wartime. To put aside history's judgment and to read Wood's editorials is to recognize that he tenaciously and often eloquently supported the Constitution and the liberties it was created to protect.

In 1866, the U.S. Supreme Court vindicated some of Wood's accusations against the Lincoln administration in a decision that set a new standard for imposing martial law. Lamdin P. Milligan had been one of five men arrested by military authorities in Indiana in 1864, charged with conspiring to steal federal weapons and to release Confederate prisoners at a prisoner-of-war camp in Illinois, and elsewhere. The five were tried before a military court and were sentenced to hang. Appeals to federal court delayed execution of the sentence. In 1866, Milligan was freed by the Supreme Court, which ruled in his case that martial law could not be imposed far from the field of battle, nor could civilians be tried by military tribunal where the civilian courts were still functioning. The opinion of the Court delivered a stinging rebuke to Abraham Lincoln, post mortem: "The Constitution of the United States is a law for rulers and people, equally in war and in peace, and covers with the shield of its protection all classes of men, at all times and under all circumstances. No doctrine involving more pernicious consequences was ever invented by the wit of man than that any of its provisions can be suspended during any of the great exigencies of government. Such a doctrine leads directly to anarchy or despotism, but the theory of necessity on which it is based is false, for the government, within the Constitution, has all the powers granted to it which are necessary to preserve its existence, as has been happily proved by the result of the great effort to throw off its just authority."[45] That is, by the recently concluded civil war.

Benjamin Wood may have taken some pleasure in publishing the Court's ruling in the *Daily News,* which he continued to edit until shortly before his death in 1900.

4

REMEMBER THE *MAINE*

The Spanish-American War and the Philippine Insurrection (1898–1902)

In the closing years of the nineteenth century, with Spain's empire in decline and all of her conquests in the New World except one having long since become independent republics, continued Spanish rule of Cuba was for the United States a vexing anachronism. The U.S. had considered buying the island from Spain in 1854, but the plan was scuttled by Northern fears that it was a scheme to extend slavery. Americans were sympathetic when Cubans revolted against Spanish rule in 1868, but it was too soon after America's Civil War to muster support for armed intervention on the rebels' behalf. The revolt continued for ten years, until 1878, when Spain promised reforms. Royal officials soon lapsed in implementing those promises, and the Cubans' impulse for independence grew stronger. By 1895, when insurgent forces again rose against the Spaniards, Americans had $50 million invested in the island and twice that in annual trade, mainly in sugar and tobacco. The revolution threatened American investments and reduced trade, but American sympathies were with the insurgents. These feelings grew stronger when Spain took harsh measures against the civilian population, herding them into "reconcentration" areas without adequate shelter, food or sanitation, where more than half died of starvation and disease. The American press gave full play to the atrocities committed by the Spanish, and sensationalist journals fanned war fever.

In 1897, Spain announced that the reconcentration camps would be abandoned, and that Cubans would be given more autonomy in their own affairs, but it was too little, too late. The rebels were demanding independence for Cuba, and Americans were running guns to the insurgents, evading the U.S. Navy's efforts to interdict them. President William McKinley, a Republican, was no more willing to intervene in Cuba than his Democratic predecessor, Grover Cleveland, had been, but riots in Havana in December 1897 prompted McKinley to send the U.S. battleship *Maine* to Havana harbor to protect American citizens and property. In Congress, pressure to aid the cause of Cuban independence was mounting.

When American newspapers printed a letter written by the Spanish ambassador to Washington that described McKinley as "weak and catering to the rabble, and, besides, a low politician,"[1] the resulting furor further inflamed American public opinion and forced Spain to recall the indiscreet minister. A week later, on February 15, 1898, the *Maine* exploded and sank in Havana harbor with the loss of more than two hundred and fifty of her crew.

⌒

Within 48 hours of the sinking of the *Maine,* the *New York Evening Post* reported that the McKinley administration had convened a court of inquiry made up of senior naval officers, and that Secretary of the Navy John D. Long was convinced "that the Disaster Was Not Due to Design." The *Evening Post* regarded "the appalling loss of the Maine" as a test of national character: "All the antecedent circumstances were of a sort to make one dread a wild outburst of blind rage in Washington and throughout the country; but happily the event has disappointed both those who dreaded and those who desired and labored for such an outbreak." Addressing the suspicions, voiced in many quarters, that Spain was responsible, the *Evening Post* found the idea preposterous: "It is simply inconceivable that the Spanish authorities in Cuba, high or low, could have countenanced any plot to destroy the Maine. Make them out as wicked as you please, they are not lunatics; and official connivance in torpedoing the Maine, or in firing a mine under her, would have been an act

of madness far more fatal to Spain than it could possibly be to this country." The *Post* approved the restraint shown by the McKinley administration, and added, referring to those who were quick to pound the drums of
war, "despite the Jingoes, it is better to have foreign nations admire us
than dread us, better to be conscious of strength of character than strength
of muscle."[2]

From the outset, President McKinley worked to check hot-tempered
reactions, but his calming efforts were countered by two of the nation's
most influential newspapers. The *New York Journal,* one of those that had
"desired and labored for such an outbreak" of bellicose feeling against
Spain, responded to the *Maine*'s sinking with blaring headlines and published a succession of extras throughout the first day. "CRISIS IS AT
HAND," and "GROWING BELIEF IN SPANISH TREACHERY," an-
nounced "Extra No. 9."[3] The *Journal* reported that the departing Spanish
ambassador had declared, regarding the explosion aboard the *Maine,* "No
Spaniard did that!" To which the *Journal* responded, "For the sake of
Spain it is to be hoped that no Spaniard did do it. . . . Until further facts
are known we are bound to accept the accident theory."[4]

This modicum of restraint didn't last the night. The next day, the
Journal trumpeted, "DESTRUCTION OF THE WAR SHIP MAINE
WAS THE WORK OF AN ENEMY," over an announcement that Assistant Secretary of the Navy Theodore Roosevelt was "Convinced the Explosion of the War Ship Was Not an Accident."[5] A later edition claimed
that the *Maine*'s commander, Captain Sigsbee, "KNEW A TORPEDO
DID IT," but that "He Was Forced to Be Silent, Much Against His Will
by Navy Department."[6]

Few of these pronouncements represented balanced, or even considered opinion. The *New York Journal* was influential not because of its integrity but, in the manner of James Gordon Bennett's *Herald* a
half-century earlier, from the brash insistence of its visual style, its
overblown reporting, and its wide circulation. In the week after the sinking of the *Maine,* the *Journal* set a new record by selling a million copies
a day. It was one of two newspapers owned by William Randolph
Hearst, a young San Francisco publisher who had bought the *Journal* in
1895. Hearst had taken control of his other paper, the *San Francisco Examiner,* in 1887, when he was twenty-four years old. On the day the
Maine story broke, the *Examiner* reported that a telegram from Captain

Sigsbee included a plea that "Public opinion should be suspended until further report." The *Examiner* cautioned that the news of the *Maine* disaster was "apt to stir a feeling of anger, and quick public opinion will attribute it to the malevolence of the Spaniards. Captain Sigsbee asks that the American people be patient until an investigation can be made, and his suggestion is most wise."[7]

In the *Journal*, such qualifications were hard to find after the first day's issues. The top-selling *Journal* was in head-to-head competition with the second-place *New York World*, now published and edited by Joseph Pulitzer, a Hungarian immigrant and Civil War veteran who had merged two St. Louis papers to create the *St. Louis Post-Dispatch* before coming to New York, where he bought the *World* in 1883. The *World* and Hearst's *Journal* employed banner headlines and vivid illustrations liberally. They printed sensational stories of murders, crime and scandal in a fierce competition for readers. A dispute over a comic strip, "The Yellow Kid," had resulted in both papers running the strip, drawn by different artists. This comic-strip war led to the coining of the term "yellow journalism" for the style of the *Journal* and the *World*.

The *World's* first reaction to the sinking of the *Maine* was marginally more restrained than the *Journal's*. It reported, "Cause of Explosion Unknown," and "Capt. Sigsbee Wires 'Suspend Judgment'" on the front pages of succeeding editions on February 16. The next day, the *World* puffed up its coverage to match Hearst's, with a headline. "MAINE EXPLOSION CAUSED BY BOMB OR TORPEDO." Pulitzer did not want Hearst's reporting of the Cuban crisis to overshadow his own, but he was somewhat more objective in his editorial positions, while Hearst led the charge to war.

On February 17, the *Journal* attacked President McKinley for tolerating Spanish insults and the atrocities in Cuba too long. "Mr. McKinley MUST feel that he is responsible for this great calamity. He MUST realize that in shirking his duty as the guardian of the Nation's honor he has indirectly brought about this catastrophe," the paper wrote. It warned that McKinley could not ignore the fate of the *Maine:* "It seems to us that MUST have some effect. There MUST be a limit to our willingness to submit. There MUST remain somewhere in us some slight touch of the spirit that threw the tea overboard and welcomed a fight with a power that seemed bound inevitably to annihilate us."[8]

By the following day, the third since the *Maine* blew up, the *Journal* was openly calling for war: "There is nothing complicated about our national attitude. We ought to fight. As a nation we are ready and anxious for war. But we shall probably not have it if we can possibly persuade Spain to let us alone. Why?" Chiefly, the *Journal* believed, because William McKinley and the Republican party were in the pocket of big capital. The capitalists feared war, the *Journal* wrote, because "war would mean a drop in the price of all stocks, and in this blessed land stocks are more important than national honor."[9]

This sort of jingoistic propaganda infuriated E. L. Godkin, editor of the *New York Evening Post.* For Godkin, journalism was an almost sacred responsibility. Born in Ireland, Godkin had come to the United States after covering the Crimean War for the *London Daily News.* He had founded *The Nation* and made it the most respected weekly in America before selling it to the owner of the *Evening Post,* of which Godkin became an editor, then editor in chief. Within a year of taking the helm, in 1883, Godkin had disassociated the *Post* with the Republican party, which it had championed since the party was founded, and thereafter it maintained a position of political independence. Godkin could be scathing in his criticism of politicians up to and including the president, but the topic on which Godkin gave the fullest vent to his indignation was the yellow press. When Hearst and Pulitzer raised the cry for war with Spain, Godkin let his Irish temper show: "Our cheap press to-day speaks in tones never before heard out of Paris," he wrote. "It urges upon ignorant people schemes more savage, disregard of either policy, or justice, or experience more complete, than the modern world has witnessed since the French Revolution."[10]

The agitations in the press continued while President McKinley tried to defuse the crisis diplomatically. In March, Vermont's Redfield Proctor, a well-respected Republican senator who had been secretary of war for two years in Grover Cleveland's Democratic administration, went to Cuba to see the state of things for himself. While Proctor was still on the island, the *New York World* reported, "Senator Proctor Says He Visited Four Provinces, Consulted All Classes, and Found Everywhere Suffering, Starvation and Death."[11] Proctor related his findings to the Senate on March 17 in a rigorously unsensational account that did much to convince even those who rejected the alarums of the yellow press that the situation in

Cuba was intolerable. The *Wall Street Journal* reported, "Senator Proctor's speech converted a great many people in Wall street, who have heretofore taken the ground that the United States had no business to interfere in a revolution on Spanish soil."[12]

On March 28, the *New York Evening Post* published the report from the naval board of inquiry, which found that the loss of the *Maine* was not due to any negligence on the part of the ship's officers or crew, and that, in the opinion of the court, "the Maine was destroyed by the explosion of a submarine mine," which detonated her forward magazines. The report concluded, "The court has been unable to obtain evidence fixing the responsibility for the destruction of the Maine on any person or persons." The *Evening Post* observed that Washington had remained calm since the release of the report. In Godkin's view, because no evidence had been found to place responsibility for the loss of the *Maine* on any foreign agent, "Therefore the honor of the nation is not touched."[13]

The same day's newspapers reported that President McKinley had sent Spain a message proposing it announce an armistice with the Cuban insurgents, release the *reconcentrados,* and accept his good office to negotiate a lasting peace. Hearst's *New York Journal* accused McKinley of offering a "Shameful Deal" that sought "Peace with Dishonor." The *Journal* scornfully characterized the president's underlying message as, "First—We will say nothing about the Maine murders just at present. Let the dead sailors rot under water while the stock market rallies. Later, when it is half forgotten, settle the murders on a genuine McKinley cash basis." The *Journal* demanded, "Was anything more shameful ever proposed in any country? . . . What shameful cowards in charge of the Government! What a punishment for the people that chose a bought, bankrupt man for President!"[14]

Spain dithered, then announced an armistice with the Cuban insurgents, but the momentum to war in the U.S. Congress was by now irresistible, and the Cuban rebels would accept nothing less than independence. On April 11, in his annual message on the state of the union, President McKinley asked Congress for authority "to secure a full and final end to hostilities" between Spain and the insurgents, to establish a stable government on the island, "and to use the military and Naval forces of the United States as may be necessary for these purposes." He did not, however, propose to recognize Cuba's independence or to expel Spanish forces from the island.[15]

In the *San Francisco Examiner,* under a banner, "THE NATION LOOKS TO CONGRESS TO SAVE THE NATION'S HONOR," a front-page article by former Kansas Senator John J. Ingalls pointed out that the only line in the president's speech that drew applause from McKinley's listeners was "the war in Cuba must stop." Beyond that, Ingalls wrote, "there is no other phrase in the whole document that has any snap, powder or electricity in it." In one editorial, the *Examiner* declared, "The President has sounded the retreat. It is plainly not the duty of Americans to follow him." In another it charged, "The President has recognized the facts but he has had the weakness to shrink from recommending the remedy. It depends on Congress to follow the facts to their logical conclusion."[16]

Congress, feeling the pressure for war from the public and the press, stepped up to its duty. It passed resolutions declaring Cuba to be free and demanding that Spain withdraw its forces. Spain severed diplomatic relations. On April 24, Spain declared war on the United States. Congress reciprocated the following day.

News of the American declaration of war reached Rear Admiral George Dewey, commander of the U.S. Navy's Asiatic squadron, in Hong Kong within hours of the vote in Congress. (By 1898, more than 150,000 miles of communication cables had been laid on the ocean floors; almost a century before the Internet, it was already a wired world.) The Philippine archipelago had been a Spanish colonial possession since the sixteenth century. Spain's Pacific fleet was based at Manila, the capital and the principal city on the large northern island of Luzon. The *New York Times* calculated that even if Dewey's ships steamed at a "leisurely pace" of eight knots to conserve coal, they could reach Manila, "hardly 500 nautical miles" distant, in a few days. "The primary military object of the mission," the *Times* wrote, "must be to neutralize the Spanish squadron which has its station at Manila. If that squadron were left free to act it would naturally proceed to prey upon American commerce in the whole western half of the Pacific."[17]

On Monday, May 2, 1898, Americans awoke to headlines announcing that Dewey's fleet had entered Manila Bay before sunrise the day before and, as the light brightened, proceeded to destroy Spain's Pacific armada, at the cost of eight American sailors wounded. "DEWEY SMASHES SPAIN'S FLEET," the *World* announced. The *New York Journal* printed a single word across the top of the front page in enormous type: "SUR-RENDERS!" In San Francisco, the *Examiner* headlined the story "DEWEY SINKS AND BURNS SHIPS OF SPAIN," and in a subhead called the battle "The Second Trafalgar." The *New York Evening Post* headed the first column of the front page "SPAIN'S FLEET ANNIHI-LATED," and filled all seven columns with dense text on the Dewey's tri-umph and related stories.[18]

The declarations of war had united the American press. The *Evening Post* had supported McKinley's measured diplomacy after the sinking of the *Maine* and had argued against war as a remedy for the problems in Cuba, but once war began, the *Post* extolled the heroes and supported the American forces as steadfastly, although far less flamboyantly in print, as the *Journal* and the *World*.

Dewey's victory at Manila raised a question that the *Journal* addressed on an inside page of the May 2 edition: "PHILIPPINES OURS, WHAT WILL WE DO WITH THEM?" The *Journal* considered that the United States might cede the islands to Great Britain, but decided this was certain to bring protests from Germany, France and Russia, the other naval pow-ers in the western Pacific. The *World* suggested that the islands "can be held as security for our war indemnity. Japan or Germany would be glad to buy them."[19] In the view of the *Evening Post,* "We could hardly acquire them, as conquest, after the declaration we have made of our motives in beginning the war."[20] The declaration the *Post* had in mind was Congress's joint resolution of April 20, declaring Cuba independent of Spain, which had proclaimed "That the United States hereby disclaims any disposition or intention to exercise sovereignty, jurisdiction, or control over said Is-land except for the pacification thereof." The *Post* reminded its readers that President McKinley had issued a message in December, in which he declared, as the *Post* summarized it, "that forcible annexation was not to be thought of; that by our morality it would be criminal aggression." These statements concerned the future of Cuba, but the *Post* regarded them as equally binding in regard to the Philippines. In the *Post*'s view, "if we are to regard our honor we have no choice in the matter."[21]

In the weeks following the battle at Manila, the press reported on plans to send troops to Cuba, speculated on the whereabouts of Spain's Atlantic fleet, which had departed the Cape Verde Islands, off the east coast of Africa, when war was declared, and followed the formation of a regiment of "cow-boy cavalry," which became known by the name of its second in command, Theodore Roosevelt, who resigned from his position at the Navy Department to get into the fray.

The Navy found the Spanish fleet off Santiago de Cuba in late May. The American commander, Admiral William Sampson, feigned a withdrawal and then blockaded the port when the Spanish ships entered the bay.

While the attention of the United States was on Cuba, and before the first American forces arrived in the Philippines, Filipino insurgents who had been fighting against the Spanish under the leadership of Emilio Aguinaldo since 1896 declared the archipelago independent of Spain and proclaimed a provisional republic with Aguinaldo its president. Word of the declaration was not well reported in the United States until the third week of June. In the meantime, on June 15, the House of Representatives voted by a large majority in favor of annexing the Hawaiian Islands, a mid-Pacific outpost that was an important naval station for American ships, and where, as in Cuba, Americans had substantial investments in sugar. Annexation of Hawaii had been discussed and negotiated for more than fifty years; the time for the United States to complete its acquisition of the islands seemed to be at hand.

In the House vote, the *Evening Post* saw a larger design: "Hawaiian annexation, for which the House voted so strongly yesterday, is now admitted by both its friends and foes to be but a letting out of the waters. If we take Hawaii, we take the Philippines. Once hoisted over those, our flag is then to fly over the Caroline Islands, and, of course, the very name of the Ladrones ("robber" islands)[22] will impel us to take them next." The *Evening Post* considered any such intentions to be "a momentous change in policy," and warned that choosing the imperial course held particular dangers for the United States: "That is the great peril to which we are exposed in going forward on the path of conquest—the peril that we shall have to eat all our fine words in favor of freedom and self-government."[23] The *Post* charged "Republican managers" and the *New York Tribune,* which the paper regarded as McKinley's organ, with plotting to take hold of "every island that may be seized or conquered or bought in the seven seas. . . . The first taste of military glory, the first sip of national adventurousness in unknown seas, has maddened them, and they are now ready to run the whole course of the debauch. . . . Thus are Republican leaders planning to drag all our humanitarian motives in the dirt, and hold us up to the world as a nation devoured by unscrupulous greed and unblush-ingly avowing our hypocrisy."[24]

"Roosevelt's Rough Riders" and other units of the U.S. Army landed on the southern coast of Cuba in the third week of June. (The Marines had gone ashore on June 10, at Guantánamo Bay.) Within days, the Americans were fighting at El Caney and Kettle Hill and San Juan Hill as they advanced on Santiago. With American ground forces nearing the city, the Spanish admiral preferred to take his chances at sea. On July 3, the Spanish fleet left the harbor and was annihilated by the U.S. Navy's North Atlantic Squadron and "Flying Squadron" as thoroughly as Dewey had dealt with the Spaniards at Manila.

This second naval victory effectively decided the Spanish-American War in favor of the United States. Santiago surrendered to American troops on July 17. Within days, Spain requested terms of surrender. In just eleven weeks from the reports of the first ship's guns in Manila Bay on May 1, the United States had put to an inglorious end the four-hundred-year history of the Spanish Empire, and it could no longer put off the question of whether to acquire an empire of its own.

The *New York Times* declared that Spain must withdraw from the Western hemisphere. (The *Times*, nearly moribund in 1896, had been bought that year by Adolph S. Ochs; by 1898 Ochs had won new respect for the long-established name.) "This is our 'sine non qua,'" the *Times* said. "Outside of this there is nothing which cannot be made the subject of negotiation." Well, perhaps there was. "We could not, after beginning the conquest of the Philippines, agree to render them back to Spain." In the *Times*'s view, the United States had entered "perhaps not into express, but at least into implied, obligations to the representatives of the natives of the Philippines, which we cannot disown." The representatives of the natives might have taken issue with this interpretation, but the *Times* con-sidered the abilities of Filipinos to act in their own behalf limited. Aguinaldo, in the *Times*'s judgment, "is a precocious child of nature. Few of his compatriots are abreast of him. A very large part of the people of the island have not now, and perhaps never will have, any capacity for govern-ing themselves." The Filipinos might be admitted to participation in local government, the *Times* thought, as the Czar admitted Russian peasants to village councils, but "The mistake of inviting either the Filipinos or the Cubans to enjoy at once the blessings of universal suffrage we shall not, of course, commit. We did make the mistake of giving the ballot to the negroes at the close of our civil war, and it has proved a costly mistake for the blacks and for the country."[25]

At the end of the nineteenth century, the *Times*'s attitude reflected the deeply rooted racism that pervaded every level of Western society and underlay the policies of all the imperial powers. Not even those who advocated the rights of the dark-skinned races considered them to be inherently equal. Assumptions about the inferiority of those peoples were as much a part of the *Evening Post*'s mind-set as that of the *Times*. In an editorial before the declaration of war with Spain, the *Post* had spelled out its position on what constituted a just and necessary war: "If anybody cares to know our idea of a 'just and necessary' war, we admit freely that a war of a civilized nation against a barbarous one is nearly always just and necessary." The *Post* approved Russia's war against the Turks and the British conquests of India and Egypt as praiseworthy efforts "to roll back the tide of Oriental barbarism" that had overwhelmed the Roman Empire.[26] After three hundred and fifty years of harsh conversions by Spanish priests, the people of the Philippines were mostly Catholics—except for some Muslims on the southern islands—but they were not white Christians and were not expected to have the same capacities for politics and government.

These largely unexamined racial assumptions played an important role in deciding American policy toward the Philippines. The more explicit arguments in favor of keeping the islands were commercial: with Hawaii in mid-Pacific and the Philippines on the doorstep of Asia, the United States would greatly extend its influence and would be in a much stronger position to maintain and increase its trade with China. And the Philippines themselves seemed ripe for exploitation. The *Evening Post* of July 14 published a dispatch from a correspondent aboard the flagship of an American fleet carrying troops to Manila, who reported that "nearly every one on board with whom I have talked, either expects to get a permanent position in the Philippines after the war is over or intends to go into business there. Not one of them doubts that the islands will be kept by the United States, and many men have enlisted simply to be on the spot when the 'boom' in Manila real estate begins. What America was to the Spaniards three centuries ago the Philippines are now to these men—a land of gold."

An armistice protocol ending the war with Spain was signed at the White House on August 12, 1898. (On the same day, sovereignty over the Hawaiian Islands was formally transferred to the United States.) Negotiation of the final treaty terms would take place at Paris, commencing no later than the first day of October. Until then, the question of territories to be freed, traded or acquired was deferred. Hearst's *New York Journal* celebrated the armistice by declaring, "We have risen above the cramping traditions of our national infancy and have learned to survey the whole round earth without blinking. We have studied geography, and have discovered that our flag looks as well flying over distant islands to whose rescued people it is the emblem of their salvation as it does over J. Pierpont Morgan's office in Wall Street. Welcome to peace, but hail to the glorious war that has brought it."[27] As the *Evening Post* feared, "the first sip of national adventurousness in unknown seas" had awakened a vision of the next westward leap for Manifest Destiny.

In the war with Spain, Pulitzer had kept the *World* a few paces to the left of Hearst, while matching him headline-for-headline and illustration-for-illustration in coverage of the fighting on sea and land. On August 16, Pulitzer parted company with Hearst in an editorial about whom President McKinley might appoint to the peace commission that would negotiate the final treaty with Spain. The *World* took to task an unnamed but easily-identified competitor, "A rabid by-jingo journal," that had insulted McKinley by admonishing him to appoint peace commissioners who wanted to keep the Philippines. "In the first place," the *World* declared, "we do not hold the Philippines, in the next place we do not want them."[28]

With Spain ejected from the Western hemisphere, Hearst best revealed his vision of America's new Pacific imperium from his home in San Francisco. Gazing westward from the Pacific shore, the *Examiner* covered each development in unfailingly positive terms: "Spain Comes As a Beggar For Peace" on July 27. "Hawaii Hears the Great News of Her Annexation; Welcomes it With Great Joy," on the 28th. (A subhead sniffed, "Native Element Alone Refuses to Join in the Rejoicing.") "Merritt Rules the Philippines" on the 30th, five days after General Wesley Merritt and his troops had disembarked and two weeks before Merritt took Manila. On August 13, when Merritt finally secured the city after fierce fighting against the Spanish, who did not know the war was over, the *Examiner* reprinted, in a box top-center on the editorial page, a cable that Hearst had sent to the paper from Cuba (where he had gone to report for his own newspapers), near Santiago—after the land battles at Kettle Hill and San Juan Hill, but before the naval victory—in which Hearst declared that "every officer and every private in the American forces on land and sea hopes that no peace may be granted until the American flag is nailed to the flagstaffs of Porto Rico and the Philippines—NOT SIMPLY HOISTED THERE, BUT NAILED."

With Manila full of Americans, Emilio Aguinaldo took his provisional government and established a new capital at Malolos, fifteen miles distant, where he convened an assembly that ratified a constitution for the Philippines. The United States did not recognize the legitimacy of either action. Spain, feeling the wounds inflicted by the U.S. Navy sufficiently healed, announced in the negotiations at Paris that she would prefer to keep the Philippines. On November 17, the *Evening Post* reported that "Spain maintained the absolute recognition by the protocol of her sovereignty over the Philippines." With no military forces anywhere that she could bring to bear on the United States, this was a futile assertion. What was worse for the Spaniards, since the sinking of the *Maine,* William McKinley had been seduced by the siren song of empire. The president had been a reluctant warrior at first, but after Spain was vanquished he resolved, after much soul searching, in which he "prayed Almighty God for light and guidance," that the United States could not retreat from what it had gained by force of arms.[29] The *Evening Post* reported McKinley's reply to the Spanish under the headline, "Entire Philippine Group Demanded—Twenty Million Dollars Offered in Return."[30]

The *Times* gave front-page prominence to the view of Republican Senator George F. Hoar of Massachusetts, the foremost anti-imperialist in the Senate, that the Filipinos should be allowed to govern themselves: "My opinion," said Hoar, "is that if the United States acquires the Philippine Islands, to govern them as a subject or vassal state, the destruction of the American Republic will date from the Administration of William McKinley."[31]

Like Hoar, E. L. Godkin was appalled by McKinley's demand. In a *Post* editorial he traced the expansion of executive power since George Washington and accused McKinley of treading dangerous ground: "Jefferson and Jackson and Lincoln asserted the Presidential prerogative in startling and almost revolutionary ways, but none of them moved to their ends with so sheer an assumption of naked, arbitrary power as that displayed by Mr. McKinley in the present year of grace. Saying nothing now about the initiation and prosecution of the war, his action in dictating terms of peace has condensed into his own person the exercise of the whole national sovereignty in a way which would not be possible in the case of any other ruler except the Czar."[32] Thereafter, Godkin was relentless in his condemnation of McKinley's decision to launch the United States on the course of empire, alternating bitter lectures with others, no less biting, expressed satirically and with caustic humor, as in an editorial on December 1, 1898: "Suppose a man who has wasted and embezzled two estates were to apply to us for the management of another, we should at once inquire how he had managed the other two and then tell him we could not comply with his request. . . . In like manner, when the United States ask us to support them in taking charge of 10,000,000 or 12,000,000 of people, mainly ignorant colored barbarians, we, if prudent men, ask at once: How did you succeed with the last colored barbarians you had charge of? . . . The truth is, the United States have made a bad character of governing inferior races, and it will never be any better until we have governed some inferior race decently."

The Treaty of Paris, ending the Spanish-American War, was signed on December 10, 1898. In addition to the Philippines, the United States acquired Puerto Rico, which had been taken by American troops in late July, and Guam in the Ladrones (Marianas). Hearst's *Examiner* greeted the news by urging the immediate establishment of a steamship line between San Francisco and the Philippines for the economic benefit of California, but Hearst's enthusiasm for ruling Filipinos against their will did not match the pugnacious attitude he had brought to the war with Spain. "To profess to carry liberty among them as a gift from a great and benignant republic and then mow them down with machine guns should they venture to differ with us warmly on what is and is not good for them, would hardly meet with the approval of the American people," an *Examiner* reporter opined in a news column. "Besides, there is a well-armed Filipino army of between 30,000 and 40,000 men."[33] Later in the week, the *New York Journal* editorialized, "What we must avoid is any attempt at imperialism. We want no foreign colonies to be plundered by the President's favorites; to be ruled by statesmen's incompetent sons. We want our new colonies to be taught to govern themselves. That is a continuation of American policy which has won its way from Manhattan Island to the Klondike."[34]

The misgivings of the foremost propagandist for war with Spain did not sway the McKinley administration from its determination to proceed with what the president called in a proclamation to the Filipinos the "benevolent assimilation" of the Philippine Islands and their inhabitants. In the archipelago, relations between the American forces and the Filipinos were increasingly fraught, but this news came to the United States circuitously, by way of Hong Kong and European capitals. The U.S. Army command had imposed strict censorship on news dispatches from Manila, hampering the ability of American papers to report accurately on the tensions there.

In January 1899, the Filipino assembly proclaimed the Malolos constitution the governing instrument of the Philippines, formalizing the establishment of the Philippine republic. The U.S. Senate was scheduled to vote on February 6 to ratify the Treaty of Paris. Over their breakfasts on that date, the senators read in the morning newspapers that fighting between Filipinos and American troops had broken out in Manila on the evening of February 4 when an American sentry shot and killed a Filipino who appeared to have taunted the sentry deliberately.[35] The conflict had continued through the night, inflicting some two hundred casualties on the Americans, including twenty or more killed. Filipino casualties were heavy. Some American newspapers speculated that the insurgents had planned the action in the hope of influencing the Senate against ratifying the treaty. If that was in fact their hope, it failed. The Senate approved ratification by 57 to 27, one vote more than the necessary two-thirds in favor.

At the *Evening Post,* E. L. Godkin took the view that the fighting in Manila had "brought about" the vote in the Senate. He protested that the "vigorous censorship" of news reports from Manila had left Americans dependent on military dispatches, which "led us to believe that the Filipinos were quieting down and acquiescing in our rule." It appeared, Godkin wrote, "that the American people were as ill-informed about the Filipinos as the Filipinos about us," and he feared that if Spain's experience in the Philippines was any guide, "this war may last long."[36] The *World* branded the news from Manila "deplorable," and seconded Godkin's protest against the military censorship that had left us "suddenly, without warning, face to face with the actualities of empire. It is no longer possible to sugar it with bland phrases like 'benevolent assimilation.' To rule, we must conquer. To conquer, we must kill and must get used to hearing of the killing of our soldiers."[37]

In set-piece battles, Aguinaldo's forces were no match for the Americans. The Filipino capital, Malolos, fell on March 30, or rather it was occupied by American troops on that date, the insurgents having evacuated the city before the Americans entered it. The achievement produced no celebrations in the United States like those that followed news from Manila and San Juan Hill the year before. The *Evening Post* saw this as evidence that the American people felt for the Philippine war none of the enthusiasm they had demonstrated for the war with Spain. "To-day the returns from fighting quite as serious fall upon the War Department with a dull and sombre thud, and in this respect the Department is doubtless representative of the American people," the *Post* reported. "They have no heart in the Philippine war. It is contrary to the genius of their institutions."[38]

Aguinaldo had said that he would surrender if Malolos was taken, but he evidently thought better of it and retreated with his army. The insurgents established a new capital at Tarlac, some seventy miles north of Manila, while the McKinley government dispatched reinforcements to the Philippines.

The war was taking its toll on E. L. Godkin. In May 1899 he wrote to a friend, "American ideals were the intellectual food of my youth, and to see America converted into a senseless, Old World conqueror, embittered my age."[39] Godkin was sixty-seven, and his health was failing. He went to Europe for a rest, consulted French doctors, and decided that he would retire from the *Evening Post* on January 1, 1900. Horace White, who had been at the *Post* as long as Godkin, was already writing the editorials while Godkin was abroad, but readers would never have guessed that the editorial pen had passed to another hand. On June 15, 1899, White demanded to know, "Why should we have had to fight these brave Filipinos at all? The conviction is deepening on all sides that the whole thing was a hideous blunder . . . A little tact, a little grace, a little common sense in the orders from Washington, a less high and mighty tone on the part of our President . . . and all the bloodshed and bitterness might have been avoided. . . . If there is anything which deserves to be branded as 'un-American,' it is this ignoble war by which every true American feels himself and his country disgraced."[40] (With the substitution of "Iraqis" for "Filipinos," White's comment might have been written in June of 2004.)

One American who did not feel his country disgraced by the Philippine campaign was Senator Albert J. Beveridge, a young Republican from Indiana. Beveridge had entered the Senate in March 1899 and traveled to the Philippines later in the year to study the situation for himself. Already a noted orator in the style of the times, Beveridge gave his maiden Senate speech on January 9, 1900, in support of a resolution he had introduced, which declared that the United States intended to keep and govern the Philippine Islands. The speech was one of the most fervent expressions of Manifest Destiny ever made. "The Philippines are ours forever, 'territory belonging to the United States,' as the Constitution calls them," Beveridge proclaimed to his fellow senators and to the visitors jamming the galleries. "And just beyond the Philippines are China's illimitable markets. . . . We will not abandon our opportunity in the Orient. We will not renounce our part in the mission of our race, trustee, under God, of the civilization of the world. . . . God has not been preparing the English-speaking and Teutonic peoples for a thousand years for nothing but vain and idle self-contemplation and self-admiration. No! He has made us the master organizers of the world to establish system where chaos reigns. . . . And of all our race He has marked the American people as His chosen nation to finally lead in the regeneration of the world. This is the divine mission of America, and it holds for us all the profit, all the glory, all the happiness possible to man. We are trustees of the world's progress, guardians of its righteous peace."[41]

Beveridge's speech was reported on front pages across the nation. Many papers offered editorial praise, but some refused to join the chorus. The *Hartford Courant,* a leading New England paper, mused, "It's rather a pity that Mr. Beveridge did not give some elderly and judicious friend the chance to take his speech in hand and squeeze all the Columbian oratory out of it." The *Boston Globe* was one of several newspapers that reported the reply of Senator Hoar of Massachusetts, who noted that "The words 'right,' 'justice,' 'duty' and 'freedom' were absent from the eloquent address."[42]

These rebuttals aside, the emotional and mostly favorable response to Beveridge's speech suggested that however much Americans might regret the Philippine war, the urge to extend America's reach across the Pacific was strong.

In recent months, the war had undergone a change whose importance was not recognized for some time to come. The Americans had reached Tarlac, the insurgents' fall-back capital, in mid-November 1899. Once again, Aguinaldo and his men withdrew before the Americans arrived. This time they did not reappear. The insurgents established no new base for Aguinaldo's government and no longer challenged the Americans in open combat. Instead they appeared and disappeared, drawing the Americans into the jungle where they had to contend with malaria, yellow fever and cholera, as well as their human adversaries. The Spaniards had named this type of warfare *guerrilla*—little war. The name was misleading in the extreme if it was taken to mean a war that was easier to prosecute than a contest of organized forces, or less painful in its results.

In November 1900, President McKinley and his running mate, New York Governor Theodore Roosevelt, the hero of the Rough Riders, defeated William Jennings Bryan even more decisively than McKinley had vanquished Bryan in 1896. Commenting on the election, the *New York Evening Post* judged that "Anti-Imperialism cannot fairly be said to have been beaten at the polls, where the issues were so mixed." The crucial time for anti-imperialists was yet to come, the *Post* said, and it urged them not give up hope: "we have but to wait and watch and press home each evil, every burden, all the perils of imperialism as they swim into our ken."[43]

In the same editions that assessed the election, the newspapers covered a report to the War Department by Major General Arthur MacArthur, who had taken over command in the Philippines in May. Reviewing the difficulties posed by the Filipinos' change from organized tactics to guerrilla warfare, MacArthur said that it had forced the dispersal of American forces, raising the number of military stations in the Philippine islands from fifty-three in November 1899 to four hundred eighteen in September 1900. "General MacArthur says that the extensive distribution of troops has strained the soldiers of the army to the full limit of endurance," the *Evening Post* reported.[44] MacArthur now commanded 60,000 men in the Philippines.[45]

Mark Twain, currently at the height of his fame, had spoken and written often against American policy in the Philippines. In the *New American Review*'s issue of February 1901, Twain published his most extended attack to date. In his pointed satirical style, he endeavored to explain to "the peoples that sit in darkness" why it was important that they should accept the blessings of civilization. He reviewed the recent efforts to that end, the war against Spain and the acquisition of the Philippines, and he wrote, "There have been lies; yes, but they were told in a good cause. We have been treacherous; but that was only in order that real good might come out of apparent evil. True, we have crushed a deceived and confiding people; we have turned against the weak and friendless who trusted us; we have stamped out a just and well-ordered republic; . . . we have invited our clean young men to shoulder a discredited musket and do bandit's work under a flag which bandits have been accustomed to fear, not to follow; we have debauched America's honor and blackened her face before the world; but each detail was for the best. We know this. . . . Give yourself no uneasiness; it is all right."[46]

From the Philippines, General Frederick Funston commented, without naming Twain, that he thought anti-imperialist writers should be hanged for treason.

The day after President McKinley's second inaugural, the *San Francisco Examiner* observed that the principles of the American Revolution were "neatly disguised" in the Philippines: "In the United States our people are ruling themselves under the Constitution. In the Philippines the President's representatives are ruling a subject race by arbitrary power, without regard to the Constitution."[47]

On March 23, 1901, Emilio Aguinaldo was captured two hundred miles from Manila, on the east coast of Luzon. The *Evening Post* believed "that the opposition to the authority of the United States will soon cease, especially if the aid of Aguinaldo himself can be enlisted to that end."[48] Aguinaldo called for an end to the insurgency, but enough Filipinos continued fighting to keep American forces in the field for another year. On April 16, 1902, the surrender of General Miguel Malvar, the last Filipino general who commanded a sizeable following, brought an end to the insurrection on Luzon and marked the end of organized resistance throughout the Philippines, except among the Moro people of Mindanao and some other southern islands.[49]

What should have been an occasion for celebration was marred by stories that had arisen in recent weeks over allegations of torture and summary executions of Filipino prisoners by American troops. Charges had been brought in March against a Marine Corps major and a lieutenant for executing Filipino prisoners without trial on the island of Samar, midway between Luzon and the large southern island of Mindanao. In the court-martial, held at Manila, Major Littleton Waller testified that his commander on Samar, Army General Jacob H. Smith, "instructed him to kill and burn; that the more he killed and burned, the better pleased he would be; that it was no time to take prisoners, and that he was to turn Samar into a howling wilderness," by the *Times*'s account.[50] General Smith testified that "his order to Major Waller about not being burdened with prisoners meant to disarm and release those prisoners who were not charged with serious offenses,"[51] but Major Waller's account was corroborated by testimony from three other Marine officers. After a trial lasting nearly a month, Waller was acquitted. The reason for the verdict was not announced, but it was understood that he had justified his actions by establishing that he was following orders.

Since early in the Philippine war, stories had circulated sporadically about the mistreatment of prisoners and the executions of wounded Filipinos. In his *New American Review* article, Mark Twain had quoted from the letter "of an American soldier-lad in the Philippines to his mother, published in *Public Opinion,* of Decorah, Iowa, describing the finish of a victorious battle: 'We never left one alive. If one was wounded, we would run our bayonets through him.'"[52] In the course of Major Waller's court-martial, new atrocity stories surfaced in the press, from accounts given by soldiers in the Philippines and veterans in the United States. On April 15, 1902, two days after the Waller verdict and the day before General Malvar surrendered, Secretary of War Elihu Root cabled General Chaffee, the American commander in Manila, instructing him, by order of the president, that all charges of cruelty and mistreatment must be subjected to "a most thorough, searching, and exhaustive investigation." Root informed Chaffee that "The President desires to know in the fullest and circumstantial manner all the facts, nothing being concealed and no man being for any reason favored or shielded. . . . Great as the provocation has been in dealing with foes who habitually resort to treachery, murder, and torture against our men, nothing can justify or will be held to justify torture or inhuman conduct of any kind on the part of the American Army."[53]

The order came from President Theodore Roosevelt, who had assumed the presidency in September 1901, following the assassination of William McKinley in Buffalo, New York, at the hands of an anarchist. The *New York Evening Post* saw Roosevelt's personal interest in getting at the truth of the stories as a sign of a significant policy shift in Washington. While McKinley was president, the *Post* said, the atrocity stories had most often resulted in "whitewashing reports. . . . The result was that the public has been grossly deceived as to the facts." The *Post* noted that a sergeant of volunteer infantry had recently testified before the Senate Committee on Philippine Affairs, which was holding hearings on the atrocity charges, that he had witnessed a form of torture called the "water cure" being given to a local official on the island of Panay on two successive days in November 1900. The *Post* urged that the investigations into this and other charges be pressed: "The public is at last convinced that there is truth in the charges against officers in our Army, and it will heartily sustain the President in his demand that the guilty shall promptly be put upon trial."[54]

The *Washington Post* gave this description of the "water cure": "This agreeable treatment consists in pinning a person down, flat on his back, holding his mouth open by any available contrivance, and then playfully filling him with cold water through the agency of a tube stuck into his throat."[55] The *New York Times* quoted a congressman on the floor of the House describing the technique, "by which men are pumped so full of water as nearly to drown them, and then are brought back to life by thumping them over the stomach with the butts of muskets."[56] The *San Francisco Examiner* told of the water cure being inflicted on a ten-year-old boy, and headlined another treatment from which the captives were not intended to recover: "Many Natives Smothered With Mud and Then Reported as Slain in Battle."[57] In the face of these stories, the *Boston Globe* suggested that "a multitude of our people would rejoice, we believe, to see the armed forces of the United States withdrawn from the Philippines altogether, and the government of the archipelago given over to its inhabitants."[58]

After President Roosevelt's order was made public, there was speculation in the press that it would result in a court-martial for Major Waller's superior, General Jacob Smith. These expectations were borne out when the Army announced on April 21 that General Smith would face a court-martial in Manila, beginning on the 24th, for "conduct to the prejudice of good order and military discipline." On the 22nd, the newspapers reported that Smith's court-martial would be convened under the direct order of President Roosevelt. As the *Atlanta Constitution* explained, "This does not mean that there will be a change in the complexion of the court, but it means that it is to be what is known as a president's court, and the proceedings and findings are to be sent direct to Washington for review."[59]

The opening day of General Smith's trial brought a startling development. As the *Boston Globe* reported, "Col. Charles A. Woodruff, counsel for the defence, said he desired to simplify the proceedings. He was willing to admit Gen. Smith gave instructions to Maj. Waller to kill and burn and make Samar a howling wilderness, that he wanted everybody killed capable of bearing arms, and that he did specify all over 10 years of age, as the Samar boys of that age were equally as dangerous as their elders."[60]

The *New York Times* saw in Smith's willingness to admit the factual truth of the charges an intention to base his defense on the assertion that his orders were justified "under the conditions prevailing in Samar." The *Times* found some merit in the claim, as the natives of Samar were said to be "among the very worst we have had to deal with, cruel, treacherous, murderous, and to the last degree dangerous." The "anti-imperialist press," the *Times* pointed out, had written a great deal about the charges of "cruelty, torture and outrage" against American troops, whereas "Of cases of infra-human Oriental torture and mutilation of our soldiers by the savage natives the anti-imperialist newspapers give but the scantiest information." In the end, the *Times* believed Smith would lose: "He will fail in moral justification before the American people and, we believe, before the President and the Secretary of War."[61]

While Smith's court-martial was under way, Congressman Joseph Sibley of Pennsylvania declared in the House of Representatives, "That man never ought to be permitted to stay in the service of the United States until the sun goes down. He is a disgrace . . . to every man who ever wore the uniform of the United States, and he is a blot and a disgrace to our present civilization." As for Smith's justifications for giving the orders that brought him before the court, Sibley said, "That man does not live who can justify such orders." When Sibley took his seat, the

Times reported, "He was vigorously applauded by the Democrats and some of the Republicans."[62]

Smith's court-martial adjourned on May 3. The findings would not be released until they were reviewed by the president. In the meantime, the newspapers could only speculate. The consensus, formed early, was that Smith would be acquitted. The *Washington Post* warned that if the court's verdict "fails to make clear the general's innocence . . . it will rest with the President to redeem the name of the nation at large by showing that Smith must not be taken as a typical American, and that an officer of rank who so far forgets the decencies of his profession as to issue sweeping orders for slaughter and rapine will be reprimanded in the hearing of all Christendom."[63]

On July 4, 1902, by proclamation of President Roosevelt, the Philippine war was officially ended. On July 17, the president's decision in General Smith's case was reported in the press. The court-martial had sentenced General Smith to be "admonished" by the convening authority—President Roosevelt—but Roosevelt had decided that in addition to the admonishment, General Smith would be forced to retire. The president's decision sent shock waves through the military establishment. As the *New York Times* explained its import: "To retire voluntarily with the stain of a reprimand is a severe punishment, according to army ideas. But that this reprimand would be turned into a compulsory retirement from the service, instead of allowing him to wait for the regular retirement for age, was, in the opinion of army officers, beyond what the court-martial expected."

~

In the Philippine war, opposition from the press did not change the government's policy, but the newspapers effectively fulfilled their obligation to inform the debate, and those that opposed the policies of the McKinley administration invoked vital American principles in support of their objections. William McKinley agonized over his decision to take possession of the Philippines and had no wish to tyrannize the Filipinos, but he decided that it would be foolish of the United States to abandon to some other nation's mercies what the U.S. had won from Spain. Under Theodore Roosevelt a civil governor replaced the American military as the ruling authority in the islands. The "anti-imperialist" press and the body of opinion it represented encouraged this and other reforms, and those who had supported taking the Philippines did not oppose them. In this war, it seems, a majority of the American people, "imperialists" and "anti-imperialists" alike, wanted a fair government for the Philippines and a fair shake for its people.[64]

When Spain sued for peace following the destruction of its Atlantic fleet off Santiago de Cuba, no one inside the American government or out of it imagined that the victory would draw the United States into its first overseas war of colonial conquest, or that what began as a contest of conventional forces would become a protracted guerrilla war and lead to charges of atrocities committed by order of American officers. Americans had infuriated the British by adopting Indian tactics after the battles at Lexington and Concord. In the Philippines, Americans were cast in the redcoats' role, fighting far from home against men who were struggling for independence on their own ground. Like the American military, the government in Washington, the press and the people felt uncertain of their footing. It would not have comforted them to know that the related problems of guerrilla war waged by an enemy considered less civilized, incidents of prisoners tortured and executed, and the cost of the struggle sapping the spirit of the American people would return to vex future editors, publishers and presidents, and would seem then just as insoluble. (What remained to be seen was whether future presidents would follow the example of Teddy Roosevelt, who stepped in to assure that nothing was concealed, "and no man being for any reason favored or shielded.")

But these conditions would not recur for more than sixty years, and before then America would become involved in cataclysms that girdled the globe and embroiled most of the world's nations.

5

THE GREAT WAR

World War I (1914–1918)

In the first days of August 1914, as successive declarations of war from Austria-Hungary and Serbia, Germany and Russia, France, Belgium and Great Britain made clear that the new European conflict would be more far-reaching than any previous war, Americans were thankful to be safely out of it. President Woodrow Wilson declared U.S. neutrality and proclaimed that non-belligerent vessels must enjoy freedom of the seas. Great Britain declared virtually all trade goods contraband, boarded even neutral vessels bound for Germany, in violation of international maritime law, and seized some American ships.

In February 1915, Germany announced that it would conduct submarine warfare against all vessels on the sea approaches to the British Isles, drawing a warning from President Woodrow Wilson that attacks on American ships would bring consequences. In May, a German submarine sank the British passenger liner *Lusitania* with the loss of twelve hundred lives, including more than a hundred Americans. Wilson sent a message of protest to Germany so strongly worded that Secretary of State William Jennings Bryan resigned to disassociate himself from a move he feared could draw the United States into the war. When a German submarine torpedoed the Channel packet *Sussex* in

March 1916, with the loss of more American lives, President Wilson threatened to break diplomatic relations with Germany. The German government yielded, pledging that merchant vessels "shall not be sunk without warning and without saving human lives."[1]

Wilson's hope to play the role of peacemaker among the warring nations was frustrated when the Central Powers and the Allies rejected his overtures. As he moved toward active support for building up the Regular Army, which had fewer than 100,000 men at the outbreak of war in Europe, Wilson aroused opposition among isolationists and pacifists. Campaigning under the slogan "He kept us out of war," he won reelection in November 1916 by a margin so narrow that his victory was not confirmed until three days after the election.[2]

On February 1, 1917, Germany resumed unrestricted submarine warfare. On March 1, American newspapers published the text of a telegram sent by German Foreign Secretary Arthur Zimmerman to the president of Mexico, which was intercepted by British Admiralty Intelligence, proposing an alliance in the event that America entered the European war, and promising to restore to Mexico the land she lost to the United States in the war of 1848. The revelation brought demands from the American public and the press for a declaration of war. President Wilson asked for congressional authorization to arm merchant ships and called a special session of Congress for mid-April. When three American merchantmen were torpedoed and sunk off the British Isles within hours of each other on March 18, Wilson moved up the special session to April 2. On that date, just one month after his second inaugural, Woodrow Wilson appeared before the houses of Congress in joint session and asked for a declaration of war against Germany, in order that the world might be "made safe for democracy."

~

William Randolph Hearst opposed American involvement in the European war from the moment the guns of August found their voice. He scorned the perpetual squabbles of the Europeans and the shifting alliances that made allies of former enemies and enemies of former allies. "They talk big of principles and sacred rights in the chancellories, but it is territory, trade and power they covet and fight over," Hearst's *San Francisco Examiner* said on August 3, 1914.[3] Hearst saw the war as a dangerous distraction from what should be the first priority of United States foreign policy—expanding American influence and trade in the western Pacific. He advocated building up the merchant marine and the U.S. Navy and he feared the long-term aims of Japan, especially since that nation's victory in the Russo-Japanese war of 1905–1906. The fact that Japan had declared war against Germany in August of 1914 did nothing to reduce Hearst's wariness toward the Rising Sun. In response to the sinking of the *Lusitania,* the *Examiner* urged, "The United States must be so equipped with a naval force that no nation would be able to disregard its treaty obligations with safety or to attack this nation with any hope of success."[4]

The reach of Hearst's opinions had increased greatly since the sinking of the *Maine* in Havana harbor, when he had owned just two newspapers, the *Journal* in New York and the *Examiner* in San Francisco. By 1916, Hearst had newspapers in San Francisco, New York, Los Angeles, Chicago, Atlanta and in every region of the country. He had a wire service, the International News Agency, and a feature service to supply his newspapers. He published *Cosmopolitan* and *Good Housekeeping* magazines. He was established in film production and had co-produced the hugely successful *Perils of Pauline* movie serial.[5] More than half a century before the phrase came into common use, Hearst had created the first media conglomerate.

Hearst was anti-British, antimonarchist, and ardently democratic. In his campaign for strict American neutrality he repeatedly portrayed the opposing sides in the European war as equally deserving of condemnation while maintaining America's right to trade with all parties. The balanced reporting in Hearst's papers, especially reporting battles from the German point of view and constantly condemning the British blockade of German ports, aroused so much hostility in America that by 1916, Hearst's newspapers were sometimes burned in the streets. In October of that year, the British government denied his International News Service the use of its cables or postal service, for what it said was distorting the news. (Hearst retorted that the I.N.S. was *un*willing to distort the news and had defied British censors by reporting stories accurately.[6]) In the American press, support for Hearst's brand of neutrality dwindled until it was backed, among the prominent papers, only by the *Chicago Tribune,* which had also echoed Hearst's interventionist policy in the war with Spain.

In February 1917, when Germany abandoned its pledge to give warning before attacking merchant ships, the tone of Hearst's coverage shifted within days toward support for President Wilson and increased calls for military preparedness. On February 3, the *Examiner*'s editorial-page cartoon showed a determined Wilson, clad in foul-weather gear, at the wheel of the Ship of State, steering her through mountainous seas. But within weeks, this willingness to back the president as he prepared the nation for war was put at risk as the Hearst newspapers became embroiled in the most bitterly fought contest of the war years between the Wilson administration and the American press.

As sea war on the North Atlantic intensified, Congress was considering a number of preparedness measures, including separate appropriations bills for machine guns, submarines, antiaircraft guns, airplanes and the arming of merchant ships. In the third week of February, the Senate took up an espionage bill submitted by the administration that requested granting the president broad powers to control what could be published in the press relating to the nation's armed forces and fortifications. In heated debate, opponents of the bill, led by Senator Albert Cummins, an Iowa Republican, accused the administration of attempting to institute "tyranny" and "despotism." As an Associated Press account reported Cummins' protest against the bill, "Tyrants of olden times, Senator Cummins declared, never dared to exercise the authority over their people which would be given the President in the espionage bill." Cummins charged that "Such a provision delegates to the President the right of absolute suppression of free speech and absolute overthrow of a free press." The senator suggested that President Wilson would have the authority, under the proposed bill, to stop the Congress from debating war measures.[7] Another senator supported this interpretation, adding that the bill "overlooks the difference between Republican and militaristic forms of government."[8]

The spirited resistance by Cummins and a handful of supporters delayed passage of the espionage bill for only a few days before the Senate approved it on February 20, by sixty votes to ten. Seven Republicans, including Cummins, voted against the measure, together with three renegade Democrats. The *Washington Post* agreed with the espionage bill's critics to the extent that the "language of the bill can be made to appear as an unprecedented grant of power to the President, clothing him with despotic powers," but the *Post* judged that "only by forced construction can it be understood as a menace to liberty. Taken as it is reasonably to be construed and assuming that the President will take care that it does not become an instrument of tyranny, the proposed law will be effective in dealing with the real enemies of the country, and no honest or well-behaving man or newspaper need fear it." To the editors of the *Post,* the bill's intent was straightforward: "The executive branch of the government needs more authority to deal with enemies within the country. The purpose of the proposed law is to meet this need."[9]

Others in the press were less willing to assume that Woodrow Wilson, or any president that followed him in office, would take care that a law giving such broad powers to the chief executive would not become an instrument of tyranny. Hearst's *San Francisco Examiner* opened a full-page editorial by wondering innocently, "how many of you Democratic Senators who voted for this Espionage Bill know how the Democratic party originated," before thundering, "Why, Senators, the Democratic party originated in the OPPOSITION of Thomas Jefferson and James Madison to JUST EXACTLY SUCH LAWS AS THIS UNAMERICAN LAW. Those laws were the Alien and Sedition laws passed in 1798, during the Presidency of John Adams." The *Examiner* charged that these "infamous and tyrannical" acts were "copied in every detail and then broadened and made more tyrannical and destructive of all liberty in the infamous measure" just approved by the U.S. Senate. The *Examiner* called on the House of Representatives "to repudiate this attempt to plant the governmental policies of European militarism on American soil" and assured the members that if they failed in this duty, the liberty-loving American people would put an end to their political careers "and to the infamous legislation that proposes to make us slaves in our own free country."[10]

When news of the Zimmerman telegram broke, the *Examiner* published a signed editorial by Hearst, titled "When the Time Comes, Be Ready All of You With Shields on Your Arms and Swords in Your Hands to Face the Foe and Win the Victory," in which the publisher repeated his belief that the United States should keep out of the war for as long as it could, but if it must fight, then it must strive "to win the war for the glory and security of our country, the advancement of our civilization, the perpetuation of our principles and the maintenance of the welfare of the world."[11]

The House Judiciary Committee held hearings on the espionage bill but it did not reach the full House before Congress adjourned on the eve of President Wilson's second inaugural. In the following weeks, Hearst maintained two apparently unrelated editorial campaigns—supporting President Wilson as the commander in chief of the armed forces and at the same time opposing the censorship clause in the espionage bill—but in fact they were complementary, the patriotic support for the president helping to deflect lingering animosity for Hearst's pro-German reporting and lending a mantle of patriotism to the crusade to defeat the censorship clause. In the midst of orchestrating these efforts, Hearst found time to respond to a request by the *Washington Post* for his opinion on the espionage bill, which would be resubmitted to the new Congress when it met in the special session President Wilson had called for April 2.[12] The *Post* printed Hearst's reply on March 27: "In my opinion any censorship laws are justifiable in case of war, which prevent the publication of information which would be of benefit to the enemy," he wrote. "But censorship laws are not justifiable which prevent the publication of information which should be in the possession of our own people for their proper enlightenment as to the conduct and accomplishments of the war." It was the tendency of government censors, Hearst said, "to shield the government and to prevent its mistakes from becoming known to the people."[13]

On April 3, 1917, the day after President Wilson asked Congress to declare war, an *Examiner* editorial drummed up support for the war effort: "There is just one thing to do now. That is to prepare all the means of making victorious war. . . . Rally to the flag and nerve yourself to meet war's sacrifices and war's perils as every man should meet them, dauntlessly resolved to win or die."[14] Beside this column, the editorial-page cartoon showed Uncle Sam addressing a sea of citizens that filled the space to low hills in the background, exhorting them to "ENLIST!"

Congress declared war on April 6. When the legislators turned their attention to the espionage bill, the *Examiner* offered guidance on how to approach it: "It is a bill which you should never permit to become law until you have pruned it of vicious features—and that not because newspapers object to it, but because it is a bill dangerous to the country and its welfare." Beyond the censorship of "purely military and naval movements," the paper declared, "there is no possible excuse for denying the American people the fullest and most accurate news of what is occurring in the country and the World. . . . Gentlemen of the Congress, do not be either persuaded or bullied into muzzling free speech and free publication. Trim this espionage bill to the bone. Leave yourselves and your people free men, while they wage war in freedom's name."[15]

As submitted to the new Congress, the bill's press censorship clause would impose "a fine of not more than $10,000" or "imprisonment for not more than ten years," or both, for anyone who "shall collect, record, publish, or communicate, or attempt to elicit any information with respect to the movement, numbers, description, condition, or disposition of any of the armed forces, ships, aircraft, or war materials of the United States . . . calculated to be, or which might, be useful to the enemy." It authorized the president to "make and promulgate" regulations for control of the press at his discretion, without providing for judicial review or further congressional oversight.[16] The *New York Times* accused the bill's authors of giving "no heed to the necessity for discrimination" between a newspaper that published such information with intent to benefit the enemy and one that criticized the government "with the honest purpose of promoting remedial action and warning against danger." The *Times* labeled the censorship provision "a Prussian measure, consistently modeled upon those press laws and practices which have forbidden the German newspapers to tell the German people what the Government was about," and charged that such censorship would deprive the American government of "the invaluable aid of enlightened public opinion and of the guidance of the public's not less enlightened criticism."[17]

The *Times* was even stronger in its condemnation of the bill when it reported on the debate in the Senate: "The provisions of this attack on the proper freedom of the press were justly characterized as tyrannous, and likened to the abhorrent Prussian despotism." The *Times* insisted that the bill must protect "information that may be in some degree useful to the enemy, but at the same time is of transcendent importance to our own people."[18] On April 22, the *Times* published samples of editorial opinion from around the country to demonstrate that a consensus in the press opposed the measures. The *San Francisco Chronicle* stood on the First Amendment's prohibition against Congress making any law abridging freedom of speech or of the press, and it quoted the newspaper's publisher, M. H. De Young, who declared that he would look on any effort to breach those safeguards as "a step in the direction of that system of autocratic government which it is the professed purpose of those who are warring upon Germany to destroy." The *Los Angeles Times* wrote in a similar vein, "There is grave danger in enacting a censorship clause like this that the Administration is establishing a Caesarism, a Kaiserism, at home in the very era in which it is seeking to dispossess a Caesarism abroad." The *St. Louis Globe-Democrat* charged that some provisions of the espionage bill were unconstitutional: "The Senators who are striving to remove from the Espionage bill the power it would place in the hands of officialdom are not battling for publishers, but for fundamental American principles, whose preservation are essential to democracy itself." The *Philadelphia Public Ledger* stated bluntly, "America will never submit to suppression of information to which the people are plainly entitled, and the sooner the authorities in Washington understand it the better."[19]

Hearst's *Examiner* was curiously subdued after its April 10 demand that the bill be trimmed "to the bone." On the 17th, the *Examiner* reported prematurely, in a small item on an inside page, under the column head "Espionage Bill Is Tamed Down," that "Indications are that no attempt at direct censorship will be made." The item reported that a new government bureau, created by President Wilson and composed of the secretaries of state, war and the navy, together with a civilian newspaperman, George Creel, would confer with editors and publishers and draw up voluntary regulations for the guidance of the press, but the *Examiner* was wrong to suggest that the creation of this bureau, the Committee on Public Information, meant that the Wilson administration was any less determined to push the espionage bill through Congress with its censorship clause intact.[20]

On April 21, the *Examiner* reported without comment that the clause, after three days of "sharp debate," and "after decided modification," was retained by a vote of 48 to 33 in the Senate. The article said this result "was regarded as definitely forecasting final retention of the censorship provisions." On the 26th, again without the *Examiner*'s customary opinion-within-the-news, the paper reported that the bill had been reported favorably to the House of Representatives, and that "The right of newspapers to criticize acts or policies of the government or its representatives would remain unchanged."[21]

On the last day of the month, as if waking from a nap, the *Examiner* mustered all hands on deck and fired with every available gun. This sudden recommitment to the fight appeared on an inside page, but it was an impressive barrage. Under a ribbon headline, "Citizens Protest to Congressmen Against Muzzle," the *Examiner* printed five items attacking the censorship provision. The column-one header declared "House Faces Big Fight on Gag Clause," with a subhead, "Opposition Is Increasing," and a second, "Amendments Discussed by Leaders in Effort to Remove Drastic Features of the Censorship." In a three-column box atop the page, John Brisben Walker, a former editor of the *Cincinnati Commercial Gazette* and the Washington, D.C., *Daily Chronicle* who had sold *Cosmopolitan* magazine to Hearst a dozen years earlier, wrote that "The most dangerous traitor to his country is the man who would suppress free speech." Another item reported that the muckraking novelist Upton Sinclair "vigorously opposes the proposed espionage bill, which would muzzle the press of the nation." A fourth article related from Chicago that a former governor of Illinois also opposed it, and the fifth, datelined Los Angeles, carried the headline "Leading Angelenos Back 'The Examiner' in Its Stand for Freedom of Speech."

Following these preliminaries the *Examiner* rolled out the main event, an editorial in which the paper charged that "for the past fifteen years our representative government has been undergoing a steady metamorphosis" as the result of "unconstitutional and dangerous usurpation of legislative powers by the executive." Against this menace, the *Examiner* declared, "there is only one defense, which is the liberty of the press," now threatened as never before by the proposed espionage bill, "the intent and sure effect of which will be to give the President and the members of his cabinet the power to destroy the freedom of the press, to put a muzzle upon the only voice which the American people have with which to make known their sentiment and their will." The editorial printed an excerpt from a letter sent by President Wilson to the editor of Hearst's *New York American,* in which the president declared, "I shall not expect or permit any part of this law to apply to me or any of my official acts, or in any way to be used as a shield against criticism." In the *Examiner's* view, Wilson's implicit admission that the proposed law "will give him the POWER to silence criticism" proved the paper's case against the bill: "That is to say, the Espionage Bill would make Mr. Wilson a despot, but his intention is to be a benevolent despot." Mr. Wilson, the *Examiner* cautioned, had changed his mind "upon nearly every question of vital importance during his presidency," and might change it again.[22]

The next day, May 1, the *Examiner* published a front-page story, "Congress Is Awakened to Gag Menace," and grouped no fewer than nine articles about the bill on two facing pages inside the issue, followed by a full-page editorial, "What An Unjust Censorship Has Done for England, The Same Censorship Can Do for United States." Through the month of May, Hearst's newspapers followed the debate in the House of Representatives virtually speech by speech. The *Examiner* printed a petition against the measure in its pages—one of Hearst's favorite ploys to rally support for his causes—and readers by the "thousands," the paper said, mailed in the forms.

The House of Representatives stripped the censorship provision from the bill, then adopted a substitute clause that would transfer to the courts the power to define what newspapers could print. The Wilson administration continued to insist that Congress pass the original bill without modification. On May 9, the *Examiner* published a signed editorial in which Hearst refuted a claim by the chairman of the House Judiciary Committee that only Hearst and his newspapers opposed the espionage bill. Hearst called the accusation "a flattering assumption but a false one. Practically every newspaper printed in the United States which is not controlled by [a] corrupt corporation or some sinister influence . . . is fighting side by side with the Hearst papers to preserve free speech and free publication and the fundamental democratic rights and liberties which the Constitution guarantees."[23]

This was certainly true of some prominent newspapers that had little in common with Hearst or his brand of journalism. In response to a revised version of the censorship clause proposed in the House that still gave the president power to prohibit publication in wartime of anything that in his judgment, "is or might be useful to the enemy," the *New York Times* listed five points in objection, "aside from the general one that the proposal is unconstitutional and unneeded."[24] The *Boston Globe* observed that "The enemy has ways of obtaining his information besides glancing at the morning paper," and opposed any censorship at all: "In fighting for the truth, democracy must know the truth. The more completely the attempt to censor the press is killed, the better for the cause of freedom."[25] The *Washington Post* had undergone a change of heart and published a series of editorials opposing the censorship clause during the weeks of debate. The *Post* considered the House's revisions an improvement, but opposed any censorship unless it came down to "a choice between free speech and the dissolution of the United States."[26] The paper said the government could not carry on a war "without the constant sympathy and support of the people," and that the only way to obtain those things was "to make the truth universally known."[27] When the Senate voted by 39 to 38 on nonpartisan lines to strip all references to censorship from the espionage bill, the *Post* applauded the action: "It is to be hoped that the Congress will stand firmly upon the position assumed by the Senate. No step whatever can be taken toward government supervision of the public press without running grave risk. . . . The fullness and freedom of its action cannot be curtailed without injury to both the people and the government."[28]

When a House-Senate conference committee reported the espionage bill on May 25 with a further-revised censorship clause included, a correspondent for Hearst's International News Service wrote that the new version, "although a drastic modification of the original gag bill, still makes possible a dangerous limitation of free speech."[29] The *Washington Post,* perhaps hoping to attract more flies with honey, congratulated the Congress for passing "eleven great bills" in forty-five working days since it convened on April 2 to hear the president's call for war, before recommending, "The espionage bill can be kept within its proper scope by omitting the proposed censorship provision, which intensively offends public sentiment and is capable of untold mischief."[30]

The *Atlanta Constitution* attacked the clause from a different flank, listing a half-dozen secret diplomatic missions involving high officials who had recently crossed the Atlantic, all unreported by American newspapers until those travels were safely completed, although they were "in full possession of all the facts in advance." Advocates of censorship, the *Constitution* said, maintained "that ninety-nine out of every hundred newspapers are to be trusted with state secrets; but legal censorship is needed to keep the hundredth from upsetting things. But according to the record thus far, the percentage worthy of trust is a round hundred."[31]

On May 31, the House voted to strike the censorship clause from the espionage bill. "The House of Representatives," by this action, the *Washington Post* declared, "has acted wisely and in response to public sentiment."[32] Within a few days, a conference committee reported the censorship-free bill back to the House. The House approved the final version on June 7, and President Wilson signed the Espionage Act of 1917 on June 15.

By its successful opposition to the bill's censorship provision, the press preserved its right to comment on the government's conduct of the war, but it acquiesced without a fight, and even gave its support, when the Wilson administration sought an amendment to the Espionage Act, in the spring of 1918, that posed a far broader threat to constitutional liberties. Like the rejected censorship clause, the so-called "sedition bill" was a single run-on sentence providing that "whoever, when the United States is at war, shall utter, print, write, or publish any disloyal, profane, scurrilous, or abusive language about the form of government of the United States, or the Constitution of the United States . . . or the flag of the United States . . . or any language calculated to bring the form of government of the United States, or the Constitution of the United States, or the military or naval forces of the United States, or the flag of the United States . . . into contempt, scorn, contumely, or disrepute, or shall utter, print, write, or publish any language calculated to incite, provoke, or encourage resistance to the United States, or to promote the cause of its enemies" would be subject to a fine of up to $10,000, imprisonment for up to twenty years, or both.

Debate on the sedition amendment began in the Senate in the first week of April 1918, fueled by an incident in Illinois, where a man of German ancestry who was believed to be disloyal had been lynched by a mob. The news was carried by papers across the country. The *San Francisco Examiner* headlined the story "Lynching Is Blamed to Delays on Spy Bill."[33] Other newspapers argued for swift passage of the sedition amendment on the grounds that it was necessary to prevent more loyal citizens from taking violent action against those suspected of pro-German sympathies. On behalf of the administration, Attorney General Thomas Gregory, the *Examiner* reported, "sent special pleas to Senator Overman to rush through the amendments to the espionage bill."[34] Lee S. Overman of North Carolina had sponsored the 1917 espionage bill in the Senate, but his effort to push the sedition amendment to a vote was opposed by senators who objected to the administration's attempt to cut off debate.

Henry Cabot Lodge, a Republican of Massachusetts and one of President Wilson's most persistent critics, declared that the greatest danger to the country was from saboteurs who had been bombing factories and ships, "starting fires, poisoning food and such things." In Lodge's view, saboteurs and traitors had been treated altogether too leniently by the courts. "The only way to put an end to their activities is try them by court-martial and shoot them," Lodge said.[35] Senator Chamberlain of Oregon put forward a bill to do just as Lodge suggested, by providing for trying the worst offenders before courts-martial instead of in the civilian courts. The *Los Angeles Times* opposed the bill, calling it "distinctly despotic." The opposition that proved decisive, however, came from Woodrow Wilson. In a "vitriolic" letter to another senator, the *Los Angeles Times* reported, the president declared that Chamberlain's proposal was "a violation of the civil rights of citizens which is neither authorized nor legalized by the Federal Constitution."[36]

To address the concerns expressed by some senators that honest dissent or casual remarks might be punished under the sedition amendment, the Senate changed the language to require that to be punishable under the amendment, the disloyal, profane, scurrilous or abusive speech must have been uttered, printed or published "willfully." The *New York Times* thought it "extraordinary" that almost an entire day had been taken up in debating the addition of this one word, but it conceded that the bill was thereby improved because it now required proof of intent. The *Times* judged that the law would give prosecutors "plenty of latitude to frame indictments against traitors, obstructionists, and the disaffected. If they do their duty fearlessly and with intelligence, there will be no excuse or pretext for lynch law in its various forms of violence as a manifestation of Americanism."[37]

Despite the amendment's focus on any who might "write, print, or publish," seditious ideas, it was aimed at political agitation or outright advocacy for the enemies of the United States, rather than at the press. The great majority of journals judged discretion the better part of consolidating their gains when it came to standing up for the rights of anarchists and Socialists against widespread public support for the amendment. One of the few newspapermen who felt obliged to speak against it was William Randolph Hearst. Having editorialized in opposition to the Espionage Act of 1917 on the grounds that it was modeled on "the infamous alien and sedition laws" of John Adams' presidency, Hearst could hardly keep quiet in the face of a bill that unabashedly sought to punish sedition. Hearst's first concern was that laws against certain kinds of speech were an invitation to abuse by anyone who was willing to lie to injure another. "If this measure becomes law," the *San Francisco Examiner* editorialized, "there is no man in San Francisco or in the whole United States, no matter how upright and how loyal he may be, who would be safe from the accusations and the perjury of malignant and unscrupulous enemies." The *Examiner* argued that "The express prohibition of the Constitution, which is the supreme law of the land, and the interpretation of an unbroken line of great judges, put it beyond the rightful authority of the Congress to make any law at all abridging the freedom of speech. . . . If we are at war for anything in the world, we are at war for the maintenance of democratic institutions, democratic liberties and democratic guarantees. . . . Let us respect the Constitution. Let us preserve its guarantees unabated."[38]

Having expressed himself on the matter, Hearst fell silent, although the *Examiner* and other Hearst newspapers gave extensive coverage to California's recent reformist governor and newly elected senator, Hiram Johnson, who issued more impassioned attacks on the bill. "Great God!" Johnson exploded on the floor of the Senate. "Why must the safeguards of the Constitution and the rights of law be broken down?" He fought for an amendment to the bill by Senator Joseph France of Maryland, who proposed to add the provision that "Nothing in this act shall be construed as limiting the liberty or impairing the right of any individual to publish or speak what is true with good motives and with justifiable ends." The Senate rejected the France amendment partly in deference to a written argument from a functionary at the Justice Department who pleaded that France's amendment, "would greatly decrease the value of the espionage act as a deterrent of propaganda." This prompted Johnson to declare, "The right of free speech in this country is, by the elimination of this amendment, for the first time repudiated by Congress and denied expression in a law."[39] When the Senate gave its final approval to the sedition bill, Johnson lamented, "Measures such as this do not unite a people. They breed discontent; they cause suspicion to stalk through the land; they make one man spy upon another; they take a great, virile, brave people and make that people timid and fearful."[40]

Neither Hearst's protest nor Hiram Johnson's eloquent objections to the bill produced a swelling of opposition to the sedition amendment in the press or in the Congress. Outstripping the nearly two-to-one margin in the Senate, the House approved the bill with a single dissenting vote.[41]

The *Atlanta Constitution*'s editorial of May 7, 1918, was typical of the press's response. The *Constitution* criticized the senators who had delayed passage of the amendment and warned that once President Wilson signed the bill, "all seditionists, all loose-tongued critics of the government's war policies had best beware, because this bill provides precisely the authority that is needed to clip their wings and to hobble them." In the *Constitution*'s opinion, "The law will do much good, and it can do no injury to any man who speaks and acts the part of a thorough-going American citizen."[42] The *Washington Post* was eager for the authorities to begin "rooting out the nests of pro-Germans which are known to exist in various parts of the country." It supported a plan mapped out by Attorney General Gregory, which would enlist newspapers and the public to cooperate with their local district attorneys "to ferret out suspicious cases and get at the facts," as the *Post* approvingly described the scheme. "In this manner every loyal and patriotic citizen himself constitutes a vigilance committee for the protection of the country."[43]

The *San Francisco Examiner* did not praise the sedition bill, but found in its passage a reason to praise President Wilson. The article appeared under an *Examiner* reporter's byline, but it was closer to an editorial than a news article and might as well have been written by Hearst himself. It described the bill's passage as "a momentous and notable event," and the amendment as "the most bitterly fought of all the measures that have passed in the Sixty-Fifth Congress." The article pointed out that "the application of this measure must rest and will rest with the President of the United States. And upon this large fact rests the confidence and the tranquillity of thousands who might otherwise view its powers with the greatest apprehension. The President is the leading evangel and exponent in all this troubled world of the spirit and theory of democracy. . . . The President has in no instance held supreme power with an iron and relentless hand. Of all the evidences which the Sixty-Fifth Congress has given of its supreme faith in the motive of the President of the United States, the passage of this sedition bill will easily be ranked among the first, if not the foremost of them all."[44] (Give yourself no uneasiness; it is all right.)

When Hearst published these sentiments, his newspapers were under renewed attack for publishing pro-German opinions. After the sedition amendment became law, Hearst's enemies moved to have him prosecuted under its provisions, and in one instance went so far as to present a case to a federal grand jury, which refused to return an indictment.[45]

Hearst and most of the press continued to support President Wilson for the duration of the war, even as the administration vigorously pursued and prosecuted under the amended Espionage Act pacifists, labor organizations (most aggressively, the International Workers of the World), Socialists, radicals and others who spoke openly against the war or any aspect of the government's war effort. The postmaster general, using authority granted by the sedition amendment, denied mailing privileges to Socialist and radical newspapers, just as Abraham Lincoln's postmaster general had excluded from the mails the *New York Daily News* and other newspapers that criticized Lincoln's administration. The anarchist lecturer Emma Goldman was prosecuted and jailed for speaking against the military draft. In some case, the enforcement of the law's anti-sedition provisions became self-perpetuating, as when Eugene Debs, the American Socialist Party's founder and four times its presidential candidate, was sentenced to ten years in prison for speaking against the prosecution of others under the Espionage Act. The press followed these efforts diligently, usually with approval.

Reporting on the war in Europe was frustrating for American newspapers, as for those of the Allied nations. There were few first-person accounts from anywhere near the front lines after the early weeks of fighting. The Allied command imposed rigid censorship on all dispatches and kept correspondents miles behind the trenches. The situation for American correspondents improved somewhat after the arrival of the American Expeditionary Force in 1917, but only in so far as they got more regular briefings. It was long after the war that the public learned the horrors of trench warfare, from books written by men who experienced it firsthand.

In October of 1918, the Central Powers requested an armistice based on the peace terms President Wilson had set forth in his "Fourteen Points" speech to Congress in January. The public and the press supported Wilson when he held out for a more conclusive victory that could only follow a change of government in Germany and the abdications of the kaiser and the Austrian emperor. Hearst's chain and the *New York Times* were among the newspapers that staunchly backed the president in this, as in urging American voters to return Democratic majorities to Congress in the midterm election on November 5. (In the event, Republicans regained control of both houses.)

When the armistice came, on November 11, the *San Francisco Examiner* headlined "GERMANY SURRENDERS" below an American eagle with wings spread across the top of the page. The next day, the *Examiner's* editorial proclaimed, "Medievalism has been brought to an ignoble end. Militarism has been crushed by the might of the free peoples. THE WORLD HAS BEEN SAVED FOR DEMOCRACY."[46]

With the victory secured, Hearst led a campaign in the press to oppose President Wilson's most cherished dreams for the future peace of the world, as they were embodied in the Treaty of Versailles and the League of Nations. When the Senate rejected the treaty, and American membership in the League, Hearst rejoiced.[47]

Woodrow Wilson, like Abraham Lincoln and William McKinley before him, lacked the impulse for tyranny, but like Lincoln he was willing to encroach on First Amendment freedoms for what he considered a greater good. Wilson cited constitutional liberties to oppose trying civilians before military courts, but when he was given unprecedented powers to curtail freedom of expression in wartime, he persecuted and imprisoned thousands of Americans who advocated unpopular opinions. Wilson enjoyed widespread popular support, and majorities—often bipartisan—in both houses of Congress, that approved virtually all the wartime measures he proposed. If Wilson had been willing to establish military tribunals to try traitors and saboteurs, it is very likely that Congress would have granted him the authority. In the context of the times, the victory of the press over the censorship clause in the original 1917 espionage bill was a remarkable achievement. Proud of this accomplishment, the majority in the press turned its back when a minority of the people—fringe groups with little popular support—lost their right to speak or print their opinions, and their liberty as well.

In 1921 the sedition amendment to the Espionage Act of 1917 was repealed as part of a general repeal of emergency measures enacted during the war. At the same time, the Espionage Act of 1917 was reinstated as it was first approved by Congress that year.[48] It remains in force.

6

THE GOOD WAR

The Second World War (1939–1945)

America's involvement in the Second World War, as in the first, began on the North Atlantic. Once again England was involved in the conflict from its earliest days, her supply lines threatened by German submarines. For Franklin Delano Roosevelt, the period between the German invasion of Poland, on September 1, 1939, and the Japanese attack on Pearl Harbor in December 1941, must have seemed like a real-life nightmare from his younger days, come back to haunt him. At the start of the World War I, Roosevelt had been the assistant secretary of the Navy. He was exasperated by President Wilson's efforts to negotiate between Germany and the Allies even after German submarines sank unarmed passenger ships. Inspired by the example of his distant cousin, Theodore Roosevelt, who favored all possible aid to the Allies, Franklin became an advocate of military preparedness and did what he could to reform the operations of naval shipyards, which were under his authority.

In 1939, Franklin Roosevelt was the president of the United States. He was convinced that the Axis formed by Nazi Germany, Italy and Japan posed a mortal danger to the western democracies, but his ability to help the Allies was limited by public opinion, which was strongly isolationist. In Congress,

Republican hostility toward FDR and the New Deal reinforced the noninterventionist opposition.

When Hitler invaded Denmark and Norway, then Belgium, Holland, and France over a five-week period in the spring of 1940, American public opinion became sufficiently aroused against Germany to enable Roosevelt to send fifty obsolete destroyers to England in exchange for ninety-nine-year leases on eight British naval and air bases scattered from Newfoundland to British Guiana. The destroyers reinforced England's ability to protect merchant vessels bringing vital supplies to the British Isles, but Roosevelt wanted to do more. By the summer of 1941, American warships were convoying merchant ships as far as Iceland, where the British Navy took over. In September, a German submarine attacked an American destroyer but its torpedoes missed their target. In another incident, a torpedo hit a destroyer and killed eleven crewmen but failed to sink the ship.[1] In response to these attacks, Roosevelt gave the U.S. Navy orders to "shoot on sight" at German subs, putting America in an undeclared war in the North Atlantic.

Early on the morning of October 31, 1941, a submarine sank the U.S. destroyer *Reuben James* west of Iceland with the loss of most of her 120-man crew. The *New York Times* reported that President Roosevelt was calm when he told a White House press conference that "he did not expect the sinking of the destroyer Reuben James to affect American foreign policy or diplomatic relations with Germany. He appeared to regard the torpedoing as an inevitable incident in the Battle of the Atlantic."[2]

In Congress, the Senate was debating a request by the Roosevelt administration to arm U.S. merchant vessels, which required revising a 1939 neutrality act.[3] A front-page column head in the *Times* the day after the *Reuben James* went down said "Senate Lines Hold"; a subhead reported, "Advocates of Neutrality Revision Say Sinking Solidifies 'Majority'." On the editorial page, the *Times* made its position unmistakably clear: "The sinking of the destroyer Reuben James by a Nazi submarine near Iceland brushes away the last possible doubt that the United States and Germany are now at open war in the Atlantic. . . . If we permit a hostile Power which is the declared enemy of our whole democratic system to cut our service of supply to Britain, Britain will go down and Hitler and his European and Asiatic allies will be masters of three continents. We cannot let our last strong friend go under. . . . The very bill which the Senate is now debating would permit our Government, at long last, to arm our merchant ships and use those ships where they are needed most. The sinking of the Reuben James ought to supply the last clinching argument for the adoption of that measure by an overwhelming vote."[4]

The *Chicago Tribune* gave the story a very different emphasis in a front-page article that championed Wayland Brooks, a Republican senator from Illinois, who had succeeded, by what the *Tribune* called a "masterful speech," in blocking a vote on the bill the day before in the Senate. "Brooks held the floor against the attempts of interventionists to obtain an immediate vote on the neutrality revision bill," the *Tribune* reported. "The Illinois senator spoke for more than an hour and when he had finished his moving and eloquent plea for a consideration of the awful consequences attendant upon this nation's involvement in the war, there was a marked cooling of senatorial tempers, and a rash act prevented."[5]

For the *Chicago Tribune,* which called itself "The World's Greatest Newspaper," this editorializing within the news was a relatively subdued response. In the following days the paper stepped up its opposition to revising the neutrality act. In every edition of the paper, the *Tribune* printed two political cartoons, one on the editorial page—a custom shared with many other newspapers—and another top center on the front page, just below the headlines. It was in these drawings, as much as in the editorial text, that the paper took some of its hardest shots at the policies and politicians it most abhorred, with Franklin Delano Roosevelt heading the list. On November 6, a week after the sinking of the Reuben James, the front-page cartoon showed a courtroom scene with Lady Liberty pleading before FDR on the bench, her hand on the shoulder of a dejected figure, "America's Youth," who is slumped in a chair. A scroll hanging from the side of the bench reads "WAR sentence," and the jury is a bunch of fat-cat New Deal businessmen. The cartoon's two captions drove the point home: "A Mother Pleads For Her Son," and "The Judge is Biased and the Jury is Packed." An editorial in the same issue counted up the American sailors killed in German attacks on American ships, and declared, "Mr. Roosevelt has himself violated the law he asks congress to repeal, the law which, by his oath of office, he is bound to uphold. Every argument he used to pass the 1939 neutrality act thru congress he has re-pudiated and denounced."[6]

The next day's *Tribune* announced in a huge banner, "SENATE RE-PEALS NEUTRALITY." Beneath the headline, in a cartoon captioned "Once Gone, Our Tears Will Not Restore Him," a droop-shouldered fig-ure, chained to heavy iron balls, stands over a fresh grave with a stone in-scribed "Here Lies Uncle Sam, Buried With the Constitution of the United States—Liquidated by the New Deal Communists." The editorial-page cartoon depicted a portly Briton looking over the shoulder of a seated Uncle Sam, who is looking at a newspaper with the headline "U.S. COMMITTED TO FREE WORLD, SAYS ROOSEVELT." The Brit says, "'Don't Take That Too Literally, Sam!" Behind them, a wall map of the world shows the countries of the British Empire in black.

These themes, isolationism in the face of German and Japanese ag-gression and hostility toward imperial Britain, were constant in the *Chicago Tribune,* close behind opposition to FDR and all his works. On the eve of America's sudden plunge into war, if someone had asked Colonel Robert McCormick, the publisher and editor of the *Tribune* since 1911, to name the well springs of evil in the world, he would have an-swered "Franklin Roosevelt and the British Empire" before—maybe—pausing to consider if Hitler or Tojo should be at the top of the list. Next to FDR and Britain, Colonel McCormick despised New York, Boston and Washington, Wall Street, bankers and upper-class easterners, especially those who meddled in finance and politics.

The period of Robert McCormick's greatest influence overlapped that of William Randolph Hearst, who in the years between the wars was the living embodiment of the American press baron. By 1940, Hearst was sev-enty-seven and in decline, his papers under the control of a trustee since 1937, while McCormick, sixty years old when the *Reuben James* went down, was approaching the peak of his power. The *Tribune* had the great-est circulation of any standard-size (as opposed to tabloid) newspaper in the United States and it led the world in advertising revenue. In the First World War, the *Tribune* had been virtually alone among American news-papers in supporting Hearst when he criticized Britain's blockade policy with as much fervor as he gave to condemning Germany's submarine at-tacks on passenger vessels. In 1939–1941, the *Tribune* was no longer a fol-lower but a leader in opposing American intervention.

The *Tribune* spoke for the Midwest against the financial and political forces of the east coast, but Robert McCormick's animus toward those forces and toward his nemesis, Franklin Roosevelt, arose as much from personal as political origins. The two men were surprisingly similar in their backgrounds, which included the coincidence of their having attended the same exclusive Massachusetts prep school—Groton, thirty miles from Boston—in the golden years of the 1890s. Against our expectations, it was McCormick who was the more anglicized and the wealthier of the two. He had attended a boy's school in England when his father, a diplomat, was posted to London. He was the scion of two prominent dynasties deeply rooted in the Midwest. His paternal grandfather, Cyrus McCormick, had developed the reaping machine that made him rich. His mother's father, Joseph Medill, had helped to establish the Republican party in 1854 before buying the *Chicago Tribune* the following year. At Groton, Robert was one form ahead of Franklin Roosevelt and eighteen months older, to the day. These advantages enabled him to ignore the younger boy, who came from a family of no public renown. Franklin had been raised genteelly at Hyde Park, New York, in the Hudson River valley. His forebears had made a modest fortune in shipping and in the development of coal-bearing lands, but when he entered Groton, two years before the Spanish-American War, his only relation in public life was a fifth cousin, Theodore Roosevelt, who was president of the board of police commissioners in New York City. Young Franklin was gawky, shy, and inept at sports, but in Robert McCormick's eyes Roosevelt and his kind bore themselves with an effortless sense of belonging at Groton, the American Eton, that made McCormick feel like an outsider from the hinterlands.

As president of the Tribune Company and publisher and editor of the *Chicago Tribune*, Robert McCormick lived in a mansion, spoke with traces of an acquired British accent and took afternoon tea punctually at half-past four.[7] He held forth on the radio, on public platforms, and in the pages of the *Tribune,* expounding his philosophy of America first, last, and always, speaking on behalf of American values and the American family, native-born and immigrant alike, defending them against perceived attacks by eastern bankers and privileged pantywaists, Democratic politicos and New Deal profiteers, and the pleas of the British and French, who begged America to come to their aid every time they got themselves in trouble with Germany.

McCormick knew the horrors of war first hand. He had served as a staff and combat officer in the First World War, rose to the rank of colonel, and won a Distinguished Service Medal before returning to Chicago convinced that America should henceforth have nothing to do with the quarrels of England or Europe. When Hitler invaded Poland in September 1939, McCormick did his best to convince himself, and the rest of America, that Britain and France could contain Germany by themselves. The day after the blitzkrieg began, the *Tribune* editorialized, "This is not our war because we refrained from doing the things which would cause it. France and Britain are not weak nations. They are great empires. . . . They have adopted policies which brought them into conflict with Germany, Italy and Japan. . . . Americans will be told that this is their fight. That is not true. The frontiers of American democracy are not in Europe, Asia or Africa."[8]

As Hitler extended his control over more of Europe, the *Tribune* performed a balancing act between attacking Franklin Roosevelt's efforts to involve the United States and supporting military preparedness for America's defense. "Defense" was the operative word. Like Hearst before the United States entered the First World War, McCormick supported building up America's defenses so no nation would dare attack us directly, but he opposed extending those defenses to the border between Germany and France. On Mother's Day 1940, next to a report on the bombing of Brussels, the *Tribune*'s front-page cartoon had two panels, one portraying U.S. Ambassador Charles Pinkney saying to the French, "Millions for defense, but not one cent for tribute!" the other showing an American mother facing a group of men representing what the *Tribune* underestimated as "America's Six Percent of Entanglers," declaring, "Millions of Sons for America's Defense, but NOT ONE SON for Sacrifice in EUROPE'S ETERNAL QUARRELS."[9]

Sometimes the *Tribune*'s coverage became almost comically self-contradictory. On September 5, 1940, in a front-page story headlined "Ship Deal Foes Weigh Move to Impeach F.D.R.," the paper reported that during a debate in Congress on sending the obsolescent destroyers to England, "Republicans and some Democrats accused the President of usurping the powers of a dictator and committing an act of war." The day before, on an inside page, the *Tribune* had printed maps of the naval and air bases the United States would lease in exchange, and outlined how they would strengthen America's defenses. On September 10, the front-page cartoon, titled "The Race of the Destroyers," showed the American destroyers steaming at flank speed across the Atlantic toward England, where "The Nazi Destroyers" unleashed a rain of bombs on London through clouds of smoke and fire, while God, in the foreground, recorded "History's Grimmest Chapter" on a stone tablet.[10]

In November 1940, Franklin Roosevelt won reelection—like Woodrow Wilson in 1916—in part because the voters credited him with keeping America out of war. Unlike Wilson, it was Roosevelt's intention to get the United States into the war as soon as possible. The *Chicago Tribune* had fought tooth and nail against FDR's renomination and his re-election to an unprecedented third term. With Roosevelt returned to the White House by a landslide (though not as great as those of 1932 and 1936), whatever slight restraints McCormick may have imposed on his editors up to that point were removed. In March 1941, when Congress was considering the president's lend-lease bill, which would enable the United States to supply Britain with unlimited amounts of munitions and equipment on credit (until now, war material had been sold on a cash-and-carry basis), the *Tribune* routinely referred to the bill as Roosevelt's "war dictatorship bill" not only on the editorial page but in its news columns, headlines and cartoons as well. On March 8, under a banner headline, "VOTE TODAY ON DICTATOR BILL," the page-one car-toon showed a politician in shirt sleeves representing the "New Deal Dic-tator Bloc" crouched beside an enormous cannon with a ramrod in his hand. The cannon, labeled "War Excuse to Seize More Power," is aimed in the direction of the Capitol building, which represents the "American Form of Government." Beyond the Capitol, a sign points to "The War." With a hand on the cannon, Uncle Sam is asking the politician, "Just What Are You Aimin' At?"

The next day, the *Tribune* headlined, "PASS DICTATOR BILL, 60 TO 31." In a true dictatorship like Nazi Germany, challenges such as these would have been more than enough cause for the paper to be shut down, the presses smashed, and the publisher put up against a bullet-pocked wall. In the United States, in two previous wars, the government had acted to repress less abusive opposition, but Franklin Roosevelt did not feel the need to seek a sedition act or to ban the *Chicago Tribune* from the mails to protect his government against criticism. If it occurred to

Robert McCormick that the vituperation the *Tribune* cast daily on FDR was proof that freedom of the press was alive and well in America, he kept that thought to himself.

The Japanese attack on Pearl Harbor on December 7, 1941, silenced the isolationists overnight and enforced a temporary cease-fire in the *Chicago Tribune*'s policy toward FDR. On December 8, under enormous headlines that announced, "U.S. AND JAPS AT WAR" / BOMB HAWAII, PHILIPPINES, GUAM, SINGAPORE," a rare front-page editorial declared, "War has been forced on the U.S. by an insane clique of Japanese militarists who apparently see the desperate conflict into which they have led their country as the only thing that can prolong their power. . . . All that matters today is that we are in the war and the nation must face the simple fact. All of us, from this day forth, have only one task. That is to strike with all our might to protect and preserve the American freedom that we all hold dear." The page-one cartoon showed a single figure representing "Every American," saluting the American flag.

The onset of all-out war, paradoxically, made McCormick's balancing act easier. The *Tribune* gave whole-hearted support to the American military effort for the duration, and after a short truce resumed its familiar criticisms of President Roosevelt and his policies.

For almost a year after Pearl Harbor, Germany and Italy controlled all of Europe and the Mediterranean, except for east Africa and Palestine, where the British held out. In August 1942, following important American naval victories earlier in the year at Midway, in the north Pacific, and the Coral Sea, off New Guinea, U.S. Marines landed on Guadalcanal, in the Solomon Islands, in a first effort to roll back the farthest extensions of the Japanese Empire. In November 1942, American and British forces made amphibious landings in French Morocco and Algeria. In May 1943, these Allied troops joined up with the British Eighth Army, which advanced westward from Egypt, giving the Allies control of the whole northern coast of Africa. At this point in the war, a year and a half before the next election, the *Chicago Tribune* began an all-out campaign against a fourth term for Franklin Roosevelt. In the May 1 issue, the front-page cartoon showed Uncle Sam pointing to these words carved in stone beneath portraits of George Washington and Thomas Jefferson: "The Unwritten Law of the Republic, as exemplified by its two greatest founders, has been that the tenure of office of President of the United States shall not exceed two consecutive terms of four years each." The caption suggested, "Why not cut the 'un' and make it the 'written law'?" In the background, a group of figures representing the states held aloft a banner calling for a constitutional amendment to limit the president to two terms.

The Allies followed up their success in Africa with landings in Sicily in July and on the boot of Italy in September, but it was the spring of 1944 before the ground, air and naval forces could be mustered for the greatest amphibious assault in history, the long-awaited Allied landing in northern France. By now, the *Tribune* was distinguishing between the "nationalists" and "internationalists" in American politics, supporting the nationalists, whom it defined as those who "stand for international cooperation to preserve peace without surrender of American sovereignty."[11] The internationalists, the paper charged, would surrender American sovereignty to the new international peacekeeping organization that was proposed for the postwar world. On June 2, as Allied forces in Italy battled toward Rome and the world awaited news of the expected cross-Channel invasion, the *Tribune*'s front-page cartoon showed Uncle Sam standing in a "Den of International Intrigue," circled by pacing lions that represented "Old Hatreds and Jealousies," "Scheme to Control American Men and Arms," "World Gov't Scheme," "Control Over U.S. Resources," and "Old World Political Double Dealing."

The landings in Normandy on June 6, 1944, diverted criticism for a time as the public and the press followed the progress of Allied troops struggling to gain a beachhead. On June 7, the *Chicago Tribune* optimistically reported the casualties as "Light on beaches; naval casualties less than expected," and proclaimed in an editorial, "As a nation we are confident that glorious days are at hand. A mighty blow is being struck to free a score of peoples from slavery." In an adjoining column McCormick published a paean to the Middle West as the last dependable bastion of American freedom in an editorial that opened with a reference to the likelihood that FDR would seek a fourth term in the White House: "If Republican voters save America from New Deal totalitarianism on Nov. 7 the middle west can claim a large share of the credit. The middle west led the renaissance of Republicanism in America because its leaders adopted American principles and refused to be swayed from them. In the east there is too much bipartisanship and compromise; too much yielding to the selfish, the voracious, the un-American."[12]

In July, with the Allied foothold in France secure but the armies still bottled up on the Normandy peninsula, President Roosevelt announced that he would "reluctantly" seek a fourth term. The *Chicago Tribune* immediately declared him to be "The Man to Destroy the Republic" in a scathing editorial that accused the president of filling government offices with Communists, of conducting "a foreign policy of subservience to foreign nations," and of wanting to remain in office because he "cannot bear to think of Churchill and Stalin, his good friends, moving the nations about as pawns on a chessboard" without him. The editorial cited as an abuse of FDR's executive power the situation in Hawaii, where martial law had been declared after the attack on Pearl Harbor and was still in force. The *Tribune* charged that Roosevelt "has sought to supplant the civil courts and his department of justice for this purpose is working to deprive the citizens of their Constitutional right to the habeas corpus process as a check upon military tyranny. . . . The America which is winning the war is the unified, independent, self-reliant nation that we owe to our free system of government. The America that Mr. Roosevelt will create if his ambition is gratified is a military dictatorship."[13]

In November, the day before the election, the *Tribune's* front-page cartoon showed Roosevelt at his desk in the Oval Office, apparently asleep in his chair, with papers representing "Fourth Term Ambition" and "Communist Support" in his lap, a globe beside him labeled "Desire for World Acclaim," and another paper, representing "Broken Promises to the American People," in the wastebasket.[14]

The *New York Times,* reporting FDR's decisive victory over New York Governor Thomas E. Dewey,[15] called Roosevelt's fourth term "a hazardous precedent," but described it as one that a majority of Americans had decided to accept "because they were convinced that in this extraordinary crisis the Republican party offered them no satisfactory substitute for Mr. Roosevelt's experience in military affairs and foreign policy, and no equally good assurance that under Republican leadership the country could achieve a lasting peace."[16]

The *Chicago Tribune* responded to the election results with an uncharacteristically muted reminder that "Our country is still the only great country in the world which has dared to hold national elections in the midst of war. Of that achievement and of that proof of our faith in the Constitution and in each other, all Americans can feel proud."[17] The next day, the *Tribune* took an optimistic view of the state of the nation, although it said America had chosen "a dark and perilous course." In an editorial titled "Look at America," the paper demonstrated a progressive position on race and an abiding faith in the nation: "We have made a new people in this land, British, Mediterranean, Jew, Slav, Negro, Scandinavian, German, French—every strain has contributed from its peculiar genius and special talents to the American people. Don't be deceived by the scum on the melting pot. It always rises to the top. Beneath is the rich, fine alloy. Our people are intensely loyal to America. The annals of this war show that there are no special racial aptitudes for war."

In the months following the election and Roosevelt's fourth inaugural, the press concealed the president's declining health as it had concealed his physical disability since his return to public life following his bout with polio in 1921. He stood with the aid of painful leg braces that were concealed by his trousers. He walked with the help of a cane in one hand and the support of an aide on the other side. Newsreels and press photographs rarely showed him walking and never showed him in a wheelchair. He drove his car by means of special hand controls of which the public remained unaware. The concealment of FDR's handicap was so effective that millions of Americans had no idea the president was a cripple. What was most remarkable about this compact within the press is that it was the result not of political pressure or censorship, but of an age in which the private life of a public figure was not considered to be something the public had a right to know about or the press felt bound to reveal.

As much as Robert McCormick despised FDR and his policies, the *Chicago Tribune* never used the president's incapacity against him. It branded him a dictator in banner headlines printed in type sizes larger than anything the *New York Times* would ever use short of the end of the world, but in the *Tribune's* political cartoons, as in those of other American newspapers, Roosevelt was often shown as a vigorous figure, standing or walking, or sometimes astride a Democratic donkey. What the *Tribune* called "the silence of good taste" was broken "only when the President himself mentioned his health or some one in his official family discussed the chief executive's illness." In the spring of 1944, FDR had gone to the South Carolina estate of his economic adviser, the financier Bernard Baruch, for what was planned as a two-week rest, and stayed for a month. He returned to Washington improved, but rumors of concealed illnesses were so persistent during the fall election campaign that the Democratic chairman had felt compelled to denounce "the whispering campaign" about the president's health and the White House physician took to issuing frequent statements that portrayed FDR's condition in a positive light.[18]

On April 12, 1945, while at a spa in Warm Springs, Georgia, that he had first visited when he was recuperating from polio (and which he had subsequently purchased and turned into a rehabilitation center for polio victims), Roosevelt was stricken with a severe brain hemorrhage and died within a few hours. The news came as a great shock to the nation, including the *Chicago Tribune*. The next day, the columns on the *Tribune*'s front page were edged in black. The paper accorded the new president, Harry S. Truman, who had been FDR's vice president for less than three months, a provisional amnesty from criticism, in the expectation "that the advent of Mr. Truman to the Presidency sounds the death knell to the Roosevelt New Deal."[19] On April 14, under twin banner headlines: "ROOSEVELT SERVICES TODAY" and "GERMANY NEARLY SEVERED," the *Tribune*'s front-page cartoon showed President Truman at a ship's wheel labeled "America At War," with Uncle Sam at his shoulder, holding a cannon's ramrod, the American flag flying overhead, and the people massed behind them cheering "Onward to Victory!"

Robert McCormick would not eulogize in death the man he had so often vilified in life, but neither would he speak ill of the late departed. The *Tribune*'s farewell to Franklin Roosevelt took the form of an editorial-page cartoon, "The Final Voyage," showing FDR as a ghostly passenger standing at the rail of an ocean liner, his hat in his hand, raised in salute to the Statue of Liberty in the distance.[20]

Delegates from forty-five nations were scheduled to meet in San Francisco two weeks after Roosevelt's death, on April 25, to convene the United Nations Conference on International Organization, which was expected to establish a new world organization to replace the failed League of Nations.[21] One of Harry Truman's first acts as president was to instruct Secretary of State Edward Stettinius to announce that the conference would go ahead as planned.

The *Chicago Tribune* had no realistic hope that it could block the new organization. FDR, before his death, had taken pains to prevent the American position at the organizing conference from becoming a partisan issue. He had appointed to the U.S. delegation Republican Senator Arthur Vandenberg of Michigan, the minority whip of the Senate Foreign Relations Committee, who had revised his isolationist views after Pearl Harbor and since then had brought the conviction of a convert to his support for bipartisanship in foreign affairs and an internationalist approach to the postwar world. The *Tribune* acknowledged that the members of the delegation "all profess varying degrees of internationalism," and described Vandenberg hopefully as "a nationalist who advocates international collaboration to prevent war."[22] Instead of blindly opposing the San Francisco conference and the new organization it undertook to shape, the *Tribune* adopted a more pragmatic strategy by championing increased liberty and self-government for colonial peoples around the world. It supported former Undersecretary of State Sumner Welles, who in the spring of 1945 was conducting a debate in print with the *New York Herald Tribune* columnist Walter Lippmann, regarding the postwar disposition of colonial possessions. Welles had been among the American team that drafted the Atlantic Charter, a document signed by FDR and Winston Churchill in August 1941 that prepared the way for the United Nations Declaration, under which twenty-six nations pledged, in January 1942, not to make separate peace with the Axis powers. Welles' position, as the *Chicago Tribune* presented it in the week after FDR's death, was that "if the San Francisco conference really intends to promote peace it must go into the question of colonies." The *Tribune* agreed wholeheartedly and rejected Lippmann's argument that the United States should think twice before criticizing colonialism, in view of its relationships with its own dependencies, which included Alaska, Hawaii and Puerto Rico. The *Tribune* countered this line of reasoning by supporting independence for Puerto Rico and statehood for Hawaii and Alaska. In the paper's view, the only obstacle to Hawaii's statehood "that requires consideration is its Japanese-American population whose loyalty can no longer be seriously questioned." Turning a cold eye on the other colonial powers, the *Tribune* recognized that "Since we insist on military bases necessary to our own protection, we must concede the same right to other powers. We can make no honest objection to Great Britain's retaining such strongholds as Gibraltar or Malta, nor to her retention of the defenses of the Suez Canal. . . . But national defense has nothing to do with colonial tyranny such as Great Britain has imposed on so much of the world. We cannot lend ourselves, as the country upon which any world organization must depend for its greatest military power, to the continuing abuses in India and elsewhere by master races, be they English, French or Dutch."[23] The *Tribune* agreed with Welles that the colonial powers among the Big Five—the United States, Great Britain, the Soviet Union, France and China—were seeking to institutionalize their great-power status in the new world organization as a means of perpetuating their empires.

In the same week, the *Tribune* supported a suggestion by former president Herbert Hoover that the San Francisco conference establish a commission to promote civil liberties in countries that denied them to their citizens. The *Tribune* pointed out that "the free press, freedom of worship, freedom of assembly, habeas corpus, and kindred private rights" had been suppressed not only in Germany, Italy and Japan, but also by Stalin in Russia. It suggested that a commission such as Hoover proposed could keep lists "of the nations which do respect the rights of man and those which don't," and it advocated the position that "no nation should be obliged to fight on the side of a slave regime. That provision would spare us the humiliation and indignity of helping the Russians to suppress the Poles, Lithuanians, the Yugoslavs, etc., and of helping the British maintain their bloody despotism in all their Indias."[24]

Between the convening of the United Nations conference in April and the vote on the U.N. charter in June, Nazi Germany surrendered unconditionally to the Allies and the United States reconfigured its supply lines to shift men and material to the Pacific theater, where the island-hopping campaign begun in 1942 had brought American forces to Okinawa, less than four hundred miles from Japan. When it became clear that the new world organization would not require the colonial powers, great or small, to emancipate their colonies, the *Chicago Tribune* printed on the front page of its June 16 edition a cartoon that depicted the "Angel of Permanent Peace," a winged female figure, forging links of chain on an anvil labeled "League of Nations—Chaining the World to Its Present Masters." The native peoples huddled behind the angel, chained by their wrists and necks, include an Arab and a turbaned Indian, representing subject peoples of the British Empire. The *Tribune's* continued use of the League of Nations name was itself a form of protest, intended to invoke the failure of that organization, which the United States had never joined.

On June 26, 1945, newspapers across the United States reported the conference delegates' unanimous approval of the United Nations Charter. The *New York Times* reported that half a million people had turned out in San Francisco the day before to welcome President Truman, who had arrived to address the delegates in a speech that would formally close the conference. The same article reported that Senator Vandenberg had called the U.N. charter "the world's only chance" to enforce collective security, and promised "that he would make every effort for ratification of the charter 'with reasonable speed'" in the Senate. The next day, with the conference over and Truman's speech printed in full on an inside page, the *Chicago Tribune* questioned, in an editorial, the U.N.'s ability to fulfill its role as an international peacekeeper: "Americans after reading the charter inevitably ask themselves whether it will prevent wars. That is what it is supposed to do, but it won't. Today there are two great military powers in the world, America and Russia, and one secondary military power, Britain. Under the charter any of these nations can, with impunity, start all the wars it may care to fight. . . . If this document had been in force in either 1914 or 1939, it would not have averted the conflagrations." The *Tribune* judged the charter "definitely obnoxious in its requirement that the United States make annual reports on the condition of the natives of Hawaii, Alaska, Puerto Rico, and the Virgin Islands," while "Russia is not obliged to report on the Baltic states which it took and holds by force, and England is not obliged to report on India. In the eyes of the new league we hold Hawaii by permission, while Russia holds Estonia and England India by right." The paper characterized the charter as "a fraud," if perhaps "an innocuous one." If there should be peace for a time, the *Tribune* ventured, "it will not be because of the operation of the clumsy and self-defeating international mechanism outlined in the charter but rather because none of the great nations chooses to start a war."[25]

For much of the present war and the years preceding it, reports on the same events in the coverage of the *Chicago Tribune* and the *New York Times* had often read like accounts from alternate universes. In June 1945, the papers' initial assessment of the United Nations were variations on the same theme. The *Times* was somewhat more optimistic, but raised the same doubts. On the day the charter was signed, the paper wondered in an editorial, "Will it work? Obviously, no decision can be made to work if all the Great Powers do not accept it. . . . Under the Charter we shall see the world controlled by the Great Powers, but subject to numerous self-denying ordinances and subject also to the world opinion which can be marshaled in an Assembly where each nation, big or little, has one vote. Big Power control is not new. It is the restrictions upon such control that are new and that constitute the gains made under the Charter."[26]

Two days earlier, in an article that accompanied a chart showing how the United Nations organization was structured, the *Times* had noted among the smaller nations' concerns, "the 'little forty-five' are uneasy about big-power domination of the Security Council." The Security Council was given the responsibility under the charter with preserving the peace and security of the world. The Big Five were permanent members. Six nonpermanent members were elected periodically by the General Assembly, where all the member nations were represented. Agreement among the Great Powers was imperative in the Security Council, for at the insistence of the Soviet Union the Council could take no action beyond procedural matters without the unanimous consent of the permanent members. The system of voting had been decided at preparatory conferences among the Big Three—the United States, Britain and Russia. As Winston Churchill wrote, recalling the moment when President Roosevelt had proposed it, "Here was the Veto."[27]

Big Power unity was the key, but before the Charter was signed, before the war in Europe was won, the Big Three were splitting apart, with the United States and Britain on one side of the chasm and Russia on the other.

Two days before the Normandy invasion, the *Chicago Tribune* had accused Winston Churchill of retreating "into the 19th century" as the promise of Allied victory glowed more brightly, favoring monarchies rather than democracies in postwar Europe, and perpetuating the colonial empires: "He steps toward the future with the monarchy as his staff of oak and the empire as his guiding light."[28] Churchill was undeniably an imperialist, but if Robert McCormick had not been constitutionally unable to see Churchill as something more than the prime minister of the British Empire, he might have found common ground with the English bulldog in the spring of 1945, when it came to resisting Russian aggression in Eastern Europe. It was Churchill who pushed first Franklin Roosevelt and then Harry Truman to issue more forceful Anglo-American protests when the Russians went back on their promises and absorbed, as they rolled back the German armies, first Romania and Bulgaria, then Hungary, Yugoslavia, Czechoslovakia and Poland. It was Churchill who doggedly resisted Russian demands for a western border for Poland that went beyond a line Stalin had agreed to, and it was Churchill who fought for a broadly representative provisional government and free elections in Poland until the Soviets and their Polish puppets had so consolidated their power that Britain was forced at last to accede to President Truman's urging and recognize the Soviet-sponsored Polish Provisional Government. In Churchill's view, the failure of the western Allies to act decisively when their armies were still at their farthest line of advance was due to "the deadly hiatus which existed between the fading of President Roosevelt's strength and the growth of President Truman's grip of the vast world problem. . . . Neither the military chiefs nor the State Department received the guidance they required. The former confined themselves to their professional sphere; the latter did not comprehend the issues involved. The indispensable political direction was lacking at the moment when it was most needed."[29]

With Great Power unity broken before the end of the war, the reservations expressed by the *Chicago Tribune* and the *New York Times* about the ability of the United Nations to prevent future wars now seem visionary appraisals. But when those first evaluations of the U.N. were written, America had not yet tested its atom bomb and the ways in which the dawn of the atomic age was to change the prospects for war and peace were unimaginable.

⌒

What is most remarkable about Robert McCormick's opposition to the Roosevelt administration in the course of the Second World War is how our view of the opinions he expressed in the *Chicago Tribune* have evolved as the world has changed. At the time, to those who supported Franklin Roosevelt and even to some who did not, the *Tribune*'s attacks on the president who gave Americans hope that the Great Depression would not be the end of us, who recognized that the danger posed by Adolf Hitler and the Axis powers was of a different magnitude than the threat Germany had represented in the First World War, and who rallied the United

States to support Britain when she stood alone against the Nazi juggernaut, seemed to verge on treason against the causes of democracy and
freedom. With Hitler and Japan vanquished and the war they began
long past, even Roosevelt Democrats can reflect that before the Second
World War began, the Supreme Court had declared some of FDR's
New Deal measures unconstitutional, and Congress and a majority of
the American people had rebuffed Roosevelt when he tried to make the
Court itself more susceptible to presidential influence. The *Chicago Tribune* railed against those abuses at the time and maintained its role as
Franklin Roosevelt's leading critic until his death. From our perspective, the *Tribune*'s attacks at the end of the war on the restoration of
colonial possessions to their prewar rulers are no longer insolent assaults on the established order but a recognition of how the greatest war
in history had changed the world. (If the United States had supported
the decolonization that McCormick advocated, if we had been perceived as an ally instead of an enemy by the peoples who achieved independence as the grip of one colonial power after another was finally
broken, the history of the intervening years might be different in ways
we cannot imagine.) Robert McCormick's doubts about the grand
claims made for the United Nations were shared by many others, and if
some held higher hopes that those claims would be borne out, their
hopes had farther to fall.

McCormick outlived Franklin Roosevelt by ten years, and in that
time he saw some of his most ardently held positions vindicated. In 1946,
a case challenging the government's continuance of martial law in Hawaii
until late in 1944 reached the Supreme Court, where the majority found
that because the civil courts had been fully capable of functioning after the
attack on Pearl Harbor, martial law had not been justified. (The majority
and concurring opinions in that case, *Duncan v. Kahanamoku,* repeatedly
cited the Court's 1866 decision in *Ex parte Milligan* and applied the test of
that decision in Duncan.) The Twenty-Second Amendment to the Constitution, limiting the president to two terms, was ratified in 1951. By then,
India had become independent of Britain. McCormick did not live to see
the dismantling of the colonial empires that took place in the 1960s, but
the trend was clear enough in the fifties. It was the course McCormick had
tried to accelerate, when the delegates to the U.N. organizing conference
were still debating restoring colonial possessions seized by the Japanese to

France and other European powers, by advocating liberty and self-government for colonial peoples, whether or not they had the military might to cast off the grip of the ruling powers. McCormick saw the Berlin Blockade broken by the will of the western Allies. He saw what the United Nations could achieve, and what it could not, in a war that erupted just a few years after Hiroshima and Nagasaki, and in the fraught atmosphere of the Cold War, his warnings about Soviet Russia were confirmed.

7

HOME BY CHRISTMAS

The Korean War (1950–1953)

On August 8, 1945, two days after the first atomic bomb exploded over Hiroshima and a day before a second bomb fell on Nagasaki, the Soviet Union declared war against Japan. Soviet troops invaded Japanese-occupied Manchuria and on August 12 the Russian army crossed the border into Korea, which had been dominated by Japan since the Russo-Japanese war of 1904–05. On September 8, United States troops landed in southern Korea. To facilitate overseeing the surrender of Japanese forces, the Americans and the Soviets established zones of occupation with the dividing line at the 38th parallel, roughly in the middle of the Korean peninsula.

Here, as in eastern Europe, the former Soviet ally became an adversary. The Russians treated the 38th parallel as a political boundary, cut off communication between north and south Korea, and refused to negotiate the all-Korea elections that had been promised in wartime agreements. The United States referred the matter to the United Nations. The U.N. supervised elections in the south in May 1948 and recognized the new Republic of Korea as the only legitimate Korean government. In response, the Soviets created the Democratic People's Republic of Korea in the north and established its capital at Pyongyang.

In December 1948, the Russians claimed that all their troops had been withdrawn from North Korea. The United States completed its withdrawal from South Korea in June 1949, leaving behind five hundred military advisers, with the approval of the United Nations, to help train the Republic of Korea's army. With the American troops gone, the North Koreans sent saboteurs and raiding parties across the 38th parallel in attempts to destabilize the southern regime.

News from the Korean peninsula, if it was covered at all in American newspapers, was relegated to the inside pages. The headlines reported President Truman's announcement in September 1949 that the Soviets had detonated an atomic device, and on the success of the communist revolution in China, which culminated in the proclamation of the People's Republic of China on October 1, 1949. In February 1950, Senator Joseph McCarthy of Wisconsin charged that Communists had infiltrated the State Department. The House Committee on Un-American Activities, which had held its first hearings in 1947, scheduled more hearings for the summer of 1950.

On June 25, 1950, the North Korean army crossed the 38th parallel in force, rolled back the overmatched South Korean army, and drove toward the capital, Seoul, just thirty-five miles south of the border.

⌒

North Korea's invasion of South Korea came on a Sunday. Less than five years after the end of the Second World War, the headlines of American newspapers blared war news again. Robert McCormick's *Chicago Tribune*, ever ready to unfurl a banner, headlined "KOREAN REDS STRIKE SOUTH," but the lead sentence of the story reported that "United States military advisers said the drive was virtually stopped by this afternoon."[1] The United Nations Security Council met in emergency session and approved a resolution that declared the North Korean action "a breach of the peace," called for an immediate cease-fire, demanded the North Koreans withdraw to the 38th parallel, and requested that U.N. member states "render every assistance to the United Nations in the execution of this resolution."[2]

The next day, the *Chicago Tribune* reported a South Korean counterattack: "DRIVE BACK REDS IN KOREA." The front-page headlines of the *New York Herald Tribune* were also hopeful—"U.N. Backs U.S., Bids

Korea End War; South Checks Invasion; U.S. Rushing Arms"—but an article below the fold, by correspondent Marguerite Higgins, filing from the Tokyo bureau, offered an evaluation of the Republic of Korea's army that opened with a sober assessment: "The South Korean Army is a tough-fibered ground force, but it is seriously handicapped by a lack of equipment—especially air power, tanks, and anti-aircraft guns."[3]

The United States and its allies had no doubts that the Soviet Union was behind the North Korean invasion. Since the end of World War II, Russia had solidified her grip on Eastern Europe behind what was now called the Iron Curtain. For almost a year, from June 1948 until May 1949, the Soviets had blocked all ground transportation to Berlin. There had been Communist threats to Turkey, Iran, Malaya and Burma. A three-year insurgency by Communist guerrillas in Greece had ended in October 1949, the same month that saw the triumph of Mao Tse-tung's revolution in China. An editorial in the *Herald Tribune* of June 26, 1950, declared that the North Korean invasion had "callously stripped away the shabby pretenses in which the Kremlin has endeavored to veil its ambitions, and showed the peril in all its starkness."[4] The bold attack by a Soviet client state triggered fears of possible threats to the Philippines, Indochina, and Generalissimo Chiang Kai-shek's Nationalist Chinese government, now confined to the island of Formosa. (The Chinese called the island Taiwan, but it was not until long after the Korean war that western governments adopted this name.)

By June 27, the retreat of the South Korean army had become a rout and all optimism had vanished from American newspaper stories that told of North Korean tanks and troops entering Seoul and the withdrawal of the South Korean government to Suwon, twenty miles to the south. On that date, President Truman ordered American military forces to assist the South Korean army under the Security Council's resolution of June 25, even as the Council reinforced its earlier request, calling now for member states to "furnish such assistance to the Republic of Korea as may be necessary to repel the armed attack and restore international peace and security in the area."[5]

Walter Lippmann, senior columnist for the *New York Herald Tribune*, approved Truman's decisions to send troops to South Korea and to act under the United Nations' mandate. Lippmann cautioned, however, that "the Korean problem is not soluble by military action in any way that

would suit us. The best that military action can do—seen from our interest—is to restore the stalemate of that partitioned country. More than
that, were we to engage forces sufficient to enable the South Korean [sic]
to take over North Korea, would most probably bring about active Soviet
military intervention."[6]

This view must have given pause to some of his readers. Walter Lippmann was America's most influential columnist, and he was uniquely
qualified to offer judgments on geopolitical strategy. Just three years after
graduating from Harvard, in 1910, Lippmann had been one of the
founders of the *New Republic*. His writings there brought him to the attention of President Woodrow Wilson, who enlisted Lippmann's help in
formulating Wilson's fourteen-point plan for peace in the aftermath of
World War I. Disillusioned by the terms of the Versailles treaty, Lippmann
returned to journalism. He made a name for himself at the *New York
World* before he moved, in 1931, to the *New York Herald Tribune,* where
he began his opinion column, "Today and Tomorrow." The column was
widely syndicated from the start and by 1950 Lippmann's reputation was
enhanced by the half-dozen highly regarded books he had written on domestic and international policy, most recently *The Cold War,* in 1947,
which had played a part in establishing that phrase in common use.

Lippmann's *Herald Tribune* colleague, Washington correspondent
David Lawrence, was one of many in the press who considered that the
attack on South Korea might be only the first in a series of aggressions
planned by Soviet Russia. On July 3, as North Korean tanks drove
South Korean troops out of Suwon, Lawrence wrote, "Immediate mobilization of American armed forces on a limited but gradually growing
scale is the only certain answer that has been devised here to meet the
contingency that Soviet Russia may already be in the process of starting
a third world war."[7]

Despite Lippmann's concern about possible Soviet intervention in
Korea, he did not believe the North Korean attack was the immediate
prelude to a wider war. The U.S.S.R.'s standing policy, Lippmann noted,
was "to expand the Communist sphere by the use of satellites, without engaging and committing its own armed forces." The Kremlin had encouraged civil and anti-colonial wars, but even when efforts to enlarge what
Lippmann called "the Soviet orbit" met with defeat, as in Greece and the
Balkans, the U.S.S.R. had kept its own troops at home. Lippmann saw

this as "a policy of very shrewdly calculated risks . . . by not engaging its own forces, the Soviet Union is reasonably insured against a world war; by not engaging its own forces, its own prestige is not totally committed in any local venture." Lippmann argued that it should be "a cardinal rule of U.S. policy that at least as long as Soviet forces are not committed in any of these borderland struggles, we shall retain mobility and freedom for our own military forces. We must remember that our power is on the sea and in the air, and that we must not commit our meager infantry forces on distant beachheads, thus engaging large elements of our power in theaters that are not of our own choosing and where no decision can ever be had." In Lippmann's view, this was the greatest danger: "It would be an incalculably great Soviet success if the United States were to become involved and pinned down in a long, bloody, expensive, indecisive struggle on the Asiatic mainland with the Chinese-Korean forces."[8]

This perspective on the Soviet Union's expansionist ambitions was the basis for virtually all of Lippmann's commentary on the Korean War. From the outset he supported President Truman's intervention, but he feared it was motivated by the Truman Doctrine, a philosophy Truman had promulgated in 1947, when the United States took over from Britain the responsibility for providing military aid to Greece and Turkey. "It must be the policy of the United States," Truman had declared, "to support free peoples who are resisting attempted subjugation by armed minorities or outside aggression." In Lippmann's view, that doctrine, "were it allowed to stand as an American commitment to defend by armed force South Korea and all the places like South Korea, would be a most dangerous military entanglement and an increasing political liability." Lippmann hoped that in Korea, if the Truman Doctrine were kept "subordinate to and liquidated into the United Nations, as in the past ten days, its good purposes could be separated from its rhetorical excesses."[9]

The Security Council requested that President Truman name an American commander in chief for the U.N. forces in Korea. On July 8, Truman appointed General Douglas MacArthur, who had served since the end of the Second World War as supreme commander of Allied forces in the Far East. MacArthur was the only possible choice. He had received Japan's surrender in Tokyo Bay, he had overseen the demilitarization of Japan and guided it toward democratic government. To place another man over him was unthinkable.

On the same day, Truman authorized the armed services to call up reserves and draft 60,000 men. On July 25, with the North Korean advance a hundred miles south of the 38th parallel and reaching down the full length of the peninsula's west coast, Truman increased the draft call to 600,000 men and asked Congress for an additional $10.5 billion for defense. The president's requests received broad support from the press, the public and both parties in Congress. Senator Robert A. Taft of Ohio, who so embodied the Republican party's philosophy and positions that he was called "Mr. Republican," urged immediate tax increases to pay for the cost of the war and said, "I think the people are ready to accept it."[10]

Walter Lippmann judged Truman's proposals adequate, for the time being, but he cautioned, "Apart from the experience gained, the men and the materials submitted to the Korean campaign are subtracted from, not added to, our military power in the rest of the world." Lippmann supported mobilization so long as enough forces were kept in reserve to deter Soviet aggression elsewhere. "Mr. Truman is absolutely right in expanding U.S. military power," he wrote. "But if he keeps on expanding American political commitments, he will never be solvent, and he will be practicing at even greater risks to the free world, a deficit diplomacy."[11]

The president was not the only one expanding America's political commitments. At the end of July, General MacArthur flew from Tokyo to Formosa to confer with Chiang Kai-shek, who had offered to send 33,000 Nationalist Chinese troops to Korea. MacArthur declined the offer because, he said, the troops were needed for the defense of Formosa. MacArthur's statements to reporters after meeting with Chiang appeared to strengthen the American commitment to defend Formosa at a time when the Truman administration was trying to downplay the issue. (In his June 27 statement committing American troops to Korea, President Truman had moved to neutralize Formosa by ordering the Seventh Fleet to the Formosa Strait to protect the island but also to prevent Chiang from launching sorties against the mainland.) MacArthur had not consulted Washington about the timing of his trip, nor did he consult the administration before he responded to a request from the Veterans of Foreign Wars for a statement to be read at the organization's annual "encampment," in Chicago. MacArthur sent a letter to the VFW in which he said that it was essential to America's interests in the western Pacific that For-

mosa not fall into the hands of the Chinese Communists. He asserted that
to lose Formosa would expose the Philippines, Australia, New Zealand,
Japan "and other areas, to the lustful thrusts of those who stand for slavery
against liberty, for atheism as against God."[12] President Truman ordered
MacArthur to withdraw the letter, but the VFW had already given copies
to the press.

MacArthur's statements fueled the hopes of the "China Lobby," those
influential politicians and citizens who denied the finality of Mao's victory
and advocated continued support for Chiang and the Nationalists, in the
hope that Chiang could one day carry the war back to the mainland under
the shield of American air and naval power.

Walter Lippmann kept silent on MacArthur's VFW letter for the time
being. When he did comment on it, he praised President Truman's
"courage and decision" in rebuking MacArthur, and expressed a hope that
the day would come when the general's supporters "will admit that the
good work of MacArthur the soldier was saved from the political reckless-
ness of MacArthur the grandiose proconsul."[13]

These controversies came at a time when the United Nations forces in
Korea—the battered remnants of the South Korean Army and the Ameri-
can units MacArthur had been able to put into the field from his garrison
troops in Japan, only recently reinforced by the first new troops from the
United States—were confined to a perimeter around the vital port of
Pusan, at the southeastern tip of the peninsula. By the end of July, the
North Koreans were sixty miles from Pusan in the west, eighty miles to
the north. A month later, the allied lines were still contracting, but the
U.N. forces had consolidated their defenses and were pushing back in
some sectors. After weeks of uninterrupted bad news, most Americans, in-
cluding Walter Lippmann, expected that if the Pusan beachhead could be
held, which was by no means certain, many months would pass before the
United Nations army could take the offensive.

These estimates reckoned without Douglas MacArthur's determination not to accept prolonged confinement of his forces within the Pusan
perimeter, much less the idea of their having to quit Korea entirely. On
September 15, MacArthur personally directed an amphibious landing of
U.S. Marines and Army units in the enemy's rear at the west-coast port of
Inchon, scarcely twenty miles from Seoul. The invasion achieved complete
surprise. The Marines quickly took Seoul's airport and advanced on the

South Korean capital while the Seventh Infantry moved inland to cut the North Koreans' supply lines.

Walter Lippmann took some comfort from the improved fortunes of the U.N. armies, but he saw the threat of greater obstacles ahead: "The critical question in Korea has always been whether the Chinese and the Russians would intervene." Lippmann had never repeated his June 27 concern that the Russians might intervene and now judged it unlikely that they would, "because that would have brought on a general war. But Chinese intervention has always been possible," he wrote, "and had it occurred this would have meant at the worst a catastrophe to our troops in Korea, at best a long gruelling and indecisive war."[14]

MacArthur's landing at Inchon achieved its hoped-for objectives with breathtaking speed. The day after the landing, the U.S. Eighth Army, now composed of a British brigade and eight American and South Korean divisions, launched an offensive against the North Koreans from within the Pusan perimeter. The Allied force broke out in a week and a few days later joined up with the Seventh Infantry in its southeastern advance from Inchon. In less than two weeks the North Korean army was cut off from resupply and destroyed as an effective force. With the Allied fortunes dramatically improved, Walter Lippmann put his column on hiatus and took himself off to study what was called at this time "the Atlantic Alliance," organized by treaty in 1949 as a mutual-defense pact against Soviet aggression. At the start of the Korean war the pact's twelve member nations had not yet organized a coordinated military defense for western Europe.

With the mandate of the United Nations to unify Korea by force of arms, General MacArthur's forces crossed the 38th parallel in the first days of October. South Korean units took the North Korean capital, Pyongyang, on October 19, as the U.N. armies continued their northward advance. By the last week of October, they were spreading out across the broad base of the peninsula, in some places less than fifty miles from the Yalu River, the border between Korea and Manchuria. On October 24, the Associated Press reported that "informed sources" in Tokyo—which usually meant members of General MacArthur's staff—predicted that "most American troops may be out of Korea by Christmas."[15] It seemed that the goals of unifying Korea through military victory and demonstrating to the world that the United Nations would punish armed aggression were all but accomplished.

And then the frontline dispatches took on a different tone. "Korea Red Lines Stiffen," the *Herald Tribune* headlined on October 28, over a story relating rumors that as many as 30,000 Chinese Communist troops might have moved south of the Yalu to reinforce the fragmented elements of the North Korean army. The Eighth Army estimated that it was facing at least two Communist Chinese divisions and fell back to consolidate its line. MacArthur's intelligence put the Chinese force at 60,000, with 500,000 more held in reserve north of the Yalu River, which American planes were forbidden to cross, even for reconnaissance.[16]

In the first week of November, the allied armies lost contact with the Chinese. Homer Bigart, a veteran *Herald Tribune* correspondent who had won a Pulitzer Prize for his reporting from the Pacific in World War II, found the Chinese withdrawal puzzling, coming as it did "at a time when the United Nations forces in the northwestern sector had been thrown off balance and were very much on the defensive." Bigart was concerned by the failure of the U.N. forces to occupy the ground yielded by the Chinese. "It is sound tactics never to lose contact with the main body of enemy forces, yet this was allowed to happen," he wrote.[17] On November 20, in a dispatch from Eighth Army's position on the Chongchon River, fifty miles from the Manchurian border, Bigart reported that "the more thoughtful American officers" on the front lines understood that there was no realistic basis for the "home by Christmas" pronouncements. Some of these forward observers, Bigart related, argued against advancing to the Yalu River, "a long and vulnerable frontier with Red China and Soviet Russia," as Bigart described it, "a frontier which would require, to 'seal' it, five times as many troops as would be needed to man a defense line across the narrow neck of the Korean peninsula."[18]

The narrow neck, just a hundred miles across, lay behind the Eighth Army's position on the Chongchon River. The U.S. Tenth Corps, on the eastern front, had already advanced far beyond the narrow neck, moving along the coast to secure the ports. Ahead of the allied armies, the base of the Korean peninsula broadened to a width of more than three hundred and fifty miles, but it was far longer along the twists and meanders of the Yalu and Tumen rivers that defined the border.

On November 24, the day after Thanksgiving, General MacArthur launched a major offensive involving 100,000 American, South Korean, British and Turkish troops. MacArthur flew to the front to oversee the launch of the operation and announced that this offensive "should for all practical purposes end the war, restore peace and unity to Korea, enable the prompt withdrawal of United Nations military forces and permit the complete assumption by the Korean people and nation of full sovereignty and international equality."[19] The Associated Press reported that MacArthur told his officers: "I hope to keep my promise to the GIs to have them home by Christmas."[20]

On the second day of the advance, Homer Bigart reported that civilian refugees crossing U.N. lines from the northwest told of "a large enemy force" in that direction. "They said the force consisted of about 5,000, predominantly Chinese," Bigart wrote. "Estimates of this sort are inclined to be greatly exaggerated."[21]

Late that night, Communist Chinese troops, estimated at first to number from 40,000 to 80,000, then said by MacArthur's headquarters to be 200,000 strong, attacked the advancing U.N. troops and broke through the center, where there was a fifty-mile gap between the Eighth Army in the west and the Tenth Corps in the east. The Communists rolled back the South Koreans on the right end of the Eighth Army's line and rushed to flank the U.N. forces on either side of the break, moving to cut supply lines and block retreat.

General MacArthur declared that the massive intervention by the Chinese created "an entirely new war" and said "he never seriously intended to hold out hope that United States troops would be 'home from Korea by Christmas.'"[22]

Homer Bigart described the dire situation on the front lines bluntly for the *Herald Tribune*—"In a series of desperate rearguard actions, United Nations troops today escaped annihilation by overwhelming Chinese forces on the Chongchon bridgehead"—and criticized MacArthur without naming him: "The U.N. forces are paying the initial price for the unsound decision to launch an offensive north of the peninsula's narrow neck. This move was unsound because it was undertaken with forces far too small to secure the long Korean frontier with Red China and Soviet Russia."[23]

On November 30, President Truman declared at a press conference that the United States was fighting for "national security and survival." He said the United States might use "any weapon," including the atom bomb.[24] The president asked Congress for an additional $18 billion for defense, including $1.5 billion "to expand atomic bomb production to meet the new Communist aggression in Korea and bolster the nation's defenses against the threat of another world war."[25] The *Washington Post* headlined "Truman Ponders A-Bomb Use; Hasn't Ordered It," and reported that a Gallup poll revealed a majority of Americans in favor of using atomic weapons "in case of all-out war in China."[26]

By December 3, MacArthur estimated that his armies were falling back before a Chinese force of 600,000 men.[27] Pyongyang fell to the Chinese on December 4. The Eighth Army had managed to execute a fighting withdrawal from its farthest advance in northwestern Korea, suffering heavy casualties. Unable to form a line across the narrow neck of the peninsula, the army continued to retreat toward the 38th parallel. The Tenth Corps, cut off by the Chinese advance, fought toward the northeastern port of Hungnam to form a defensive perimeter there and prepare for evacuation by sea.

On December 5, Homer Bigart filed a dispatch from Seoul that expressed his sharpest criticism to date: "The most questionable decision of the last few weeks was General of the Army Douglas MacArthur's abortive offensive, which the enemy quickly turned into a defeat." Bigart characterized MacArthur's decision to expand the U.N. line along the long course of the Yalu river as "an invitation to disaster." Taking a broader view, he wrote, "The overall strategic picture is even more depressing. Two-thirds of the existing trained professional troops of the United States Army are pinned down in a part of the world where little damage can be inflicted on the arch enemy—the Soviet Union. This is not a place where the west can achieve victory."[28]

Bigart's stark assessment was among the first from correspondents in the war zone to criticize General MacArthur so directly, but the magnitude of the military reversal had set the American press on a search for someone to blame and the supreme commander was the obvious target. *Time* magazine and *Look,* which was second only to *Life* in popularity, were among the many publications that put MacArthur at fault for the debacle, which the *Herald Tribune* called "one of the greatest military reverses in the history of American arms."[29]

In the first week of December, *Herald Tribune* correspondent Marguerite Higgins was with the Fifth Marines at the Changjin (Chosin) reservoir in north central Korea, encircled by a Chinese army. Since the beginning of the war, Higgins had written mostly about the day-to-day

lives of the troops, but her present circumstances moved her to consider
the strategic implications of the Chinese intervention. "The Allies, under
the present military conditions in Korea face at best a severe bloodletting
or at worst a Dunkerque," she wrote. "The point is that it is the Chinese
Communists who will decide whether the United Nations forces go or
stay in Korea." As much as the bitter cold, Higgins felt in her bones the
threat posed by the limitless manpower of Asia. In a tone very different
from her usual matter-of-fact style, Higgins warned, "Disaster threatens,
whether or not America chooses to recognize it as a nation. . . . Some
American military men are expressing the view that if China continues an
all-out war offensive, the United States will have to pull its forces out of
Korea and prepare to fight a third world war."[30]

Reporting from the front lines of the Korean conflict, Marguerite
Higgins and Homer Bigart had arrived at the same conclusions about the
far-reaching effects of America's involvement in this Asian conflict that
Walter Lippmann had found while sitting at his desk, or padding about
the confines of his study, six months earlier in Washington and had articulated so forcefully ever since: Korea was only one part of a much more far-
ranging struggle; to lose sight of the larger strategic necessity was to risk
losing both the smaller and the greater contests.

Lippmann himself, back in Washington after two months studying
the North Atlantic alliance, regarded the Korean predicament more criti-
cally than ever through the lens of the imperative strategy. The objective
of the Russians and the Chinese, he believed, was to force the United
States out of Eastern Asia and western Europe, and their method was to
"bring about a showdown in the Far East where they have military superi-
ority." "My own view," Lippmann wrote, "is that our paramount and immediate preoccupation should be the preservation of our forces, and that
our aim should be to effect an orderly withdrawal to Japan. Then, with
salt water between us and the Chinese-Soviet masses, there will again be a
military equilibrium between the infantry of the Asian mainland and the
naval and air power of the United States."[31]

Lippmann's greatest concern was that the conflicting strategic views of
General MacArthur and the Truman administration had not yet been resolved. Truman's position from the outset had been that the war must be
confined to the Korean peninsula. Red China's intervention had
prompted MacArthur's advocates to become vocal in support of giving

him free rein to do whatever was necessary to protect his forces in Korea. In Montana, two local draft board members were suspended for refusing to draft men to fight *unless* the United States used the atomic bomb in Asia. Four veterans' groups—the American Legion, Veterans of Foreign Wars, Disabled American Veterans, and Amvets—sent a letter to President Truman urging that MacArthur be given authority to bomb military objectives in Manchuria.[32] MacArthur himself had repeatedly referred to Manchuria as a "privileged sanctuary" for the Chinese; in an interview with *U.S. News & World Report,* he described the prohibition against striking across the border as "an enormous handicap, without precedent in military history."[33]

Walter Lippmann saw the Truman Doctrine as the core of the problem: "For our inability to make good on the global promises of the Truman Doctrine precipitated the fearful quarrel within the nation and between the parties over where our limited forces should be committed. In the course of that quarrel the constitutional system for the conduct of United States foreign policy has been so seriously shaken that it is no longer clear where, if anywhere, resides the authority to conduct the foreign relations of the United States."[34] Lippmann's concern was President Truman's inability to determine and conduct foreign policy without interference from the Army's most prominent general. Lippmann blamed President Truman and his secretary of state, Dean Acheson, for choosing "not to face candidly, not to debate openly, and not to make Congress and the people judge decisively the great issues of foreign policy which arise out of our conflicting interests in Asia and Europe."[35] Lippmann called for Acheson's ouster, but he was only the latest in a long line of Acheson's critics to demand it, from the *Chicago Tribune* to the Communist-hunting Senator Joseph McCarthy. Like the earlier cries for Acheson's head, Lippmann's did not persuade President Truman, whose loyalty to Acheson was unswerving.

On December 15, President Truman declared a national emergency in the face of Communist aggression that he said was pushing the world "to the brink of a general war." He imposed wage and price controls and called for raising U.S. military strength to three and a half million men, up from the two million he had requested in late July.

In Korea, the Chinese juggernaut slowed as it approached the 38th parallel, then came to a halt to consolidate its gains. The last units of the

Tenth Corps held back the encircling Chinese and safely embarked from Hungnam on Christmas Eve, ending a two-week amphibious operation in which 105,000 troops and 100,000 Korean civilians were evacuated from the beachhead. The U.S. Navy described the extraordinary achievement as "Inchon in reverse."[36]

On New Year's Day, 1951, the Chinese attacked across the 38th parallel and broke through the allied lines north of Seoul. By January 6, Seoul was in Communist hands once more.

The *Herald Tribune's* Homer Bigart, back in the United States after six months of covering the war in Korea, wrote an opinion piece for the January 30 issue of *Look* magazine. "The harsh and unassailable fact of the Korean campaign," Bigart said, "is that a fine American Army, powerfully supported by the Air Force and Navy, was defeated by an enemy that had no navy, virtually no air force and scarcely any armor or artillery." This came about, Bigart charged, because "Unsound deployment of United Nations forces and a momentous blunder by General MacArthur helped insure the success of the enemy's strategy." MacArthur had complained, Bigart noted in a barbed aside, "that the enemy moved 'surreptitiously,' as though this were an unclean and indecent way of playing the game. But, of course, these stealthy maneuvers were no more novel or immoral than the tactics our Minute Men used against British Redcoats on the road back from Lexington in 1775." Bigart criticized MacArthur for disbelieving his own intelligence, for persistently misinterpreting the intentions of the Chinese, and for underestimating their capabilities. "It is a great tragedy that a man who served his country so nobly should be hounded and disparaged in the final hours of his career," Bigart wrote. "But that is one of the occupational hazards of being a general."[37]

When President Truman and Secretary Acheson forced a vote in the United Nations General Assembly to brand Red China an aggressor in Korea, Walter Lippmann argued that this was a monumental mistake because the administration had failed to make clear "what is to follow from the condemnation: whether the war against the Chinese aggressor inside Korea is to be expanded into a general war with the Chinese aggressor."[38] This was the heart of the still-undecided dispute between President Truman and General MacArthur.

Inside Korea, the war against the Chinese aggressor had taken a turn for the better. The farthest advances by the Communist forces had been reached in mid-January, some sixty miles below the 38th parallel, and then they advanced no farther. MacArthur and General Matthew Ridgway, the new commander of the Eighth Army, marshaled their American and Allied forces into a line that held, and then began doggedly to regain lost ground. For the first time since November 25, MacArthur's troops were advancing.

In March 1951, President Truman and Secretary Acheson secretly drafted a statement they proposed sending to the Communist government in Peking from the United Nations allies with troops fighting in Korea, suggesting terms under which a cease-fire might be negotiated. While the Allies were considering the statement, the Joint Chiefs of Staff sent a copy to MacArthur, cautioning him against the movement of any major forces north of the 38th parallel.[39] Within days, MacArthur issued a statement of his own in which he declared that Communist China had failed in its attempt to conquer all of Korea, that it lacked the industrial capacity to conduct modern warfare, and that if the United Nations were to expand its operations to the enemy's "coastal areas and interior bases," the Communists would be at risk of "imminent military collapse." With these "basic facts being established," MacArthur offered to meet in the field with the commander in chief of the Chinese forces in Korea to negotiate a cease-fire.[40]

These pronouncements, which MacArthur issued without notifying or seeking approval from Washington, scuttled any chance of success for the administration's peace initiative and infuriated President Truman. That MacArthur would suggest direct negotiations with the Chinese commander added insult to injury.

The Joint Chiefs of Staff fired off a message instructing MacArthur to clear all future statements with Washington and leaked the contents of the directive to the press.[41] MacArthur, however had already dispatched his next bombshell. One of his strongest supporters was House Minority Leader Joseph Martin, of Massachusetts, who had spoken in the House in February in favor of using Chiang Kai-shek's troops to open a "second front" on the Chinese mainland. Martin had subsequently written to MacArthur, seeking his views on the speech. MacArthur replied that Martin's proposal regarding the use of Nationalist troops conflicted neither with logic nor the tradition "of meeting force with maximum counter force as we have never failed to do in the past." Alluding to his civilian superiors, MacArthur said, "It seems strangely difficult for some to realize that here in Asia is where the Communist conspirators have elected to make their play for global conquest, and . . . that here we fight Europe's war with arms while the diplomats there still fight it with words; that if we lose the war to communism in Asia the fall of Europe is inevitable, win it and Europe most probably would avoid war and yet preserve freedom."[42]

On April 5, Martin read MacArthur's letter to the House of Representatives. These opinions were exactly what MacArthur's most zealous champions wanted to hear, because it echoed their deeply held belief that Communism and democracy were fundamentally incompatible and that the Communist powers must be destroyed by any means before they could destroy the Western democracies. Pro-MacArthur newspapers rallied to the cause. The *Chicago Tribune* described the proposals to loose Chiang's troops on mainland China and to use air and naval strikes to "destroy the military and economic power of the Red Chinese government," as "the only sound doctrine for ending the Korean war by military means."[43]

The *New York Times* expressed concern that the MacArthur furor "begins to affect our cause in Korea and even the solidarity of the United Nations and the North Atlantic Alliance." MacArthur, the *Times* said, "is wrong in some of his assumptions and especially in the manner in which he has presented his case. He is wrong in taking his case to the public over the heads of the civilian authorities and in violation of the orders of his own superiors."[44]

Walter Lippmann ventured that MacArthur's statement "must be a godsend to all the Chinese and Russians who are mobilizing the troops and mounting the offensive."[45] As for the notion that Chiang Kai-shek could invade the Chinese mainland with any hope of success, Lippmann observed tartly, "The argument about Chiang is an argument about whether to enlarge the Korean war into a general war. Those who believe in a general war with China know perfectly well that if Chiang's army were able to invade China it would be only because there was an American army in front of it."[46]

The *Washington Post* characterized MacArthur's recent pronouncements as "a course of conduct that the President, out of sheer protection of his office and his prerogatives, simply cannot ignore. Any reassertion of the President's authority as the country's commander in chief and initiator of its foreign policy would win him, we feel sure, the support of the American people. That's what they are crying out for—leadership."[47] The next day, April 11, the *Post* made its position even more explicit in an editorial titled, "Bring MacArthur Home!" Overtaken by events, the editorial ran in the same issue whose front page bore the three-word banner, "TRUMAN FIRES M'ARTHUR."

In a radio and television address to the nation on the evening of April 11, President Truman said that he had relieved MacArthur of his command because it was the aim of the United States to prevent a new world war, while the actions of General MacArthur had posed a "very grave risk of starting a general war."[48]

The next day, in a front-page editorial, the *Chicago Tribune* demanded, "President Truman must be impeached and convicted. His hasty and vindictive removal of Gen. MacArthur is the culmination of a series of acts which have shown that he is unfit, morally and mentally, for his high office."[49] The *Tribune*'s sentiments were seconded in some editorials around the country, but most of the major newspapers recognized the danger to the constitutional system that MacArthur's challenge to the president's authority represented.

The *Herald Tribune* approved President Truman's action: "In high policy as in war there is no room for a divided command. With one of those strokes of boldness and decision characteristic of Mr. Truman in emergencies, a very difficult and dangerous problem has been met in the only way it could have been met."[50] Walter Lippmann's reaction was subdued. Recognizing the essential role of Secretary of Defense George C. Marshall in Truman's decision, Lippmann wrote, "The President and the Secretary have done their duty. They have been faithful to their trust."[51]

Congressional Republicans denounced Truman and passed a resolution proposing to invite MacArthur to address a joint session of Congress. Truman and the Democrats recognized that opposing the invitation would only make MacArthur more of a martyr to his disciples. MacArthur was welcomed in San Francisco by half a million people on his return to the United States, (perhaps many of them the same people who had turned out to welcome Harry Truman in June 1945, when he came to close the U.N. organizing conference). Other cities offered to receive MacArthur and provided tumultuous welcomes. His appearance before

Congress on April 19 provoked displays of emotion rarely seen in the
Capitol chamber. In his speech, MacArthur recapitulated all the reasons
he believed that Sino-Soviet Communism must be confronted not just in
Korea but all along its borders, but it was best remembered for his remark
about the fate of old soldiers, and his promise that he would now "just
fade away."

He faded from the front pages within a few weeks, although he lin-
gered longer in memory. With MacArthur gone, the controversy over the
limits of the Korean conflict did not end, but Harry Truman had convinc-
ingly asserted the primacy of the civilian government and he had removed
from the stage the looming persona of the five-star general who had advocated a wider war. The act of firing MacArthur was persuasive evidence
that the United States was committed to containing the military contest
on the Korean peninsula.

On May 7, 1951, among the Pulitzer Prize recipients announced by
the Pulitzer board were Homer Bigart and Marguerite Higgins of the *New
York Herald Tribune* for their reporting on the Korean War. Higgins was
the first female reporter honored for international reporting.

In Korea, the contest underwent a metamorphosis from dynamic to
static. The U.N. forces pushed the Communists back to the 38th parallel,
and across it in the early days of April. The Chinese pushed back. Thereafter, the opposing armies continued to grind away at each other, but their
advances and retreats were incremental, with neither side prepared to
commit enough additional troops to upset the balance of forces achieved
at such great cost to both sides.

Marguerite Higgins had judged correctly that it was the Chinese who
would decide if the United Nations forces stayed in Korea. The Chinese
evidently judged, probably correctly, that if they annihilated MacArthur's
armies, no power on earth could have limited the American response to
the Korean peninsula, and a wider war, possibly involving the use of
America's atom bombs, would have been inevitable. And so Red China
sent into Korea enough troops to throw back the United Nations forces,
but not to overwhelm them. Once the lines stabilized close to the 38th
parallel in the spring of 1951, the Chinese maintained enough troops to
enforce a stalemate.

Six weeks before the Allied armies regained the parallel, in a column
that took the long view of the Korean situation, Walter Lippmann wrote

that it was no longer possible for the United Nations armies "to pacify the whole of Korea and unite it under an independent government." The current objective would be "to render the Chinese intervention indecisive and costly." He guessed this would mean a stalemate. An "indecisive struggle in central Korea is better, of course, than the forced withdrawal" that had only recently seemed likely, he wrote, but a military deadlock posed its own problems: "A stalemate without prospect of victory or defeat, and with no end in sight, is not the kind of activity to which Americans are by temperament well suited. We do not like getting nowhere at great trouble."[52]

Truce talks began in July 1951. In 1952, Harry Truman became the first president of the United States who declined to run for reelection in wartime. The Democrats nominated Governor Adlai Stevenson of Illinois. General Dwight D. Eisenhower, whom Truman had appointed in December 1950 to be the military commander of the North Atlantic Treaty Organization, was persuaded to seek the Republican nomination. Ike campaigned on a promise to end the Korean War and won in November in a landslide that returned both houses of Congress to Republican control.

Backed by this electoral mandate, Eisenhower was able to accept terms for an armistice in Korea that would have been politically impossible for Harry Truman. The armistice signed on July 27, 1953, partitioned the country along the current battle lines, a little north of the 38th parallel at the east end, a little south of it in the west. To arrive at this impasse after more than three years of war had cost the United States 140,000 casualties, including 33,000 dead.[53]

Six months into the war, as the Chinese hordes were advancing below the 38th parallel, Walter Lippmann had pronounced the United Nations a failure in its original purpose as a peacekeeping organization, but Lippmann supported preserving it as "an invaluable, indeed an indispensable diplomatic meeting place."[54] For the rest of the war, and thereafter, he found no reason to change this opinion of the international organization.

Lippmann offered no end-of-the-war commentary at the time of the Korean armistice . Within forty-eight hours of the North Korean attack in June 1950, he had written, prophetically, "The best that military action can do—seen from our interest—is to restore the stalemate of that partitioned country." On the ninth day of the war, he had written that Korea was a theater "where no decision can ever be had." Events had proved him right and he was ready to move on.

Walter Lippmann's commentaries on the Korean War were not dictated by partisan politics or philosophy, but by his personal view of a strategic crisis that the war posed for the United States at a time when Western Europe was all but defenseless against the military power of the Soviet Union. Lippmann preferred to counsel rather than criticize, but he was willing to take on the president of the United States and the nation's most revered military leader when their actions put the country at risk. Because he took pains to stay focused on the policies that he considered essential for America's survival, his criticisms were more influential and harder to dismiss than those of his less thoughtful and less experienced contemporaries. As part of his commentary, he formulated a strategy of his own, the Lippmann Doctrine, in effect, about the need for the United States to maintain a strategic reserve of ground forces in order to preserve its options in responding to Soviet aggression. (With the Soviets gone, that doctrine continues to provide valuable references against which to measure America's military involvements.) Lippmann's writings on the United Nations' action in Korea provide a singular example of the free press helping to frame the debates on the most crucial questions facing the country in wartime. They also demonstrate once again that even when the press produces exceptional commentary and the government makes no effort to suppress criticism, there is no guarantee that the most well-reasoned opposition will have the hoped-for result.

The Truman Doctrine's sweeping promise of help for peoples resisting "attempted subjugation by armed minorities or outside aggression" was never repudiated by its author or by any later president. Although it is no longer invoked by its original name, this seductive doctrine still appeals to American idealism and incites a desire to spread the blessings of liberty. Since the Korean War it has led us down other roads, paved with good intentions, that terminated far from the intended destinations.

8

QUAGMIRE

Vietnam (1954–1975)

In the immediate aftermath of the Second World War, the Vietnamese League for Independence, which had been organized during the war to resist the Japanese occupation, proclaimed the Democratic Republic of Vietnam and established a provisional government before France could reestablish its colonial authority in French Indochina. France reached an agreement with Ho Chi Minh, the leader of the Viet Minh, as the League for Independence was commonly known, that recognized the Democratic Republic of Vietnam as a member of the French Union. Difficulties arose over the extent of France's continuing role in the region and the disagreements proved insoluble. In December 1946, the Viet Minh attacked French garrisons throughout Vietnam, launching an effort to expel the colonial power. The war lasted until May 1954, when a long siege of the strategic French fortress at Dien Bien Phu, in northern Vietnam, ended in victory for the Viet Minh. An international conference at Geneva arranged a formal end of hostilities and the temporary division of Vietnam at the 17th parallel, with the Viet Minh administering the northern and the French the southern section of the country.

The United States, which had given military aid to the French in Indochina since early in the Korean War, soon replaced the French in providing direct aid and support to South Vietnam. In 1955, Ngo Dinh Diem became the first president of South Vietnam—which was formally established as the Republic of Vietnam—in an election of questionable integrity that produced a virtually unanimous mandate. Under the Geneva agreements, all-Vietnam elections were to be held by 1956 to unify the country under a new national government. Diem, supported by the United States, refused even to discuss arrangements for elections with the North Vietnamese government, and the elections were never held.

Throughout the remaining years of the Eisenhower administration, the United States provided economic and military aid to South Vietnam. In December 1960, a number of South Vietnamese groups opposed to the Diem regime, including Communist and non-Communist elements, organized as the National Liberation Front under a program calling for the neutralization of Vietnam and the withdrawal of foreign troops. Among the NLF's supporters were some, including former Viet Minh, dedicated to the overthrow of Diem's government by guerrilla warfare. The military arm of the NLF became known as Viet Cong, shortened from the Vietnamese for "Vietnamese communist." As the Viet Cong's anti-government campaign gained ground, more American advisers were brought in to train the South Vietnamese armed forces and more American reporters arrived to cover the expanding story.

Homer Bigart arrived in Saigon in January 1962, now writing for the *New York Times*. For the next six months he covered South Vietnamese operations against the Viet Cong, early uses of defoliant to reduce the guerrillas' cover in the jungle, the government's "strategic hamlet" program to protect rural peasants from being taxed and recruited by the Viet Cong, and American efforts to reform the authoritarian ways of President Ngo Dinh Diem and his brother, Ngo Dinh Nhu. When Bigart returned to the United States in July, he wrote a wrap-up in which he judged that victory in the struggle against the Communist insurgency was remote. "The issue remains in doubt because the Vietnamese president seems incapable of winning the loyalty of his people," he wrote. "Should the situation disintegrate further, Washington may face the alternative of ditching Ngo Dinh Diem for a military junta or sending combat troops to bolster the regime."[1]

As in his reporting from Korea, Bigart showed a talent for cutting to the heart of the matter and a gift for prognostication. At this point in the American involvement, blame for poor progress in the counterinsurgency attached mostly to the Diem government, but as the American role increased, so too did America's responsibility.

A few months after Bigart's departure from South Vietnam, the *Times* sent to Saigon a junior reporter named David Halberstam. Halberstam accompanied South Vietnamese troops into the field and became intimately familiar with the Mekong Delta, a fiercely contested battleground between the government and the guerrillas. On January 2, 1963, the Viet Cong shot down five U.S. helicopters and damaged nine others while the Americans were landing South Vietnamese troops to engage the guerrillas. "This was by far the worst day for American helicopters in Vietnam since the American buildup began here more than a year ago," Halberstam wrote.[2] The next day, he reported that "Communist guerrillas, refusing to play by their own hide-and-seek rules, stood their ground and inflicted a major defeat on a larger force of Vietnamese regulars yesterday and today. . . . What made this defeat particularly galling to the Americans and the Vietnamese alike was that this was a battle initiated by the Government forces in a place of their own choice, with superior forces. . . . Today the Government troops got the sort of battle they wanted and they lost."[3]

Halberstam's dispatches, more in their vivid factual narratives than any overlay of opinion, often contradicted the official statements by the American military mission that the Diem government was making progress against the insurgency. His reporting upset President John F. Kennedy so much that Kennedy told *Times* publisher Arthur Ochs Sulzberger he wished he would get Halberstam out of Vietnam. James Reston, a columnist and associate editor of the *Times* who had recruited Halberstam to the paper, successfully insisted that the *Times* could not bow to political pressure and that Halberstam must remain.

At the same time, the Kennedy administration was wrestling with Ngo Dinh Diem's obstinate refusal to institute political reforms and his lack of aptitude for rallying popular support to his government. On September 2, 1963, to mark the expansion of the *CBS Evening News* broadcast from fifteen to thirty minutes, President Kennedy granted an interview to Walter Cronkite, the program's anchorman, in which Kennedy complained that the Diem government had "gotten out of touch with the people." When Cronkite asked if the government "has time to regain the support of the people," Kennedy said, "I think with changes of policy and perhaps with personnel, I think it can."[4]

Walter Lippmann doubted that Kennedy really believed the war against the Viet Cong guerrillas could be won even if Diem's government reformed. Lippmann had left the *New York Herald Tribune* at the end of 1962 and was now writing for the *Washington Post*. He didn't question Kennedy's desire to win, but Lippmann was convinced that "it is for all practical purposes impossible to win a guerrilla war if there is a privileged sanctuary behind the guerrilla fighters. . . . We can be sure that it is quite beyond the capacity of Diem's government, or of any other Saigon government, to cut the supply lines to the North. Only the United States could do that, and then only if we were willing to pay the price." That price, in Lippmann's view, was "higher than American vital interests can justify." He considered that China might intervene in Vietnam as it had done in Korea, but judged it unlikely because "we have made it manifest that Indo-China is not a paramount interest for the United States by keeping our intervention in Indo-China limited and more or less undeclared."[5]

Perhaps motivated in part by the departures of her fellow Pulitzer honorees (Lippmann had been recognized twice, in 1958 and 1962), Marguerite Higgins quit the *Herald Tribune* in October 1963 and signed with Long Island's *Newsday* to write an opinion column three times a week. Higgins launched the column by traveling to Bonn, West Germany, where she secured a scoop of the first order by getting an exclusive interview with the recently retired Konrad Adenauer, West Germany's first and much revered postwar chancellor. The first of Higgins' two articles on Adenauer was published in *Newsday* on November 1, 1963. Earlier the same day, in South Vietnam, a group of generals overthrew the government of Ngo Dinh Diem and murdered both Diem and his brother Nhu. Two weeks later, Higgins was in Saigon, where she interviewed Major General Duong Van Minh, the key man in the military junta that had brought down Diem. General Minh told Higgins it would take "at least two or three more years" to defeat the Viet Cong.[6]

The U.S. State Department issued a flat denial that any American officials had been involved in planning the coup, but many American newspapers assumed that American encouragement had been decisive. The

Washington Star said that the people who believed the State Department denial "can be comfortably housed in a telephone booth."[7] The *Chicago Tribune,* now under the direction of the late Robert McCormick's ideological heirs, went farther in its criticism: "The record of incitation, both open and covert, in support of a change of political management in Saigon is too extended to support any belief that the Kennedy administration was an innocent bystander."[8] The *New York Herald Tribune* was more politely skeptical of State's denial, but the paper observed that the American government had made its displeasure with Diem so well known "that the effects of the revolt for good or ill, its success or failure, its impact upon the war against the Reds will be laid on the doorstep of the White House."[9] Several newspapers pointed to President Kennedy's remark about changes of personnel in the South Vietnamese government as encouragement to those who wanted to remove Diem.

The *New York Times* responded favorably to the coup and suggested that America's recommitment to the South Vietnamese government should be piecemeal, contingent on "rapid movement toward a broadly based government capable of enlisting wide popular support." The paper urged a redefinition of American goals to include support for political and social reforms as well as the military effort, and it advised, "Such concepts as a negotiated settlement and 'neutralization' of Vietnam are not to be ruled out."[10]

David Halberstam reported that most Americans in Saigon believed the political favoritism that had flourished under Diem was over. There was a feeling, Halberstam wrote, "that promotions will now be based on ability; that troop commands are already going to aggressive, proven officers and that this is likely to infuse the entire army with a new spirit."[11] In his post-coup dispatches, Halberstam reflected the euphoric mood of Saigon and revealed his own hopes that the fortunes of South Vietnam would improve as a result. But in his last overview of the conflict before he left Vietnam, Halberstam gave a more hard-headed assessment of where the war was going. The article has a melancholy tone, perhaps reflecting the fact that Halberstam wrote it the day after President Kennedy was assassinated in Dallas, Texas. Recalling his experience in the Mekong Delta, Halberstam described the region as a "discontented paradise" where "the most vicious war in today's world shuttles back and forth in front of peasant huts." Over the last year there had been, he wrote, "a slow and subtle erosion of the government position," with the government blindly repeating its own mistakes, while it was "the Communist side which reacted more flexibly to changing developments and which has so far shown the most motivation and discipline."[12]

In the aftermath of the coup, Marguerite Higgins expressed caution seasoned with a glimmer of optimism. "It is clearly Uncle Sam's team that is at bat now in Vietnam," Higgins wrote. She judged that "the military junta has at least a 50–50 chance of making a historic score for itself."[13] Within a few weeks Higgins felt compelled to revise the odds as she contemplated "the paralysis, confusion, and sharp downturn in the war that has plunged Vietnam in the past two months into precisely the straits from which the coup d'état was supposed to have saved her."[14] In March, 1964, Higgins wrote that the anti-Diem coup had "led to chaos and near-disaster" in its effects on the war effort.[15]

Between November 1963 and July 1965, the government of South Vietnam changed hands ten times. In this period of instability, the U.S. Congress passed legislation that verged on a declaration of war, and America's role in Vietnam evolved from one of advice and support to that of an active combatant.

On August 2, 1964, North Vietnamese torpedo boats attacked the American destroyer *Maddox* in the Gulf of Tonkin, off the coast of North Vietnam. The United States did not react militarily to the August 2 attack, but when Washington received reports of new attacks on August 4, directed against the *Maddox* and another destroyer, President Lyndon Johnson ordered American planes to bomb North Vietnamese PT-boat bases and fuel supplies. In a televised address to the nation that evening, Johnson emphasized the limited extent of the U.S. military response. The following day he appeared before Congress to ask for a resolution authorizing him to take whatever actions might be necessary in response to further attacks against U.S. forces in Southeast Asia.

Editorial reaction in American newspapers was generally supportive of the president's retaliatory strike against North Vietnam. The *San Francisco Chronicle* voiced an opinion expressed in many other quarters when it judged it "incredible" that the attacks could have been carried out "without the knowledge, and consent, and indeed at the instigation of Red China."[16]

On August 7, the Senate passed the Tonkin Gulf Resolution, granting President Johnson the authorization he had requested, by 88 to 2. In the

House of Representatives, the vote was unanimous. The *New York Times* noted that "Several members thought the language of the resolution was unnecessarily broad and they were apprehensive that it would be interpreted as giving Congressional support for direct participation by United States troops in the war in South Vietnam."[17] These reservations were buried in the text of the *Times*'s report, their significance apparent only in hindsight.

Marguerite Higgins saw the resolution as an important milestone: "President Johnson has signaled the beginning of the end of the American policy of allowing its Communist enemies in Asia to enjoy privileged sanctuaries," she wrote on the day of the votes. As Walter Lippmann had done the year before, Higgins deliberately used Douglas MacArthur's phrase to evoke the Chinese Communist sanctuary in Manchuria, which had never been violated. In Vietnam, Lyndon Johnson had just changed the rules. Higgins also reported that Maxwell Taylor, the U.S. ambassador to South Vietnam and former chairman of the Joint Chiefs of Staff, was "on the official record inside the government" in favor of keeping open the option of using tactical nuclear weapons if Communist China intervened with ground troops in Vietnam.[18]

James Reston observed in the *Times* that "the debate in Congress on the proposed resolution . . . demonstrates just how much the powers of the presidency have grown and how those of Congress have declined in foreign affairs." Congress, Reston wrote, could not deny Johnson's request "without seeming to weaken and repudiate the President in the emergency." By first committing the U.S. to a course of action, Johnson had left the Congress "free in theory only," as Reston put it. "The result is that the United States has now proclaimed that the maintenance of peace and security in all of Southeast Asia is 'vital to its [the United States'] national interest and to world peace.'"[19]

Reston was twenty years Walter Lippmann's junior and he was considered by many observers to be taking over the mantle as the most influential political commentator of his generation that Lippmann, then seventy-four, would eventually yield. Lippmann was Reston's patron and friend and they shared the political philosophy of the center-left. Reston had been writing for the *Times* since 1939, with a leave of absence in the Second World War to the Office of War Information in London. His column, like Lippmann's in the *Washington Post,* ran on the editorial page.[20]

Lippmann saw the naval incidents in the Tonkin Gulf as evidence that America's "invincible and well-nigh invulnerable" sea power assured that the United States could remain in Southeast Asia "without being on the ground." He noted that the presence of thousands of U.S. troops in Vietnam in the role of advisers departed from "the established American military doctrine that we should not engage the American army on the mainland of Asia." (This was not so much established military doctrine as Lippmann's doctrine.) But he was more tolerant than was his custom when it came to criticizing the neglect of this strategic imperative: "We have departed from the old doctrine perhaps because we had to. But the main line of American policy should be to return to it. For it is based on a true understanding of our position on this globe."[21]

By early in 1965, the Viet Cong controlled much of the countryside in South Vietnam. Since 1961 the U.S. military mission had grown from a few hundred to 23,000 men, still officially advisers, but the Americans were increasingly drawn into the fighting when bases where they manned defensive positions were attacked. In February 1965, General William Westmoreland, the American commander in South Vietnam, requested two battalions of U.S. Marines to guard the American air base at Da Nang, on the coast a hundred miles south of the 17th parallel. President Johnson approved the request and the Marines landed on March 8 in classic fashion, delivered to the beach by landing craft, where they were greeted by Vietnamese school girls offering garlands of flowers.

Westmoreland's request was prompted by the presence of a large concentration of Viet Cong near Da Nang. The American command took this as a sign that the enemy might be moving from guerrilla war to conventional war with massed-force tactics when they judged the conditions favorable. There were reports of uniformed troops among the guerrillas, possibly North Vietnamese regulars. Marguerite Higgins referred to these troops as "organized Viet Minh army units," but the term was anachronistic and most of the American press called them NVA, for North Vietnamese Army.

Since the Tonkin Gulf incidents, American planes had struck at North Vietnam in retaliation for specific provocations. On March 2, 1965, the United States began bombing military targets in the southern third of North Vietnam as part of an air campaign that was proactive rather than reactive. The motive for the campaign, as the *New York Times* viewed the government's purpose, was the hope that the attacks "will induce North Vietnam to recognize the advantages of a mutual cessation of hostilities through negotiation." The *Times's* immediate concern was the possibility of Chinese intervention. "The situation in some respects parallels that of the Korean War," the paper noted. "So long as the American and United Nations troops remained well below the dividing line between North and South Korea, the Chinese held back. When American troops moved up, China entered the war. This time, Washington's calculation is that so long as the Americans do not attack Hanoi and the industrial centers in the North, China will not intervene."[22]

At this point in the conflict, the American experience in Korea represented a paradigm that encouraged two assumptions. First, that the guerrilla struggle in South Vietnam was instigated and directed by Peking or Moscow, and second, that if the survival of the client state were threatened, the sponsoring power might intervene militarily to preserve it. (Since the Korean War, the Soviet Union had deployed its troops outside its borders for the first time, in Hungary in 1956, to put down a popular uprising there.) From the beginning of the American buildup in Vietnam, another divided country that shared a northern border with China, the possibility of Chinese intervention had been raised repeatedly by policymakers and the press.

Marguerite Higgins took the view that "Vietnam is a war that never would have happened if Peking had not decided during the war in Korea that the United States and its allies were merely paper tigers."[23] In a column on Walter Cronkite's September 1963 interview with President Kennedy, Walter Lippmann wrote, "Our intervention in Indo-China is to prevent Red China from absorbing the great natural resources of Southeast Asia."[24]

In Vietnam, the new element was the conviction that the failure of the United States to sustain the independence of South Vietnam would encourage other wars of national liberation throughout Southeast Asia, and that one by one those countries would topple like dominoes. The "domino theory," like the Korea paradigm, was an assumption reflected in most of the reporting from Vietnam, as in David Halberstam's farewell to Vietnam, when he considered the consequences of the struggle there: "The stakes could hardly be higher, for what happens here may decide not only what happens in this country but perhaps what happens in much of Southeast Asia as well."[25]

These assumptions affected planning at the highest levels of the American government. In February 1964, in a telephone conversation with Secretary of Defense Robert McNamara, Lyndon Johnson had considered the options of withdrawing from Vietnam or escalating the war: "We could pull out of there, the dominoes would fall, and that part of the world would go to the Communists," Johnson said. "We could send our Marines in there and we could get tied down in a third world war or another Korean action."[26] In this Hobson's choice, as Johnson saw it, the Korea paradigm pointed to the risk of a wider war but the domino theory ruled out alternative choices that might have led to neutralization rather than escalation.

In March 1965, a week into the new air campaign against North Vietnam, James Reston's thinking reflected the same preconceptions: "We are not at the end, but only at the beginning, of a very long struggle to block the aggressive expansion of Communist China. It is in the interests of all nations that this technique of military subversion be stopped, but it will take time to organize effective international forces for the purpose and meanwhile the United States must bar the gate."[27]

Those who accepted these assumptions accepted implicitly not only the goals of the Truman Doctrine, but also the policy advocated during the Korean War by General Douglas MacArthur, of confronting Communism everywhere along its periphery. There were some, however, who were questioning the underlying assumptions that were driving American policy toward escalation. Even as James Reston accepted that the United States must bar the gate, the *New York Times* took editorial positions that rejected the Korea paradigm. In 1963 the paper had urged that the United States should consider a negotiated settlement and the neutralization of Vietnam. In 1965, a week before the first Marines dug in around the airbase at Da Nang, the *Times* reiterated this view and advocated that victory should not be America's goal in Vietnam: "There was no victory or defeat in Korea," the *Times* pointed out. "The threat of a great war over Vietnam can be avoided if neither victory nor defeat becomes involved—which is to say, if there is neutralization under satisfactory terms and guarantees."[28]

In the third week of the bombing campaign, Walter Lippmann urged "a serious reappraisal of our policy in Indo-China . . . because the policy is not working and will not work. It will have to be reappraised in order to avert disaster: the disaster of our expulsion from the area leaving China supreme over it, and the disaster also of an escalation to a Chinese-American war." Lippmann saw the same choices President Johnson had considered the year before, but Lippmann regarded the conflict in South Vietnam as a civil war, one that "is going from bad to worse despite the bombing in North Viet-Nam." He considered the bombing campaign to be "only half a policy . . . all stick and no carrot," because "we are not telling the North Vietnamese what kind of future there would be for them and the rest of Indo-China if the war ended as we think it should end." In the absence of a cease-fire and peace negotiations, Lippmann foresaw worsening military and moral dilemmas for the United States. "As the military situation continues to deteriorate," he wrote, "the cry will be raised for an attack on the populated centers of North Viet-Nam around Hanoi and Haiphong. There we would be killing women and children. . . . I do not think that we shall stoop to that. And if we did stoop, it could land us in a war not only with the 16 million Vietnamese but with 700 million Chinese."[29]

Lippmann still believed in the threat of Chinese intervention, but he no longer credited the idea "that this war . . . will decide the future of 'wars of liberation.'" He called the notion that revolutionary uprisings like the one in South Vietnam were manufactured in Peking or Moscow "a profoundly and dangerously false notion," and proposed instead that they were motivated by "violent discontent with the established order and a willingness of a minority of the discontented to die in the attempt to overthrow it." He believed the time had come "to abandon the half-baked notion that the war in Southeast Asia will be decisive for the future of revolutionary upheavels [sic] in the world."[30]

In April 1965, when President Johnson announced that two more battalions of Marines would be sent to Vietnam and that American troops in Vietnam were now eligible to receive combat pay (this had not been the case so long as they were classified as advisers), Lippmann wondered why Johnson didn't propose an unconditional cease-fire, and he reasoned that the president rejected that option because "a cease-fire today would leave the Viet-Cong with the upper hand in the eventual negotiations with Saigon and Washington." Lippmann believed Johnson's goal was "to reverse the existing balance of power in South Viet-Nam before the negotiations for the eventual settlement begin," but he saw this as a futile endeavor. He pointed to "two great forces which we must and can rely on when eventually we bargain out the terms of our leaving Saigon. They will help us preserve the independence of Viet-Nam against Chinese conquest." One was America's "unchallenged supremacy at sea"; the other was "Vietnamese nationalism which, whether communist or not, is deeply, and it would appear permanently, resistant to Chinese imperialism."[31]

In Lippmann's view, the real reason America was fighting in Vietnam was "to avoid admitting a failure—to put it bluntly, we are fighting to save face" by continuing to insist that the United States could protect other countries against the Communist menace. Lippmann believed the effort would have the contrary result: "it is more likely that in making Viet Nam the test of our ability to protect Asia. . . . We are allowing ourselves to be cast in the role of the enemy of the miserable and unhappy masses of the emerging nations."[32]

In these and other dissents written over several months in the spring and summer of 1965, Walter Lippmann challenged bedrock assumptions that underlay the Johnson administration's justifications for the war, and he agitated the debate as few other journalists had done to that point in the conflict. As the American involvement in Vietnam deepened and as the rate of combat deaths rose, other voices joined what became in time a chorus of opposition to the war, but Walter Lippmann was one who led the way, persistently and persuasively, as the major escalation began. (In contrast, Marguerite Higgins, Lippmann's former colleague at the *New York Herald Tribune,* never abandoned her belief that Peking was the puppet master behind Hanoi, or that the Viet Cong, whom she referred to as infiltrators or invaders in the south, were entirely Hanoi's creatures. She continued to believe in the Korea paradigm and the light that American military commanders and government officials professed to see at the end of the tunnel. In October 1965, Higgins began one of her last dispatches from Saigon, "Once more in Vietnam, there is light at the end of the tunnel. But it will take at least 100,000 more Americans to break through to real daylight."[33])

At the end of 1965, there were more than 180,000 American troops in South Vietnam. A year later, the American troop level was nearing 400,000. The number of Americans killed in combat since 1954, which had reached only about two hundred by early 1965, topped 5,000 by the end of 1966. Expressions of opposition in the press increased as the cost of the war rose. In December 1966, an editorial in the *Saturday Evening Post*, which was considered to be conservative editorially and out of touch with the politics and mores of the 1960s counterculture, must have stunned many of the magazine's regular readers. "The essence of democracy is that the citizens of a nation shall have the right to vote on the major issues confronting them," the *Post*'s editors wrote. "The essence of our tragedy in Vietnam is that no such right has ever been exercised, either in Vietnam or in the United States." In the 1964 presidential election, the editorial said, the American people had overwhelmingly rejected the hawkish rhetoric of Barry Goldwater, but as soon as the election was over, "President Johnson adopted Goldwater's policy as his own." The *Post* branded Johnson's assertion that North Vietnam was guilty of aggression against South Vietnam "virtually worthless," and declared: "Vietnam is one country, torn by the agony of civil war, and the major outside intervention is our own."[34]

In the spring of 1967, a story arose from Vietnam that stirred the ghosts of the Philippine insurrection. Homer Bigart covered for the *Times* the court-martial, at Fort Jackson, South Carolina, of Captain Howard Levy, an Army doctor who was tried on charges of refusing to obey an order to train Special Forces aid men in Vietnam. Levy justified his refusal by accusing the Special Forces of torturing Vietnamese prisoners. The defense elicited testimony from three former Green Berets that established a tradition of brutality among Vietnamese irregulars who worked with the Special Forces, and admissions that Americans were sometimes present when prisoners were tortured, but as Bigart reported, the defense "failed to produce a witness with first-hand knowledge of torture or any atrocious act by any American in Vietnam."[35] The military court found that there was no basis for Levy's defense that the men he trained would "prostitute their medical training by employing it in crimes against humanity."[36] Levy was sentenced to three years at hard labor and dismissal from the service.[37]

In May 1967, Walter Lippmann retired from writing his column "Today and Tomorrow" (but not, he told his readers, from writing "occasional articles . . . without fixed schedules and with no deadlines to meet"). Despite his recognition that resistance to Chinese imperialism was central to Vietnamese nationalism, Lippmann never fully discounted the possibility that one or both of the two great Communist powers might intervene in Vietnam. In his next-to-last regular column (the last was a personal farewell), Lippmann wrote that President Johnson was playing "a kind of Russian roulette" by guessing how many and what kind of targets he could bomb in North Vietnam without provoking intervention by Red China or the Soviet Union. There was no certainty the Korean experience would be repeated in Vietnam, Lippmann conceded, "But what we do know is that President Johnson has war aims in Asia that cannot be achieved against the offensive power of China and of Russia."[38]

Lippmann's criticisms of Johnson's war policy stung the president and his advisers. In a comment on Lippmann's retirement, James Reston condemned the "vicious vendetta" President Johnson had conducted against Lippmann by leaking remarks about him to the press, and he called Lippmann "the greatest journalist of the present age."[39]

From the Tonkin Gulf incidents in the summer of 1964 through 1967 the major story in the Vietnam War was the escalation of America's war effort—the number of troops in South Vietnam and the intensity of the air attacks on North Vietnam. Because so much of the focus was on the deployment of American forces and their combat operations, the press coverage gave the impression that the United States, through the massive military power it was bringing to bear on a small Southeast Asian nation, had the initiative in the contest. When this impression proved false, the shock was seismic.

On January 31, 1968, the Viet Cong and their North Vietnamese allies launched an offensive during Tet, the lunar new year, simultaneously attacking more than one hundred and fifty objectives, including the American embassy in Saigon and virtually every provincial capital in South Vietnam, as well as most American military bases. The Tet offensive, as it was called, demonstrated vividly that any claims to the effect that American and South Vietnamese forces were "pacifying" the countryside and gaining ground in the war were wishful thinking. A month into the offensive, the Associate Press reported that 1,829 Americans had died from January 28 to February 24, 1968, more than were killed in the first five years of the U.S. involvement in Vietnam.[40] Stunned by the grim statistics and the scope of the Viet Cong's offensive, the American press undertook sober reappraisals of the war. The *Boston Globe* looked back to President Johnson's military response to the Tonkin Gulf incidents, which the paper had supported at the time, and judged the bombing of North Vietnam on that occasion "out of all proportion as a retaliation for an attack, which, if it did occur, did no damage." The *Globe* now urged "a willingness to accept an honorable compromise instead of victory."[41]

Walter Cronkite went to Vietnam in February, at the height of the offensive. On his return, he presented his experiences in a half-hour news documentary that aired on February 27. At the end of the program, Cronkite offered a personal comment: "To say that we are mired in stalemate seems the only realistic, if unsatisfactory, conclusion," he said. "But it is increasingly clear to this reporter that the only rational way out then will be to negotiate, not as victors, but as an honorable people who lived up to their pledge to defend democracy and did the best they could."[42]

In the days following the broadcast of the documentary, Cronkite made further comments on the *CBS Evening News*. He said pacification efforts in South Vietnam had come to "a complete stop." Of the still-rising U.S. troop levels and the continuing bombing of North Vietnam, he warned, "with each escalation, the world comes closer to the brink of cosmic disaster."[43]

When Lyndon Johnson heard of Cronkite's commentary, he is reported to have said, "If I've lost Cronkite, I've lost the nation."[44]

Events bore out Johnson's doleful judgment. March 1968 proved to be a fateful turning point in the war and in its effects on politics and public opinion in the United States. (Polls showed a solid majority of Americans already in favor of a phased withdrawal from Vietnam and a near-majority who considered the U.S. involvement a mistake.[45])

On March 10, 1968, the *New York Times* reported that General William Westmoreland had requested 206,000 more troops for Vietnam, a 40 percent increase over the half million U.S. troops already there, in order "to regain the initiative" from the enemy. In its response, the *Times* argued that "the policy of military escalation in Southeast Asia which President Johnson and his Pentagon advisers have followed for more than three years is futile—and worse." The effect of Westmoreland's latest request, the paper feared, "will be to push off negotiations, not advance them. The time has come to abandon this bankrupt policy. . . . The fate of the nation depends on it."[46]

On March 11, Secretary of State Dean Rusk appeared before the Senate Foreign Relations Committee, which was examining the administration's

Vietnam policy. The committee chairman, Arkansas Democrat J. William Fulbright, was a confirmed opponent of the Johnson administration's war policy. A majority of the Democrats and Republicans on the committee joined Fulbright in contending with Rusk. James Reston, in the *Times,* contemplated Rusk's failure to convince men who were "not only his natural political allies but his natural personal friends," and concluded, "He is a good man stuck with a bad case, which he cannot sell even to his old friends and allies."[47]

The second day of Rusk's testimony fell on Tuesday, March 12, the date of New Hampshire's first-in-the-nation presidential primary. Minnesota Senator Eugene McCarthy had announced in November that he would challenge Johnson in the Democratic primaries as an antiwar candidate. As recently as Sunday, March 10, the *Times* had headlined a front-page story, "Johnson and Nixon Given Big New Hampshire Edge," but McCarthy came within a few percentage points of defeating President Johnson. The unexpected strength of McCarthy's showing, like the Viet Cong's in the Tet Offensive and the American revolutionists' at the Battle of Bunker Hill, turned what was technically a defeat into a moral and psychological victory for McCarthy and the antiwar movement. The *Wall Street Journal* warned, "We think the American people should be getting ready to accept, if they haven't already, the prospect that the whole Vietnam effort may be doomed; it may be falling apart beneath our feet."[48]

On March 16, Senator Robert F. Kennedy entered the presidential race. McCarthy's partisans claimed that the Minnesota senator had done the hard work of opposing a sitting president for the nomination of his own party and attacked Kennedy for reaping the benefit of that labor. The *San Francisco Chronicle* rebutted this objection on the grounds that the two senators together, "each working on the Anti-Vietnam issue, have a much greater chance of getting it seriously weighed by the people as an alternative to the Johnson policy than McCarthy alone would have."[49]

As the three-way race for the Democratic nomination accelerated, editorials declaring opposition to the war marched apace. In a special sixteen-page section on the war that was bookended by sober editorial commentary, *Newsweek* declared, "After three years of gradual escalation, President Johnson's strategy for Vietnam has run into a dead end. . . . Only the deluded can console themselves with the comforting feeling that suddenly the war will turn a corner and the enemy will wither away." Recent events, *Newsweek* said, had underlined a grim truth: "the war cannot be won by military means without tearing apart the whole fabric of national life and international relations."[50]

On March 31, Lyndon Johnson addressed the nation to announce an unconditional halt in the bombing of North Vietnam and a diplomatic effort to initiate peace negotiations. At the end of his address, Johnson dropped a bombshell. He did not feel, he said, that he should devote an hour or a day "to any personal partisan causes" or to any duty other than his duties as president. "Accordingly, I shall not seek and I will not accept the nomination of my party as your president."

Johnson's peace initiative marked the end of official talk about victory in Vietnam, but the end of the war lay seven long years in the future. Johnson's successor in the presidency, Richard M. Nixon, had been an early and vocal advocate for bombing North Vietnam. As president, while pursuing a policy of "Vietnamization" of the war and gradually withdrawing U.S. troops, Nixon conducted a secret bombing campaign in Cambodia, authorized ground incursions into Cambodia and Laos, mined the harbors of Haiphong and other North Vietnamese ports and, in December 1972, soon after his reelection to a second term, unleashed the heaviest bombing of Hanoi and its surroundings in what was known as the Christmas Bombing. Almost half the Americans who died in the war fell on Nixon's watch, and more bombs were dropped on Vietnam and its neighbors during his presidency than were expended by all combatants in the Second World War.

In 1971, Nixon intervened, in a manner reminiscent of Theodore Roosevelt's intervention in the 1902 court-martial of General Jacob Smith, in a scandal over the murder of Vietnamese civilians by American troops, but with an outcome far less favorable for Nixon. The story of the "My Lai massacre," in which more than three hundred Vietnamese civilians were killed by American troops on March 16, 1968, was broken by journalist Seymour Hersh in November 1969. An Army investigation produced charges in March 1970 against more than a dozen officers, but only one officer, Lieutenant William Calley, was eventually convicted. When Calley was found guilty in March 1971 of the premeditated murder of not less than twenty-two Vietnamese civilians and was sentenced to life at hard labor, there was an outpouring of public support for Calley that tended to overlook his personal guilt in the My Lai murders because of a widespread perception that he was a scapegoat for higher-ranking officers who had ordered the attack on the hamlet and covered up the murders for more than a year. The day after Calley's verdict was announced, President Nixon ordered Calley released from the stockade and confined to his quarters at Fort Benning, Georgia, where the court-martial took place, pending a review of his case. The *New York Times* called the intervention "precipitous" and "an unfortunate interference with the processes of military justice." On April 8, the *Times* responded more fully to Nixon's action, commenting on a letter written to President Nixon by Captain Aubrey M. Daniel, the Army prosecutor in Calley's case. In his letter, Daniel defended the trial process and the verdict against Lieutenant Calley, and said that Nixon's intervention had, in his opinion, "damaged the military judicial system and lessened any respect it may have gained as a result of the proceedings."[51] The *Times* supported Captain Daniel and called Nixon's action "outrageously political." "Mr. Nixon's entrance into this matter," the *Times* declared, "was an affront to the American judicial process and has already done untold damage to respect for American law as well as justice, civil as well as military."[52]

In this instance, as throughout his conduct of the war, the press subjected Nixon to intense scrutiny. For his part, Nixon took a far more aggressive attitude toward the press than either John Kennedy or Lyndon Johnson. Nixon's attorney general, John Mitchell, authorized wiretaps on Hedrick Smith of the *Times* and Marvin Kalb of CBS News, and instructed the FBI to investigate CBS newsman Daniel Schorr.[53] The *Times* and the *Washington Post,* as well as scores of individual journalists from those and many other publications, ended up on what became known as Nixon's "Enemies List," and the two newspapers were at the center of a momentous confrontation with the administration over freedom of the press that took place in June 1971.

On Sunday, June 13, the *Times* published the first of what it planned as a series of ten articles, to be published on consecutive days, about a secret report that had been commissioned by Secretary of Defense Robert S. McNamara in June 1967. The report was formally titled "United States—Vietnam Relations, 1945–1967." It was prepared within the Department of Defense, drawing on the documentary records of the U.S. government to examine the course of U.S.-Vietnamese relations since the end of World War II, and the origins of the Vietnam War. The report had been brought to the *Times* by Daniel Ellsberg, a former Marine Corps officer and one of the Defense Department employees who worked on the report. Of all those who produced it, Ellsberg must have been one of very few who read most of the report's 7,000 pages. Convinced that the report should be made public, Ellsberg had first tried to convince several members of the U.S. Senate to release it. When the senators refused, Ellsberg offered the report to the *Washington Post,* which declined to publish it, before he found a warmer reception at the *Times.*

Within forty-eight hours of the appearance of the first article in the *Times,* Attorney General Mitchell requested that the newspaper cease publishing the articles. When the *Times* refused, Mitchell obtained a temporary restraining order in federal district court in New York City. This was the first time an American court had ever approved prior restraint, prohibiting in advance the publication of specific material by an American newspaper. James Reston acidly observed, "For the first time in the history of the Republic, the Attorney General of the United States has tried to suppress documents he hasn't read about a war that hasn't been declared. This is one of the final ironies about this tragic war, but it won't work for long."[54]

At the *Washington Post,* publisher Katharine Graham and editor Ben Bradlee reconsidered their earlier decision not to publish the Pentagon report. The *Post* began its own series on June 18 and was restrained by the federal district court in Washington, D.C., on the same day. The *Boston Globe* and the *St. Louis Post-Dispatch* were similarly enjoined when they too attempted to publish commentary and excerpts of the report, which by now was called "the Pentagon papers."

Because of the seriousness of the constitutional issue, the case moved through the courts with exceptional speed. When the respective district courts issued rulings in favor of the *Times* and the *Post,* the Justice Department appealed to the Supreme Court, which combined the two cases, heard arguments, and announced its decision on June 30. By six to three, the Court ruled in favor of the newspapers. The majority found that the government had failed to meet the burden of proof that publication of the report would cause "irreparable injury to the defense interests of the United States."[55]

In a concurring opinion, Justice Hugo Black wrote that even if such injury had been shown, he would still oppose prior restraint: "The government's power to censure the press was abolished so that the press would remain forever free to censure the government. . . . In my view, far from deserving condemnation for their courageous reporting, *The New York Times, The Washington Post* and other newspapers should be commended for serving the purpose that the Founding Fathers saw so clearly. In reveal-ing the workings of government that led to the Vietnam war the newspa-pers nobly did precisely that which the Founders hoped and trusted they would do."[56]

The *Times* declared the Court's ruling "a ringing victory for free-dom under law," but the *Washington Post* found little to celebrate. It noted that the door to prior restraint of the press had been opened by the temporary orders of the district courts and had not been closed de-cisively by the Supreme Court's decision. In the *Post*'s view, "there is not all that much comfort, let alone clearcut law, to be found in yesterday's outcome."[57] The *Times*'s columnist Tom Wicker reviewed a series of policies the Nixon administration had instituted or advocated—"Pre-ventive detention, preventive eavesdropping . . . and preventive sup-pression of the news"—and wondered, "what will they seek to prevent next, and by what dubious or extraconstitutional means? It is a sad question, made unavoidable by this ominous and continuing search for loopholes in the Bill of Rights on the part of a Government solemnly sworn to uphold it."[58]

The *Times* and the *Post* resumed their series on the Pentagon papers, joined now by many other newspapers around the country. Among the revelations in the report was confirmation that the United States had "variously authorized, sanctioned and encouraged the coup efforts of the Vietnamese generals" against Ngo Dinh Diem in 1963.[59] Possibly the most damning disclosure was that in the summer of 1964, before the Tonkin Gulf incidents, the United States had supported secret attacks on installations on the North Vietnamese coast and offshore islands by South Vietnamese torpedo boats and had conducted electronic surveil-lance of shore-based communications by specially equipped U.S. Navy destroyers, including the U.S.S. *Maddox*. In light of this admission, it was apparent that the North Vietnamese had responded to these provo-cations, and that the Tonkin Gulf Resolution, passed in response to what President Johnson had termed "open aggression the high seas," was based on a lie.

In the Vietnam war, the press demonstrably played a key role in shifting public opinion from supporting the government's war policy to opposing it. In the Korean conflict, the public had turned against the war once the contest lapsed into stalemate and there was no longer any chance for victory, but before the public became disenchanted with the war the American government had renounced the United Nations' original goal of unifying Korea by force and was committed to a negotiated settlement. There, the press affected public opinion by reporting the ongoing cost of the struggle, which was too much to bear for no visible purpose, rather than by opposing an ongoing government policy. In Vietnam, the press and the public turned against the Johnson administration while the president was still committed to a military victory, forcing Johnson to change course in Vietnam and take himself out of the running for reelection. The positions endorsed beginning early in the war by the *New York Times* and by Walter Lippmann in the *Washington Post* became part of a gathering consensus that produced the historic shift. There were others who expressed early dissent, but Lippmann and the several voices of the *Times*—especially David Halberstam, Neil Sheehan and Charles Mohr among the correspondents and James Reston in his column, as well as the editorial page—articulated the opinions of what was at the start a small minority, and by passion and persuasion expanded the opposition into a majority.

Writing of the dramatic helicopter air-lift from the roof of the United States embassy by which the last Americans left Saigon on the last day of April 1975, the *New York Times* saw the "scenes of agony and tumult" as "one more sorrowful episode at the conclusion of an American—and Vietnamese—tragedy."[60] On May 4, 1975, while the dust raised by the final Communist offensive was still settling in South Vietnam, the *Times* put the war to rest and looked ahead: "Past errors must not now be compounded by a misreading of their meaning for the future. . . . For the long term, we as Americans need to regain enough confidence in ourselves to spurn both isolationism and the temptation to improve the world by forcing it into the American image."[61]

9

DESERT STORM

Iraq (1991)

In September 1980, Saddam Hussein, the president-dictator of Iraq, launched his military forces into neighboring Iran to secure the waterway that separated the two countries, and with the aim of controlling an oil-rich area of western Iran. The Iran-Iraq War lasted for eight years. It inflicted a million casualties on the two nations. Iraq's use of poison gas against Iran provoked international condemnation, as did Iran's attacks on Kuwaiti oil tankers in the Persian Gulf. The two nations accepted a cease-fire negotiated by the United Nations in July 1988.

On August 2, 1990, Iraq attacked another neighbor, this time the tiny kingdom of Kuwait, in a dispute over oil production, over a shared oil field on the Iraq-Kuwait border, and over Kuwait itself, which Iraq claimed as an errant province. The U.N. Security Council condemned the invasion, imposed a trade embargo on Iraq, and demanded that Iraq withdraw from Kuwait. President George H. W. Bush launched a diplomatic campaign to assemble a coalition of nations to oppose Iraq's aggression and restore Kuwait's sovereignty. Saddam Hussein ignored the U.N. resolution, declared the annexation of Kuwait, and was reported to be massing his troops along Kuwait's border with Saudi Arabia. Osama bin Laden, a Saudi-born millionaire who had fought beside and helped to finance the mujahidin in Afghanistan in their ten-year struggle against the Soviet army, offered to provide an army of mujahidin to protect his native land. The Saudis rejected bin Laden's offer and requested American troops to guard their oil fields. The first U.S. contingent arrived in Saudi Arabia within a week of Iraq's invasion of Kuwait as the vanguard of an operation called Desert Shield. Within a few weeks the United States had dispatched more than 200,000 troops to the Persian Gulf. The American Navy blockaded Iraq's ports, enforcing the U.N. trade embargo and shutting off shipments of Iraqi oil.

In October and November 1990, as Saddam Hussein built up his forces in Kuwait to half a million men, President Bush doubled the number of American troops in the region to more than 400,000. The U.S. force was augmented by contingents from the United Kingdom, France, Egypt and other members of the coalition, which now included more than thirty nations. On November 29, the U.N. Security Council set January 15, 1991, as a deadline for Iraq to withdraw its forces from Kuwait, after which the American-led coalition was authorized to use military force to eject the Iraqis. By early January, there were more than 700,000 coalition troops in the Gulf, with the American contingent at half a million.

<hr />

The 1991 war in the Persian Gulf acts as a two-sided mirror, reflecting back to the war in Vietnam and casting a premonitory light forward to America's present difficulties in the Middle East, for which, at this writing, there is no end in sight.

The American response to Saddam Hussein's aggression against Kuwait was virtual unanimity in condemning it. President Bush stated flatly, "This will not stand." The *New York Times* declared, "Without warrant or warning, Iraq has struck brutally at tiny Kuwait, a brazen challenge to world law."[1] Other newspapers exercised variations on the same theme.

As the buildup of forces in the gulf began, it soon became clear that the American military, still bitter over what it saw as betrayal by the press in Vietnam, was resolved not to allow any similar misbehavior in this theater, whether or not the massive deployment led to war. The U.S. military's Central Command (Centcom), whose authority included the Middle East,[2] established a headquarters for the American press corps at

Dhahran, Saudi Arabia, on the western shore of the Persian Gulf, three hundred kilometers from the Kuwaiti border. Press access to the coalition troops was strictly controlled by Centcom. Correspondents in Dhahran could sign up for field trips on which they might see tanks practice-firing, have lunch with the frontline troops, and possibly interview a battalion commander.[3] At the press headquarters in Dhahran, press pools—groups of reporters from the various media—were formed and assigned to military units in the desert staging areas near the Kuwaiti border. Typically, a pool team would include a reporter from the print media, one from radio, a still photographer, and a two- or three-man television crew. Competition to get assigned to a pool was intense, despite the reporters' loathing for the pool system, under which all dispatches filed by pool correspondents were shared with the reporters who were not assigned to units in the field. An added aggravation was the requirement that all reports filed by press pools in the desert, as well as television and radio reports sent from the pool headquarters at Dhahran or from the Saudi capital, Riyadh, were subject to "security review" by military censors—that is, censorship.[4]

There was no single newspaper or commentator, either before or during the war, that set a standard for others in the press to follow, but three newspapers—the *New York Times* and two important regional papers, one in New England, the other in the deep South—expressed misgivings and criticisms that were representative of those put forth in other journals widely separated by geography and philosophy.

On January 8, 1991, with the United Nations January 15 deadline looming, President Bush sent a letter to the leadership in Congress, requesting a resolution to support the use of "all necessary means" to enforce the U.N. resolution if Iraq did not withdraw voluntarily from Kuwait. The *Times* urged Congress to consider "what best serves the vital interests of the United States." It suggested that "At this time those interests would not be served by the offensive use of military force to expel Iraq from Kuwait." The *Times* noted that it supported President Bush's successful creation of the coalition to oppose Iraq's aggression, it supported deploying troops to protect Saudi Arabia, and it supported the trade embargo against Iraq. "Nor do we shrink from the ultimate prospect of war," the paper assured its readers. "There are circumstances that justify, even compel, the sacrifices of war. But those circumstances are not now present." For now, the *Times* advised the Congress, "the wise, brave vote on war is no."[5]

The *Boston Globe* declared, "The blank check that Bush seeks will be dangerous and politically divisive, yet he may well get it." The *Globe* expected a close vote in the Senate, not so close in the House, where "many Democrats have caved in to the administration."[6]

The *Globe*'s prediction was on the money. The House approved the resolution authorizing the president to use force by 250 to 183 and the Senate by 52 to 47. Ten Democratic senators, including Al Gore of Tennessee and Joseph Lieberman of Connecticut, voted to back the president.[7] The *Globe* pointed to the results as proof that "the country is deeply divided about the wisdom of President Bush's policy and about the necessity of war at this time." The paper branded the votes "a grave misstep," and said, "They represent the Congress' final acquiescence in an unconscionably risky resort to violence that is not only not warranted at this time, but that is likely to reap a whirlwind of grim consequences."[8]

In the *Times,* columnist Anthony Lewis observed, just as James Reston had observed after the vote on the Tonkin Gulf resolution in 1964, "how dominant is the power of the modern President." Like Reston, Lewis pointed out that the president—in this case George H. W. Bush—"had framed the question so that it was extremely hard for the Congress to say no." Lewis noted that Bush had ordered the increase in the size of the American contingent in the gulf in late October but had only revealed that decision after the midterm election in November. Bush then persuaded the U.N. Security Council to authorize the use of military force if the Iraqis did not withdraw from Kuwait. "He made delay equal to an American defeat," Lewis wrote. And only then, having framed the issue in these terms, did Bush put the question to the Congress: "The wisdom of George Bush's course will be tested soon. It may be that Saddam Hussein will give way. I hope he does. But it may also be that the President has so successfully destroyed all other options that he and we will find ourselves at war, with incalculable consequences."[9]

The January 15 deadline came and went. Another day ticked past. Early in the morning of January 17, Peter Arnett, Bernard Shaw and John Holliman, three reporters for the Cable News Network who had remained in Baghdad when most American reporters left, reported the start of the aerial bombardment to the world half an hour ahead of the official Pentagon announcement that the war had begun. In those thirty minutes, Operation Desert Shield became Desert Storm and the dominant influence in television news shifted from the traditional networks' evening news broadcasts to CNN.

The first Centcom briefings on the air war included edited video clips from cameras aboard "smart" bombs and missiles and jet fighter-bombers. The images and the technology were dazzling. The briefings bypassed the press corps and went directly to the United States and the world. Of all the top-ranking Centcom briefers, none was more masterful than General Norman Schwarzkopf, the supreme commander of the coalition's military forces. In the judgment of veteran CBS newsman Morley Safer, Schwarzkopf "made journalism redundant."[10] The television networks had no film of their own to augment what was provided by the U.S. military or borrowed from CNN's team in Baghdad.[11] Short of live images, the networks made extensive use of computer-animated graphics to show maps of Iraq and the locations of air strikes. The combined effect on the public of the computer graphics and the military's video clips, in the view of John R. MacArthur, the publisher of *Harper's* magazine, was "deadening. . . . It made them think that war was a game."[12]

The *Boston Globe* protested that the Pentagon was offering an incomplete picture of the conflict. "Far more important elements—human and political—are being lost."[13]

The *New York Times* said of the military videos, "The camera doesn't lie. . . . But the camera doesn't necessarily tell the whole truth, any more than the home team's highlight film adequately depicts a football game." The *Times* reported that a Centcom briefing officer said B–52 bombers had been striking targets "across both Kuwait and Iraq," but he offered no film and gave no further information on targets or results. Students of the Vietnam War, the *Times* observed, "may shudder at the memory of the sights and sounds of a B–52 dropping 50 tons of bombs on 'free-fire zones,' wreaking indiscriminate havoc."[14]

The *Atlanta Journal and Constitution* criticized the Pentagon for withholding from the public "a real picture of the hell that is war." Refuting the military's lingering resentment over Vietnam as a rationale for the restrictions on the press in the Persian Gulf, the *Journal and Constitution* declared, "Accurate news reporting did not make Vietnam a national disaster; government deception about the actual nature of the war did."[15]

To avoid the censorship and travel restrictions imposed in Saudi Arabia, some reporters elected to report from Jordan, on Iraq's western border. Marcia Kunstel, a correspondent for Cox Newspapers, drove two hundred and fifty kilometers from Amman to the Iraqi border with other reporters to interview the refugees who were fleeing Iraq in expectation of the American-led assault. These included Kuwaitis who escaped their country during or after the Iraqi invasion, and foreign nationals who were ejected from Kuwait by the Iraqis. (Iraqis were not allowed to leave.) The people emerging from Iraq told tales of "buildings being destroyed and people being killed," Kunstel related, "and then you'd go back to your hotel [in Amman] and you'd look at CNN and they'd have all these sort of antiseptic reports about 'surgical strikes' and how wonderfully the military's doing, and nobody's getting hurt." In contrast to the picture the refugees gave of the air war, Kunstel said, the television news accounts "did seem to be really controlled."[16]

The controversy over the Pentagon restrictions, argued at length in the print media and reported by television news programs mostly as if it didn't involve them, generated little sympathy in the American public. The *Boston Phoenix,* an alternative weekly, summed up the prevailing attitude neatly: "The American public is far more interested in giving the Pentagon unfettered powers to do what's necessary to win the war than it is in having reporters present an unvarnished picture of what's going on—and, thus far, the military has very skillfully used the national-security argument."[17]

In addition to offering its own views of America's role in the Gulf War, the alternative press also critiqued the performance of the mainstream media.[18] New York's weekly *Village Voice,* which had confined its coverage of the Vietnam War mostly to antiwar events that took place in and around New York City, now felt comfortable taking a less parochial viewpoint. In the second week of the air war, in a piece titled "The Mobilization the Media Won't Let You See," the *Voice* charged that the mainstream press was underreporting or entirely ignoring many well-attended antiwar protests. Robert Hennelly reported for the *Voice* that "tens of thousands of Americans in towns, regional hubs, and cities have turned out to protest the Persian Gulf War. . . . While mass demos in San Francisco and Washington were barely acknowledged, the national media entirely blacked-out several other major actions." Hennelly pointed to gatherings of 40,000 demonstrators in San Francisco, 30,000 in Seattle, and protests in other major centers, including Los Angeles, Chicago, Atlanta and Boston.[19] In its next issue, the *Voice* reported on a march organizers claimed brought 250,000 protesters to Washington, D.C., and it criticized the mainstream media for giving no notice to large antiwar demonstrations abroad, in "Paris, Madrid, Nice, Copenhagen, Sydney, and Bonn."[20]

As it reported on the demonstrations, the *Voice* called attention to an important difference between these protests and those in the Vietnam era. Then, protesters had vilified the troops as well as the government. Now, the *Voice* reported, "Most activists are going to great lengths to distinguish that they support the troops though not the war."[21] The paper's coverage of the quarter-million-strong demonstration in Washington, D.C., on the weekend of February 2–3, 1991, noted, "In a concerted effort not to alienate American troops abroad, the march was led by military families, backed by some 3,000 vets, waving American flags."[22]

The *Atlanta Journal and Constitution* and the *Boston Globe* were among the big-city newspapers that covered local demonstrations. The *Globe* ran front-page coverage of a march that shut down parts of downtown Boston on the second day of the air war; in the same issue an editorial countered charges—another echo of Vietnam—that the protesters were unpatriotic: "Such dissent is not disloyal," the *Globe* declared. "It is as American as the Bill of Rights and should be respected."[23]

Some newspapers feared that the United States might find itself in a Vietnam-like quagmire in Iraq, but the great majority expected the war to be short. Even before the bombing began, editors were looking beyond the impending conflict with concern for the long-term effects on the Middle East and the region's relations with the United States and the rest of the world. On January 10, the *Times* expressed fears that war with Iraq would create new problems in the future, however it might play out: "A limited war that left most of Baghdad's military capability intact would only inflame future crises with a heightened sense of Iraqi grievance. Yet an all-out war that destroyed Iraq's military potential would create a destabilizing power vacuum adjacent to both Iran and Syria."[24]

The *Atlanta Journal and Constitution* expressed a similar caution: "If we destroy Iraq as a functioning nation, we create a dangerous vacuum in a dangerous region."[25] When the air war began, the paper warned that it was up to President Bush "to construct a peace" when the war was over. "The trouble is," the paper said, "not once in the long domestic debate over whether to wage war with Iraq did the president describe clearly the shape peace in the Middle East would take. . . . He has made a critical omission; military doctrine preaches against entering into conflict without a keen idea of the desired outcome."[26]

In the *Times,* Anthony Lewis wrote, "The danger is clear: that millions of Arabs, whether they liked Saddam Hussein or not, will react to an Iraqi defeat with feelings of despair, anger, resentment of America and the West. There is a real chance that radical Islamic fundamentalism will surge through the Persian Gulf Arab states." To prevent such an upsurge, Lewis felt, the United States would have to turn "seriously to the question of relations between Israel and its Arab neighbors." He expressed guarded optimism that "the worst consequences may be avoided. A quick war just might lead Arabs and Israelis to see how urgently they both need stable security arrangements." It all depended, in Lewis's view, on whether President Bush had "the courage to tackle the great political problem of the Middle East. He must try."[27]

A week into the air war, Lewis had become convinced that "the political consequences in the Middle East will be extremely dangerous." He saw the air campaign converting Arab allies, like Egypt, into adversaries, because the intensity of the bombing demonstrated "a carelessness about the value of Arab lives." Turning to the more immediate question of whether Saddam Hussein would be left in power when the war was over, Lewis was convinced that "the United States has no real choice now but to go on to the end—the end of Saddam Hussein's power."[28] The *Atlanta Journal and Constitution* considered Iraq without Saddam and wondered, "what is to happen to Iraq? Assuming its defeat and Saddam Hussein's fall, will what remains be so weakened it will be torn apart by feuding between its Sunnis and Shiites, not to mention its long oppressed Kurdish minority?"[29]

These questions and concerns recognized the importance that the Middle East, both for its oil reserves and as the focal point of conflict among three of the world's great religions, would continue to hold for the foreseeable future. At the start of other wars there had been proclamations by politicians and the press about America's war aims—to teach the Kaiser, or Hitler, or Santa Anna a lesson; to unify Korea, or Vietnam, under a democratic government—but always before, victory in the war and the certain achievement of the hoped-for goals were seen to go hand in hand. What is noteworthy about the speculations in the press before the Gulf War was that so many of them envisioned results that boded ill for the United States even in the aftermath of a military victory.

In the second week of the air war, William Pfaff, writing in the *New Yorker,* traced the divergence between Islamic societies and the West that had begun during the Enlightenment and continued ever since, the West becoming more secular while Islam remained "an integrally religious society." As Pfaff saw it, "The proposition that a victory over Iraq will constructively change the relations between the Islamic states and the West ignores the sources and the nature of their differences, which will endure long after Saddam Hussein—and George Bush—have quit the mortal scene."[30]

Mark Jurkowitz, reporting on the Iraq war for the *Boston Phoenix,* reached a similar conclusion based on his appraisal of the political forces at work in the present day. Jurkowitz predicted failure not just for the military intervention in the Middle East, but for President Bush's proclaimed vision of a new world order: "George Bush has justified his big-stick approach to Saddam Hussein by claiming he is working for a new post–Cold War world order. According to this vision, the old bipolar superpower rivalry will be supplanted by a broad coalition of nations that will act in concert to deter—and if necessary punish—rogue aggressors. Even with the collapse of communism, this seems a utopian concept, one destined to crash against the rocks of realpolitik." Contemplating the Middle East, Jurkowitz wondered, "Will the US military involvement seriously destabilize the region by uniting traditional foes—Arab leftists and nationalists and their fundamentalist brothers—in a potent anti-Western alliance?"[31]

In the Persian Gulf, press protests against the Pentagon restrictions continued as the air war lengthened. "More than 1,000 journalists have been accredited to cover the war," the *Times* reported, but "Only 126 are in Pentagon pools." The effect, the *Times* said, was that reporters couldn't do their job: "Without access to American troop units, correspondents are unable to verify statements made at press briefings in Riyadh, the Saudi capital."[32]

With the daily briefings producing little that was new about the ongoing air war, Mark Jurkowitz suggested, futilely, in the *Boston Phoenix,* that television reporters refuse to cover the briefings, or at least add some vigorous commentary: "Instead of simply parroting Lieutenant General Thomas Kelly's blithe assertion that good weather paved the way for 'a healthy day' of Baghdad bombing, how about having the on-air talent stare sternly into the camera and declare: '"Healthy bombing," folks? Isn't that one of the most obscene oxymorons you've ever heard? What the hell's going on here?'"[33]

On February 20, in testimony before the Senate Governmental Affairs Committee, Walter Cronkite, now the dean emeritus of CBS News, advocated giving many more journalists access to the frontline troops: "With a rational censorship system in place," Cronkite said, "the press should be free to go where it wants when it wants, to see, hear and photograph what it believes is in the public interest." Cronkite accused the U.S. military of limiting the American people's right to know "with an arrogance foreign to the democratic system." He insisted that the military "has the responsibility of giving all the information it possibly can to the press and the press has every right, to the point of insolence, to demand this."[34]

Saddam Hussein's seizure of the oil field that Iraq shared with Kuwait and his threat to the fields of Saudi Arabia had been the catalysts that sparked the Saudis' call for American help. Since then, oil had hovered under the surface of the news as a minor theme. With the air war under way, the *Village Voice* charged that President Bush's son, George W. Bush, the director of the Harken Energy Corporation of Dallas, Texas, "stands to profit directly if Desert Storm does its job. Not only will our boys be protecting the oil-producing infrastructures of Saudi Arabia and Kuwait, but also those of Bahrain, where Harken Energy has obtained an exclusive concession."[35]

The mainstream press made few accusations this pointed, although it was well known that President Bush, as well as some prominent members of his administration, including Secretary of State James Baker and Commerce Secretary Robert Mosbacher, were oil men. But when President Bush put forth, on February 20, a conspicuously oil-dependent energy policy, it was roundly criticized in mainstream editorials that drew a direct connection between America's dependence on foreign oil and the war in the Middle East. The *New York Times* called the energy policy "distressingly blind to the oil addiction that underlies the dispatch of 500,000 American troops to the Persian Gulf," and criticized Bush for "paying only lip service to efficiency and conservation."[36] The Allentown, Pennsylvania, *Morning Call* joined the call for conservation and said, "the energy policy demonstrates that outside of foreign affairs, Mr. Bush lacks vision."[37] The *Seattle Times* declared, "Bush's refusal to seize the moment for conservation is a disgrace."[38]

In the *Times,* columnist Tom Wicker wrote, "Mr. Bush has produced an energy policy that demands no energy conservation, demands no consumer sacrifice, imposes no energy taxes, sees no threat in heavy reliance on imported oil. . . . President Bush's continuing energy myopia raises the hard question whether the bloodshed and sacrifices of Desert Storm may have to be undertaken anew, when some future oil crisis finds the U.S. still dependent on hostile potentates, far-off sheikdoms and its own gas-guzzling addiction."[39]

The difficulty of foreseeing favorable outcomes intensified as the air war lengthened with no indication from the Bush administration about when, or whether, a ground war would follow. As late as February 23, the *Boston Globe* dared to hope that a ground war might be avoided. It had no doubt that the coalition would win such a contest, "maybe easily and maybe not. But the cost in blood would be extremely high for Iraqis. A resort to disproportionate violence would surely reap Americans a harvest of hatred and shame."[40]

An eleventh-hour effort by Soviet president Mikhail Gorbachev failed to negotiate a solution, Saddam Hussein thumbed his nose at a final ultimatum from President Bush, and the disproportionate violence was unleashed in the early hours of Sunday, February 24. The half-million-man Iraqi army in Kuwait was a significant force, at least numerically, but it was staffed by an officer corps chosen for political and sectarian reasons and it lacked a cadre of professional non-commissioned officers.[41] As the coalition forces rolled into Kuwait and Iraq, they were never seriously challenged.

The *Boston Globe* marked the launch of the ground assault with an accusation: "It was not necessary for Bush to abandon the promising economic sanctions in January in favor of massive bombing. Nor was it necessary for him to move to a ground war last night."[42] The *Times* urged that the war's objectives and duration be limited: "Limiting the war serves long-term U.S. interests in three pronounced ways: by leaving Iraq enough force to defend itself against ambitious neighbors; by avoiding the quagmire of a U.S. occupation, and by avoiding needless friction with the Soviet Union."[43]

As the ground war began, Secretary of Defense Dick Cheney ordered a twenty-four-hour news blackout that one reporter later characterized as "the most comprehensive news blackout in American military history."[44] Pool reporters with American forward units found that many of the stories they filed simply didn't get through during the ground war. In part, the rapid advance was to blame, creating difficulties in conveying dispatches to the rear, but correspondents in Riyadh, Saudi Arabia, saw military censors there exercising heavy-handed control over the reports they received from the field, sometimes erring on the side of caution and censoring entire dispatches rather than taking the time to excise sensitive information.[45] As the coalition troops advanced and Iraqis began retreating from Kuwait, some American correspondents traveled with Kuwaiti and Saudi units to escape the rigid control of the U.S. military. Satellite uplinks, still cumbersome enough at this stage of their development to require a vehicle to transport them, enabled a few television crews to send uncensored reports directly from the battlefield.[46]

With coalition troops forging into Iraq, whether Saddam Hussein should remain in power became the question of the moment. The *Boston Globe* believed that the coalition's "first goal is to expunge, for as long as possible, a military threat that Iraq's neighbors find intolerable. The political corollary of this aim is to get rid of Saddam." The *Globe* warned, however, that "American forces cannot afford a protracted occupation of Iraq. Nor will the coalition forces be able to impose a government of their choosing in Baghdad."[47]

For experienced correspondents in the war zone, the assumption that the world would be a better place without Saddam Hussein gave way to an appreciation of hard realities. Marcia Kunstel, of Cox Newspapers, traveled from Jordan to Saudi Arabia by way of Cairo during the air war. In Cairo, as she had done in Amman, she spoke with experts on the Middle East, including academics from the universities, about the merits of deposing Saddam Hussein, "and they all said, 'Don't do it. This would be really disastrous. The whole country's just going to implode.'"[48]

As the ground assault rolled toward certain victory, it became clear that the Bush administration had arrived at the same conclusion and was not willing to embroil itself in creating a new government for Iraq. On February 26, on the heels of an announcement by Saddam Hussein that he had ordered Iraqi troops to leave Kuwait (he did not announce that he had ordered them to set fire to all of Kuwait's oil wells before they left), the *Atlanta Journal and Constitution* reported that President Bush "hopes to undermine President Saddam Hussein's authority to the point that he might be overthrown or assassinated by his own people."[49] The report did not suggest how Bush hoped to achieve that end, beyond continuing the war until Iraq agreed to abide by the Security Council resolutions on Iraq.

On February 27, the *New York Times* warned that an effort by the coalition to impose a new government in Baghdad "would plunge the West into direct and lasting responsibility for maintaining a government in the explosive heart of the Arab, Islamic Middle East."[50] That evening, in an address to the nation, President Bush declared Kuwait liberated, and announced that at midnight, Washington time, "all United States and coalition forces will suspend offensive operations." In his speech, the president did not mention Saddam Hussein. He listed Iraq's immediate obligations to comply with all Security Council resolutions and to release prisoners of war and other detainees, and he declared that "Coalition forces fought this war only as a last result and look forward to the day when Iraq is led by people prepared to live in peace with their neighbors."[51]

One hundred hours after it began, the ground war was over. The *New York Times,* which had forcefully stated its objections just a few weeks before to what it saw as President Bush's premature resort to warfare in place of diplomacy, gushed a congratulatory editorial that withdrew those earlier misgivings. Bush's "choices at treacherous junctures proved as successful as they were bold," the *Times* wrote. Reevaluating the air war, the *Times* ventured the opinion, "To judge by the evidence so far, the crushing air assault achieved its objectives of demolishing military targets while holding civilian casualties to a remarkable minimum."[52] (The *Times* was forced to reassess this too-rosy judgment a few weeks later. When a United Nations inspection team characterized the damage caused by the air war as "near-apocalyptic," the paper conceded, somewhat meekly, that "The findings raise questions about how much of that bombing was needed, or justified."[53])

The *Boston Globe* congratulated President Bush and the American military on the coalition's victory, but cautioned its readers, "As the nation looks ahead, it should recognize that the gulf war was a special case. The strategic importance of the region and the 'defining' nature of the moment helped President Bush acquire uncommonly broad international support. We repeatedly argued—and continue to believe—that he could have used that support to craft an effective diplomatic and economic response to the Iraqi aggression. Yet we acknowledge that having chosen to move to combat, he and the military did it well." The *Globe* warned that Americans' enthusiasm for the war "may be because so much of the experience of this war was electronically disembodied, almost indistinguishable from a game. Only on a few occasions—a shelter bombed in Baghdad, tragic Scud strikes in Saudi Arabia and Israel—did the television coverage show a body or carry a cry of 'Medic!'"[54]

It was not only in the war zone that images of bodies were rare. In marked contrast to the frequent images shown on television in the Vietnam War of flag-draped coffins being unloaded from military transport planes at air bases in the United States and greeted by honor guards in full-dress uniforms, the Pentagon banned reporters and cameras from Dover Air Force Base, where the dead from the gulf arrived, and conducted no ceremonies on the tarmac. The *New York Times* questioned this decision in an editorial titled "Homecoming, Without Honor." The *Times* disputed the Pentagon's assertion that the policy was intended to respect the privacy of family members, charging, to the contrary, that "relatives of those now serving in the Persian Gulf have repeatedly petitioned the Government to allow public ceremonies. They may wonder just whose feelings are being spared." The president and a great majority of Americans might celebrate the end of the Gulf War, the *Times* said, "But the ghosts of Vietnam will not rest until Presidents and the nation have the courage to confront the dead."[55]

After the cease-fire, the American media continued to express criticism of the Pentagon's press policies in the hope of forcing better access in the next war. Leslie Kaufman, writing in the *Boston Phoenix,* reviewed the lack of public sympathy for the press's complaints about the restraints imposed by the military, and she found simple, persuasive reasons to explain it. The war had been so short that the traditional public support in the early stages of a war had not had time to wane, Kaufman pointed out, but the main reason, as she saw it, was "that the Pentagon, which has been experimenting with censorship policies for years, may have finally come up with a system that controls the information it wants controlled and, at the same time, provides the press with so much information that it looks silly when it demands more." Kaufman warned, "The media better re-group after Desert Storm if they want to retain their rights. The irony here is that, of course, the military wants press coverage when things are going well. General Norman Schwarzkopf, not able to contain himself at the success of the start of the ground operation, stepped in front of the cameras, breaking Cheney's [news] embargo himself. That merely adds fire to the press's argument that the military is silent only when there is nothing to brag about. It is exactly at those times when the public needs to know."[56]

CNN's Christiane Amanpour saw the press as complicit in the Pentagon's achievement: "The military won a major round when it managed to control the press. By kowtowing and bowing to the Pentagon's desire to control the image of the Gulf War, we, the press, presented war as a risk-free, casualty-free operation, as a surgical operation. It was a lie, because there is no such thing as a casualty-free war."[57]

A week after the cease-fire, the *Washington Post* still harbored hope that Saddam might be overthrown. "The United States presses actively for Saddam Hussein's ouster,"[58] the *Post* said, but the most accurate assessment of Saddam's postwar prospects came from the Jordanian journalist Mona Ziade, of the Associated Press, who reported that Saddam "has grown in stature in the eyes of many Arabs." Despite his military defeat, Ziade wrote, "Saddam can still claim wide support from Arabs who view him as a hero who stood up to America and other world powers."[59]

As for the immediate and long-term future of Iraq, the *Washington Post* noted "signs of a budding fundamentalist Islamic uprising in southern Iraq, home of a majority Shia population heretofore ruled by Saddam Hussein's Sunni-Baath party-military clique." In the *Post*'s view, "the American government has simply not thought through the political transition that Iraq must make now that the guns are silent. Washington necessarily hesitates to intervene directly, and it holds itself apart from the exiles not because it's indifferent but mostly because it's unprepared."[60]

The publisher of the *Boston Phoenix,* Stephen M. Mindich, saw Washington not so much as unprepared, but simply reverting "to business as usual—a depressing thought. For if all parties do not seize upon the window of opportunity that exists as a result of our victory over Iraq, and move quickly and boldly toward substantial changes in the politics and policies of the region, they shall have only themselves to blame when the next regional war occurs. And that war will be an inevitable consequence of letting this window close."[61]

Within weeks of the cease-fire, reports came out of Iraq that Saddam Hussein was viciously suppressing uprisings against his regime that the United States had actively incited. Despite this evidence that the Iraqi military, however battered in the recent war, was still capable of oppressing the Iraqi populace, the *New York Times* favored rapid withdrawal of American forces. Coalition forces "could have kept up the pounding for weeks without eliminating Iraq's military capacity to repress its own people," the *Times* wrote. The paper also believed that President Bush was right "to extricate U.S. troops from Iraq's civil strife. However much Americans want Saddam Hussein to be toppled, his fate is best left to the Iraqi people."[62]

It would have been more accurate to say that the fate of the Iraqi people was left to Saddam. Tens of thousands of Kurds and Shiites died in the aftermath of the Gulf War. Some responsibility for those deaths clearly rested with the United States, which encouraged uprisings against Saddam, provided air support and medical aid to some of the insurgents, and withdrew it as Saddam reorganized his army after the war. But the Security Council's resolution of November 29, 1990, had authorized the use of force to eject Iraq from Kuwait, not to oust Saddam Hussein and install a successor regime in Baghdad.

The *New Yorker* magazine was one of the few publications that dared to suggest that the United States should have considered exceeding the Security Council's mandate: "The real irony of the current situation," Lawrence Weschler wrote in a "Talk of the Town" commentary on April 15, "is that many of those who opposed the war (and were chided for their isolationism) subsequently came to feel that, having gone this far, we had incurred a moral responsibility to those whose rebellion we had encouraged—a responsibility that would have to be addressed, even at the risk of further United States entanglements and casualties." In the American disengagement, Weschler saw an unhappy parallel to an earlier withdrawal: "And it's a further irony that, despite protestations to the contrary, our present situation in the Gulf all too disturbingly recalls the end of our involvement in Vietnam. This time, we are in military control, of course, and can withdraw on our own schedule, but we are nevertheless trying to hurry away from a disaster in which we are heavily implicated, while acting as if we'd never had anything to do with it."[63]

Long after the troops sent to the Persian Gulf in 1990 and 1991 had returned home (but before it became apparent that the United States would return to Iraq) Philip Taubman looked back in a Sunday *Times* piece and concluded that George H. W. Bush had made the right decision when he chose not to oust Saddam Hussein. Taubman couldn't know that as he wrote about the past, he was also writing about the future: "If American forces captured Baghdad, they could not turn around and go home a week later, even if they were welcomed as liberators, which was far from certain. The United States, without strong international support, would have faced a long, expensive stay as it tried to install a new government and help reconstruct a country traumatized by war and years of murderous dictatorship."[64]

The press coverage of the 1991 Gulf War is distinguished by the many foresighted predictions about the consequences of American military involvement in the Middle East that were written before, during and after the war. In the light of subsequent events, the accuracy of many of these prognostications is stunning. The warnings began with inchoate premonitions—the "whirlwind of grim consequences" foreseen by the *Boston Globe,* the "incalculable consequences" predicted by the *Times*—before the war began, and evolved to more specific admonitions that foresaw the threat of another, similar, war in the not-too-distant future. The sense of a job unfinished, as Saddam Hussein resumed the torture and slaughter of his own people, damped the proud spirits that normally followed a military victory and left many in the American government, the public and the press looking back to see what might have been done differently, as well as forward to divine the consequences of failed opportunities. Whatever their viewpoints, the postwar forecasts rose from a recognition that the coalition's victory had done nothing to resolve the underlying causes of the war.

For Joseph Albright, the biggest mistake made by the press corps in the Gulf War was that it turned its back on Iraq too quickly when the war was done. In the first days and weeks after the cease-fire the travel restrictions were lifted, the press minders were gone and the usual routines of crossing international borders were not yet reestablished. "We were driving around without any escorts or anything," Albright remembered. "But partly under budget pressure from the papers, and partly because we were exhausted, we left the scene too quickly. . . . There should have been an effort to have a second wave of press to go up there, people who were fresh, when you could still get across the borders, and really document what happened."[65]

10

SEPTEMBER 11TH
AND AFGHANISTAN

The War on Terrorism (2001–2003)

The web of events that led to the war against the Taliban government of Afghanistan in 2001 was woven in part of strands spun from American decisions taken in the preceding decades that were seen at the time as being in the overriding national interests of the United States. The degree to which the U.S. military engagement in Afghanistan followed from those events is difficult to gauge, but it is hard to look back on the earlier policies without seeing them as contributing in some measure to the causes behind the terrorist attacks of September 11, 2001.

Fought over for more than two millennia by Macedonians, Indians, Greeks, Turks, Chinese, Arabs, Uzbeks and Mongols, among others peoples, Afghanistan emerged as a nation in the eighteenth century in the lands that lay astride the trade routes connecting the peoples of the Mediterranean, India and the Orient. The British fought three wars in Afghanistan, the first in 1837, but even Britannia at the height of her power could not hold the harsh terrain of the Hindu Kush for more than a few years against the resistance of the peoples who lived there. In 1919, Britain recognized Afghanistan's independence.

Afghanistan maintained neutrality during the world wars, but from its position on the southern border of the Soviet Union it could not avoid being drawn into the rivalry of the Cold War. A Marxist political party, the People's Democratic Party of Afghanistan, gained strength in the 1950s and '60s and seized control of the government in 1978. The new, pro-Soviet regime's social programs and repression of religion aroused strong resentment among the deeply traditional Afghan people, the inheritors of a thousand years of Islam. Mujahidin—Islamic religious warriors—began armed resistance against the government, which led to intervention by Soviet troops in late 1979.

Even before the Soviet intervention, the United States had acted to draw the Russians into Afghanistan—by providing support to the mujahidin insurgents so covertly that the rebels themselves were often not aware of its American origin—in the hope of entangling the U.S.S.R. in a Vietnam-style quagmire that would strain its economy and hamper its strategic mobility. As the Soviet involvement in Afghanistan deepened, American aid to the mujahidin escalated, increasing by an order of magnitude under the Reagan administration. (The cost of the 1979–1989 war is credited with contributing to the collapse of the Soviet Union two years after the last Soviet troops withdrew from Afghanistan.)

Among the mujahidin who benefited from the American support—perhaps without his knowledge—was Osama bin Laden. In 1988, bin Laden founded a group called "al Qaeda" (most often translated as "the base") to conduct a holy war whose aims were to establish a transnational community of fundamentalist Muslims and unite them in opposing Western influence in the Islamic lands. The presence of American troops in Saudi Arabia—where the holy sites of Islam are located—during the 1991 Persian Gulf War fueled bin Laden's hostility toward the United States. After he was stripped of his Saudi citizenship, bin Laden returned to Afghanistan in 1996, where the Taliban—the most conservative elements of the former mujahidin—were emerging as the victors after years of civil war that had followed the Soviet withdrawal. Protected by the Taliban government, bin Laden established training camps for al Qaeda and turned his attention to the United States, whose troops had remained in Saudi Arabia since the Gulf War.

⌒

On the evening of September 11, 2001, George W. Bush addressed the nation from the White House. In his brief speech, Bush vowed to take revenge on those responsible for the attacks on New York and Washington, but he said nothing about who they might be.

The day after the president's speech, the *New York Times* reported, "Intelligence officials said they strongly believed that Osama bin Laden's terrorist organization is behind the attacks."[1] When Mr. Bush addressed a joint session of Congress on September 20, nine days after the attacks, he announced, "The evidence we have gathered all points to a collection of loosely affiliated terrorist organizations known as Al Qaeda." The president linked al Qaeda and bin Laden to Afghanistan—as government officials and the press had done in the days since September 11th—where they were supported by the ultra-fundamentalist Islamic government of the Taliban. The president made clear that the wrath of the United States was directed at al Qaeda and the Taliban, not the Afghan people: "The United States respects the people of Afghanistan. After all, we are currently its largest source of humanitarian aid. But we condemn the Taliban regime." Bush demanded that the Taliban hand over bin Laden and close al Qaeda's terrorist training camps. "These demands are not open to negotiation or discussion," he declared. "The Taliban must act and act immediately. They will hand over the terrorists or they will share their fate."[2]

The American press, like the rest of the nation still reeling from the shock of the September 11th attacks, was able nevertheless to rally its critical faculties and warn against the hazards of an indiscriminate military response. The *Atlanta Journal-Constitution* credited the president with "near perfect pitch" in his address to Congress, but the paper called attention to the fact that Bush "asked us to take it on faith that investigators have evidence that al Qaeda and its bases in Afghanistan were behind the recent attacks. By all accounts, though, no firm links have yet been established." The *Journal-Constitution* noted that the president did not spell out what would happen if the Taliban did not meet his demands, but it had no doubt the response would involve armed force: "Whatever the military response, it must avoid terrorizing regular Afghans, for whom Bush rightly professed 'respect.' The Taliban, he noted, is one in a succession of forces that have 'brutalized' the Afghan people. We must not be yet another."[3]

The *Washington Post* urged, "The United States must make clear to other countries why it is sure that al Qaeda and Osama bin Laden were behind the attacks in New York and Washington, and it must work hard to line up allies for a potential battle with the Taliban."[4] The *Post* was concerned that "in this new kind of war, civilian casualties and suffering probably would strengthen rather than weaken al Qaeda, winning it new recruits both in Afghanistan and elsewhere in the Muslim world."[5]

The *New York Times* issued a similar warning: "It is a reasonable presumption that the terrorists who attacked New York and Washington aimed not just to kill American civilians," the *Times* said, "but also to draw the United States into an indiscriminate and brutish military response that might attract Muslims around the world to their cause." To avoid this outcome, the *Times* advised, "Washington must be smart in selecting targets and cognizant of the political consequences that its military operations are likely to produce in the Islamic world." The president, the *Times* believed, would have to choose between narrowly targeting the "terror groups and governments that Washington can demonstrate were complicit in the World Trade Center and Pentagon attacks," and a broader response that would "extend the fight to countries more broadly linked to international terrorism, possibly including Iraq." For now, the *Times* advised Mr. Bush to choose the narrower course, and it reminded him that "Military means alone will not assure success."[6]

The *Boston Globe* predicted that it would be much more difficult for Secretary of State Colin Powell to assemble a coalition to fight the amorphous enemy of global terrorism than it had been to oppose Saddam Hussein's brazen invasion of Kuwait in 1990: "The countries Powell has been courting do not all perceive the terrorist threat in the same way, and they have divergent or conflicting interests in this fight," the *Globe* observed. "Despite these considerable difficulties, it is crucial that the administration strives to bring together as many governments as possible for a perilous conflict."[7] The *Globe* reminded its readers that "both the Taliban and bin Laden's terrorist network, Al Qaeda, owe their perch on power in Afghanistan to feckless American past policies." The CIA, the *Globe* said, had been "unconcerned" with the mujahidins' "political projects—overthrowing secular regimes in their own countries. In CIA jargon, the calamities that ensued were an unfortunate example of 'blowback,' the boomerang effect of unintended consequences." In Afghanistan, the *Globe* said, "the consequences of blowback included human suffering and cruelty on a scale that is almost unimaginable to comfortable Americans." The *Globe* called for expelling the Taliban regime: "the only way to deprive bin Laden of Afghanistan as a staging area for more mass murders here in the United States is to topple his Taliban protectors from power," but it warned the Bush administration to "avoid the blunders of their predecessors, who ignored the human and political dimensions of an alliance with bin Laden and his like."[8]

On October 7, President Bush addressed the nation to announce that American and British forces had launched air attacks against al Qaeda and Taliban camps in Afghanistan. In response to the start of the military campaign, the *New York Times* declared that the American people "will support whatever efforts it takes to carry out this mission properly." It noted that "Mr. Bush has wisely made providing humanitarian assistance an integral part of the American strategy," but it also pointed out that the air campaign was being conducted only by American and British forces, and that some administration officials, before the strikes began, "had expressed a preference for a relatively narrow coalition. . . . That seems shortsighted," the *Times* commented. It emphasized that "combating international terrorism effectively requires sustaining a wide network of cooperating countries."[9] This opinion supported what was already a broad consensus in the press.

On the ground in Afghanistan, American Special Forces units were doing their best to create a network of anti-Taliban warlords and tribesmen to help find Osama bin Laden. Once the air campaign was under way, the Green Berets spotted for the bombers and organized their Afghan allies to fight against the Taliban and al Qaeda. The strategy of deploying only very small American units in the assault had the effect of limiting press access to military operations much more severely than in the Persian Gulf War. No reporters at all were allowed in the initial phases and very few until some of the cities were secured. The press accepted these limitations for the most part because this was plainly a new kind of war, more like supporting partisans in German-occupied Yugoslavia in World War II than the Normandy landings. The strategy kept American casualties low, which helped to mute the protests, and in the United States the watchdogs in the press perceived more serious threats to freedom at home.

Before the Bush administration presented its first proposals for new legislation to combat terrorism, the *Boston Phoenix* anticipated an assault on civil liberties. "Herein lies the greatest challenge to our democracy," publisher Stephen M. Mindich wrote on September 14 in a prescient commentary: "The temptation will be great to accede to those who insist on ceding our civil rights for the need of security. We will be asked to yield to restrictions on our freedom to travel, to enter public buildings and monuments. We will be asked to give government broader authority to invade our privacy—to look up our records, listen in on our conversations, read our e-mail, and otherwise circumscribe our liberties. . . . But if we want to remain the nation we have paid dearly to become . . . we cannot in knee-jerk fashion react to even this heinous attack by closing up and shutting down our free society. . . . We must make certain that when the debris from the buildings that once stood as symbols of our national pride is cleared away, the real foundation of our nation's being—our freedom— is not left in the rubble."[10]

The government's initial proposals seemed relatively innocuous. The *New York Times* reported on September 16 that "Attorney General John Ashcroft and Congressional leaders opened talks today on an emergency package of antiterrorism legislation that would expand the Justice Department's ability to use wiretaps in cases of suspected terrorism or espionage."[11] A comment by Vice President Cheney on *Meet the Press* suggested that the government would seek powers that went beyond roving wiretaps: "We've got to spend time in the shadows. We have to work toward the dark side, if you will. . . . It is a mean, nasty, dangerous, dirty business out there, and we have to operate in that arena. . . . We need to make certain that we have not tied the hands, if you will, of our intelligence communities."[12]

As the government put forward proposals to enable the attorney general to detain legal immigrants indefinitely with little judicial review and to admit in United States courts evidence obtained overseas under conditions (such as torture) that would exclude it under the American legal system, the criticism gained strength. On September 23, the *New York Times* worried that "many of the ideas being shopped by the Bush administration would reduce constitutional protections with no obvious benefit to national security." The *Times* approved Attorney General Ashcroft's roving wiretap proposal, and another to remove the statue of limitations on terrorist acts, but the paper opposed other requests, which the *Times* said "amount to a wish list of things that the Justice Department and the Federal Bureau of Investigation have unsuccessfully lobbied for in the past and that do not make sense now."[13]

The alternative press was vigorous in making early objection to the White House's antiterrorism package and to the jingoism used to justify it. The *Boston Phoenix*'s reporter Dan Kennedy and frequent contributor Harvey Silverglate warned in the September 28 issue, "Part of the job we all have to do in order to win this war is to prevent the barbarians who seek to exterminate the Western notion of individual liberty from causing us to do a good part of the job ourselves. . . . At this time of national crisis, many Americans take some comfort in waving the flag, and rightly so. But the flag is not the only symbol of our culture of liberty. So, too, is the Constitution."[14] In the *Village Voice* of October 2, Cynthia Cotts wrote, "Something is burning this week, but it's not the site of the former World Trade Center. It's what's left of the First Amendment." In place of free speech, Cotts saw the rise of "a heinous kind of propaganda in which anti-war sentiment is dimmed and right-wing pundits denounce their counter-parts on the left as madmen and enemies-from-within." The *Voice*'s senior columnist, Nat Hentoff, feared that the administration's roving-wiretap proposal went too far and would involve too little oversight. "If we do not spread the word of this bipartisan attack on the Bill of Rights—and insist on our First Amendment right to protest—" Hentoff wrote, "we will become accomplices in this war against the Constitution."[15]

In the second week of October, under intense pressure from the administration, both houses of Congress passed preliminary drafts of the administration's antiterrorism legislation. The *Washington Post* took a harsh view of the way the bill had been rushed through the House: "The House Republican leadership made a mockery of the normal legislative process last week in forcing a vote on a major antiterrorism bill that had been anonymously written only the night before and that not even most members of the Judiciary Committee had had more than a fleeting chance to read. The bill has enormous implications for civil liberties, on which it arguably infringes in a number of serious ways while conferring additional powers on law enforcement officials to combat terrorism." The *Post* reported that the substitute bill had replaced a bipartisan measure with broad support, which had been unanimously approved by the "normally deeply divided Judiciary Committee," and it scolded members of both parties for approving the substitute bill despite their ignorance of what it contained. "They call this the PATRIOT act, for 'Provide Appropriate Tools Required to Intercept and Obstruct

Terrorism.' The politics are pretty obvious," the *Post* noted dryly. "But some of the tools in this bill are not appropriate, and in the long run those who ignore the risk to civil liberties in seeking to meet the risk of terrorism do the country a disservice."[16]

The reconciled legislation, now retitled the USA Patriot Act, passed in the House on October 24, by 336 to 66, and in the Senate on October 25, by 98 to 1, with Wisconsin Senator Russ Feingold casting the lone dissenting vote. President Bush signed the act on October 26.

On November 13, 2001, President Bush signed an executive order providing that terrorism suspects could be tried in secret before military tribunals, possibly to be held aboard ships at sea. Under the terms of the order, the accused could be sentenced to death by a simple majority of the tribunal, with no right of appeal to the federal judiciary.

The press reaction to this order was prompt and vehement. The *New York Times* called it a "travesty of justice," and "a dangerous idea, made even worse by the fact that it is so superficially attractive. In his effort to defend America from terrorists, Mr. Bush is eroding the very values and principles he seeks to protect, including the rule of law."[17] The *Boston Globe* called it "a panicky, unnecessary abandonment of the legal rights and protections that distinguish a true rule of law from the arbitrary law of the ruler, such as defines the Taliban regime in Afghanistan."[18] The *Washington Post* warned, "History offers too many examples of responses to legitimate danger that escalated into shameful excesses. It wasn't a very long road from the attack on Pearl Harbor to internment of Japanese Americans. Cold War fears fed blacklists and McCarthyism."[19] The *Atlanta Journal-Constitution* reminded its readers, "The justice of an open society is the most important message we can send to an Islamic world in which democracy is still a stranger."[20] The *Christian Science Monitor* wrote, "That question has to be asked: The terrorism threat appears openended, but must counterterror infringements on civil liberties also be open-ended?"[21]

While the White House's antiterrorism legislation was pending in the Congress, the Senate Judiciary Committee had repeatedly requested that Attorney General John Ashcroft appear before the committee to answer questions about the government's strategy in the war on terrorism. In late November the administration finally agreed to allow Ashcroft to testify and his appearance was scheduled for December 6. As the date neared, the

Los Angeles Times proposed that the senators should "pepper him with questions," such as: "The U.S. convicted the 1993 World Trade Center bombers in federal court, so why have you proposed military tribunals for suspected terrorists now? Why limit defendants' choice of attorney? Why let juries convict with a lower burden of proof than in regular criminal trials? Why no right of appeal?[22] The *New York Times,* alarmed that the government was creating "a parallel criminal justice system, decree by decree, largely removed from the ordinary oversight of Congress and the courts," issued its most forceful criticism of the Bush administration since September 11th: "The Founding Fathers, properly wary of an unrestrained executive branch, created our system of checks and balances precisely to guard against a president and his aides grabbing powers like these without Congressional approval or the potential for judicial review."[23]

In an opening statement before the Judiciary Committee, Ashcroft took aim at the administration's critics: "To those . . . who scare peace-loving people with phantoms of lost liberty, my message is this: Your tactics only aid terrorists, for they erode our national unity and diminish our resolve." In high dudgeon, the *Washington Post* admonished, "It is the attorney general's function, or should be, to ensure that a lively debate over policy is protected—even during wartime. . . . Mr. Ashcroft may not like the criticism. But his job is to defend dissent, not to use the moral authority of his office to discourage people from participating in one of the most fundamental obligations of citizenship."[24]

On December 8, the *Post* and the press celebrated the collapse of the Taliban regime in Afghanistan following the withdrawal of the Taliban from Kandahar, the last city where they had clung to a foothold. Since October, as they lost ground to the coalition forces, the Taliban and al Qaeda fighters had retreated to the mountains along Afghanistan's eastern border with Pakistan, where Osama bin Laden had built a complex of deep tunnels and caves at Tora Bora during the Soviet war, financed by money from the CIA, with heavy equipment "from his father's construction empire," as Mary Anne Weaver later related in the *New York Times Magazine.*[25] The Tora Bora redoubt had been bombed throughout November by American bombers, guided by U.S. Special Forces spotters. The ground assault, by Afghan warriors of the Eastern Alliance, began in the first week of December. Philip Smucker, writing from Afghanistan for the *Christian Science Monitor,* reported that where once there had been

"1,500 to 2,000 of Arabs, Afghans, and Chechens" in the mountains at Tora Bora, "yesterday, after tribal fighters said they captured the last of the Al Qaeda positions, killing more than 200 fighters and capturing 25, there was still no sign of the world's most wanted terrorist–Osama bin Laden. And there were far fewer fighters both captured and killed than were originally thought present." According to al Qaeda prisoners, Smucker reported, "bin Laden had left Tora Bora almost two weeks ago."[26]

Bin Laden's escape from Tora Bora with most of his al Qaeda warriors was a serious setback. "The war in Afghanistan," the *New York Times* said, "not to mention the war against terrorism, will never seem complete without the capture or confirmed death of Osama bin Laden and his two top surviving deputies, Ayman al-Zawahiri and Abu Zubaydah."[27]

The country was far from pacified. The warlords and warriors the United States had enlisted to drive out al Qaeda and topple the Taliban were now free to pursue agendas of their own, which included stealing relief supplies intended for Afghan civilians and consolidating their control of fiefdoms remote from Kabul and Kandahar. New fighting broke out among those who had been formerly united in common cause. In the 2000 presidential campaign, Mr. Bush had declared himself opposed to "nation-building," but on December 22, 2001, on the heels of what seemed at the time to be a convincing victory, the *Boston Globe* warned the president to guard against the return of "warlordism, drug trafficking, and civil war," and it urged that the United States should take a leading role "in helping build a stable, self-sustaining Afghanistan."[28]

In the absence of further military operations overseas, the rights and the treatment of captive "enemy combatants" took over the front pages and editorial pages of American newspapers. Concern over President Bush's plan for military tribunals, far from fading after the initial outburst of critical editorials, grew more intense. On December 6, 2001, the day Donald Rumsfeld appeared before the Senate Judiciary Committee, the *Washington Post* published an op-ed piece by Walter Dellinger and Christopher H. Schroeder, law professors at Duke University and former Justice Department officials, insisting on the need for judicial oversight for the military tribunals. "Even if the president were validly exercising his power to suspend the privilege of habeas corpus, it cannot be constitutional to exclude the courts altogether," Dellinger and Schroeder wrote. "Independent review outside the executive branch is essential if the nation

is to be assured that such military commissions are fairly designed to as-
certain guilt and are limited to the extraordinary circumstances that alone
can justify their use."[29]

The *New York Times* argued strenuously for trying the detainees in
federal courts, declaring that "No other type of judicial proceeding could
offer Americans and the rest of the world as satisfying a verdict, or a more
resounding vindication of American justice and freedoms."[30]

Treatment accorded the detainees became controversial in January
2002, when a "chorus of criticism over the US treatment of Al Qaeda and
Taliban prisoners held in Cuba arose yesterday from European governments and international human rights organizations," as the *Boston Globe*
reported on January 23. The *Globe* related that several "British outlets"
had alleged that prisoners at Guantánamo were being tortured. A proxi-
mate cause of the controversy was a recent statement by Donald Rumsfeld
that the detainees were "unlawful combatants" and had no rights under
the Geneva Conventions. The *Globe* called attention to the fact that much
of the "extraordinary sympathy" expressed around the world for the
United States after September 11th came from a reaction against what was
seen as the terrorists' violation of international morality. "It would be a
terrible mistake," the *Globe* said, "for the United States to reverse the positions of violator and violated by refusing to abide by the Geneva Convention governing prisoners of war." It branded Rumsfeld's position as
"utterly wrong," and declared, "it is as important to honor international
agreements and the rule of law as it is to capture or kill the criminals who
murdered some 3,000 in cold blood."[31]

The *Times* declared, "It is in America's interest to afford all the prisoners humane conditions of detention and basic standards of due
process. The United States should stand for the rule of law, even when it
comes to prosecuting violent enemies committed to carrying out terrorist
attacks."[32]

In February, after weeks of conflict within the administration over
the issue, with Secretary Rumsfeld and Vice President Cheney arguing
against Geneva Convention protections for the detainees and Secretary of
State Colin Powell—the only top administration official with military
service in a war zone—in favor of giving them full protection, President
Bush decided that the Geneva Conventions applied to the Taliban, but
not to al Qaeda prisoners. Bush's reservations and qualifications

prompted the *Washington Post* to protest, "the president has interpreted the convention so narrowly that he will not receive, nor does he deserve, the credit he seeks, and the risk to U.S. fighters in future conflicts may increase as a result."[33]

The discovery of two Americans among the Taliban taken captive in Afghanistan added loathing for traitors to the emotional response to the 9/11 attacks, but it also focused concern for the rights of prisoners on individual captives for the first time. John Walker Lindh, twenty years old, gaunt and bearded, was captured by Northern Alliance forces in November 2001. Dubbed "the American Taliban" by the media, he was denied access to counsel and interrogated for almost two months in Afghanistan and aboard U.S. Navy ships before he was brought to the United States and charged in federal court with ten crimes, including conspiring to kill Americans and supporting terrorist organizations. In a plea agreement that saved the administration the embarrassment of having details of Lindh's rough treatment at the government's hands aired at trial, Lindh was allowed to plead guilty to two charges in July 2002 and was sentenced to twenty years without parole.[34]

Charging Lindh in federal court proved an awkward precedent for the government when it treated other American suspects differently. Yaser Esam Hamdi, born in Louisiana of Saudi parents, was captured in Afghanistan at the same time and place as Lindh. Like Lindh, Hamdi was just twenty at the time of his capture; unlike Lindh, who grew up in Washington, D.C., and Marin County, California, Hamdi had been taken to Saudi Arabia as a child and was raised there. After his capture, the government brought Hamdi to Guantánamo, where he revealed his citizenship, then transferred him to the United States and held him without charges, fighting off attempts by the federal public defender to gain access to his client, while the Lindh case made its way through the courts and that of another American citizen, Jose Padilla, attracted far more media attention.

Padilla was arrested by the FBI at Chicago's O'Hare International Airport on May 8, 2002, on his return from travels that had taken him to several Muslim countries, including Afghanistan and Iraq. His arrest received no public notice until June 10, when Attorney General Ashcroft announced, during a visit to Moscow, that the government had detained Padilla (who had adopted the Muslim name Abdullah al-Mujahir) in connection with an alleged al Qaeda plot to detonate a "dirty" bomb in the United States. In the *Boston Phoenix,* the political satirist and monologist Barry Crimmins suggested that "Kaiser Ashcroft" had traveled to Moscow "to lay a wreath on Joseph Stalin's grave," and gave a critical view of the government's position: "According to the USA Patriot Act of 2001, Abdullah al-Mujahir needn't be charged with anything for the duration of the Purported War on Terrorism. In other words, so long as there is a terrorist on planet earth, this American citizen is relegated to rot in confinement with no defense, trial, or contact with the outside world."[35]

Because Padilla had been raised in Chicago and was arrested at O'Hare, the *Chicago Tribune* took a special interest in the case. Clarence Page, a member of the *Tribune's* editorial board, demanded to know, "why is Padilla being held indefinitely without charges while other alleged combatants like John Walker Lindh, the so-called 'American Taliban,' and Zacarias Moussaoui, the so-called '20th hijacker,' are tried in federal court? Is Padilla that much more dangerous? Or is the government merely holding him because they don't have enough evidence that would hold up in court? Failure to ask such questions and our failure to hold the government accountable in such cases endangers all of our rights." Page declared, "When the executive branch targets and detains its own citizens without access to a lawyer, it is up to Congress and the courts to provide oversight and safeguards to make sure those powers are not abused. Wartime does not require us to abandon the rules that define America as a civilized society."[36]

On June 23, Doug Cassel, head of the Center for International Human Rights at Northwestern University Law School, warned in the *Tribune,* "The tree of liberty is not about to topple, but it is being steadily chipped away." Cassel found Padilla's case more troubling than those of the other American detainees because, unlike Lindh and Hamdi, "Padilla was arrested far from combat or a war zone—in the U.S.—and is publicly accused of criminal conduct. In law, then, his legal entitlements to due process are the strongest to date. Yet . . . Secretary of Defense Donald Rumsfeld claims the right to hold him until the 'war' on international terrorism is over." American citizens were protected from being imprisoned without a hearing, Cassel noted, by the due-process clause of the Fifth Amendment. "Some say that in the world after Sept. 11, we cannot afford such constitutional luxuries. But as the Supreme Court answered long ago, in rejecting the military trial of a civilian during the Civil War, 'The Constitution . . . is a law . . . equally in war and peace, . . . at all times, and under all circumstances. No doctrine, involving more pernicious consequences, was ever invented . . . than that any of its provisions can be suspended during any of the great exigencies of government. Such a doctrine leads directly to anarchy or despotism.'"[37]

The *New York Times* was similarly concerned about the executive branch's claims of extraordinary power in the Hamdi case. "The Bush administration seems to be using the Hamdi case to establish the principle that it has the exclusive power to decide who is an enemy combatant," the *Times* editorialized on August 8, 2002. If the government prevailed in the Hamdi case, the *Times* feared, it could "seize anyone it wants simply by saying the magic words 'enemy combatant,' and the courts will be powerless to release such people from prison." The *Times* saw a fundamental flaw in this rationale: "This was not what the founders had in mind. They established a system of checks and balances so no one branch of government would have unrestrained power."[38]

It was inevitable as the first anniversary of September 11th drew near that the press would offer perspectives on how the world had changed since the Twin Towers fell. Looking to Afghanistan, where much of the country was still beyond the effective control of Hamid Karzai's government and there were signs that al Qaeda and the Taliban were regrouping, the *Boston Globe* made a plea for nation-building: "The current US military effort to rid Afghanistan of the Taliban will be squandered," the *Globe* said, "if the central government of President Hamid Karzai is not supported with hard cash for reconstruction and Afghans are not protected from rapacious warlords. This mission demands a full-hearted US commitment—along with international donors—to the work of nation-building in Afghanistan."[39]

The *Washington Post* recalled the "unprecedented global outpouring of support and sympathy" that had followed the attacks and concluded that by rebuffing NATO's offer of military help, by withdrawing from international treaties, and by failing to support democratic values among its allies, the Bush administration had "failed to take full advantage of a rare international opportunity." The *Post* suggested that the White House would do well to learn some lessons from the past year: "One is that it is better to include allies in military campaigns than to exclude them, especially if their political and material support will be needed off the battle-field. The second is that American engagement abroad must shift some weight back toward insisting on the democratic values that are the best an-tidote to terrorism—the values that made Mexico, and not Uzbekistan, a close U.S. friend before 9/11."[40]

One of the more bitter assessments of the state of the nation a year after September 11th appeared in the *Boston Phoenix*. The approach of the anniversary found Clif Garboden, the senior managing editor, in a pes-simistic mood. It seemed to Garboden that too many Americans of his ac-quaintance sought ways to excuse the excesses of the Bush administration: "Over the past year, I've humored these positions from seemingly intelli-gent people who've been driven, by fear and emotionalism and myopic pri-orities, to falling in line with a corporate-centered foreign policy presided over by a right-wing administration that is, at best, a laughably transparent puppet of militaristic racists. . . . I expect no better of hypocritical mon-eyed toadies like G.W. Bush and unconvincingly closeted fascists like John Ashcroft. If feeding the public's jingoism makes them popular, they'll ex-ploit it; if war protects their cronies' investments, they'll wage it; if an inter-national crisis gives them the excuse to rob uppity citizens of their civil rights, they'll deport foreign labor and frisk babes-in-arms at airports until we all get the message. But the rest of us should know better. . . . Amid our passive acceptance, simple truths have been lost: war is evil and always should be resisted; religion, race, and nationality are artificial distinctions; and rights are just that and must not be relinquished."[41]

On the eve of Thanksgiving 2002, Nat Hentoff offered in the *Village Voice* a clipping gleaned from commentaries on the 9/11 anniversary, one from deep in the heartland. "On September 8 of this year," Hentoff wrote, "the *Journal Gazette,* a daily newspaper in Fort Wayne, Indiana, published a full-page, five-column editorial, its first such broadside in nearly twenty years. The headline was 'Attacks on Liberty': 'In the name of national security, President Bush, Attorney General John Ashcroft and even Congress have pulled strand after strand out of the Constitutional fabric that distinguishes the United States from other nations. Actions taken over the past year are eerily reminiscent of tyranny portrayed in the most nightmarish works of fiction. . . . The sudden suspension of due process for immigrants rounded up into jails is familiar to readers of Sin-clair Lewis's *It Can't Happen Here.*'"[42]

Hentoff had seized on the case of Yaser Esam Hamdi and he would follow it over the course of two and a half years to its ignoble conclusion. As they were exemplified in the case, Hentoff saw George W. Bush's claims of virtually unlimited powers in wartime as so pernicious that they threatened the foundations of the republic. "It is not mere rhetoric to point out that the future of the Constitution for generations to come is at stake," Hentoff wrote in January 2003. He drew on the *Federalist,* No. 47, for James Madison's view that "The accumulation of all powers, legislative, executive, and judiciary, in the same hands . . . may justly be pronounced the very definition of tyranny."[43] In a dark moment, Hentoff believed that American citizens no longer cherished their most essential freedoms: "The imprisonment of 'enemy combatant' Yaser Esam Hamdi in a naval brig in the United States is not a matter of concern to most Americans," Hentoff wrote, "since they do not know of Mr. Hamdi's isolation from the Bill of Rights, and might not care if they did. But the Supreme Court will ultimately decide whether George W. Bush's Constitution will replace—in significant parts—the Constitution that most Americans are also not familiar with."[44]

In February 2003, Hentoff appeared on PBS's *NOW with Bill Moyers.* Moyers, playing a genial devil's advocate, asked, "Does the Constitution extend to terrorists who want to kill us?" Hentoff responded that habeas corpus, the right of a suspect to challenge his detention in court, "is the oldest English-speaking right. It goes back to the Magna Carta." But must such protections apply to everyone, "Including terrorists who are trying to kill us?" Moyers asked again. "Suspected terrorists," Hentoff shot back. "If you have somebody you believe is a terrorist under our system of law, you have to prove it."[45]

In January 2002, the *Washington Post* had brushed off early charges that detainees were being tortured at Guantánamo, attributing them to "America-bashers in the European press and human rights community."[46] On December 26, 2002, Dana Priest and Barton Gellman reported in a front-page article in the *Post* that the United States had detained and interrogated "nearly 3,000 suspected al Qaeda members and their supporters" since September 11, 2001. Priest and Gellman related that interrogations of the captives took place at the Baghram air base in Afghanistan, on Diego Garcia island in the Indian Ocean (which the United States leases from Great Britain), and at secret CIA detention facilities located elsewhere abroad. Before the interrogations began, the article reported, captives in American custody were "'softened up' by MPs and U.S. Army Special Forces troops who beat them up and confine them in tiny rooms. The alleged terrorists are commonly blindfolded and thrown into walls, bound in painful positions, subjected to loud noises and deprived of sleep." Priest and Gellman's informants told them that pain medication was withheld from captives wounded in battle until they became more cooperative.[47]

In the same article, Priest and Gellman introduced the phrase "extraordinary rendition" to the post-9/11 lexicon when they reported that in some cases, "usually involving lower-level captives, the CIA hands them to foreign intelligence services—notably those of Jordan, Egypt and Morocco—with a list of questions the agency wants answered. These 'extraordinary renditions' are done without resort to legal process and usually involve countries with security services known for using brutal means."[48] In an editorial, the *Post* declared, "there are certain things democracies don't do, even under duress, and torture is high on the list. Some of the alleged tactics straddle the line between acceptable and unacceptable conduct. Without knowing more about what exactly is happening, it's hard to judge. But beating prisoners is entirely out of bounds." The *Post* urged the Bush administration "to clarify what tactics it is using and which are still off limits," so the American people and their representatives could debate the issue. Of one thing the *Post* was certain: "It shouldn't be the administration's unilateral call."[49]

The revelations in the *Post* provoked curiously few responses from the press at large in the weeks that followed. Nat Hentoff viewed the failure of the *New York Times* to follow up independently on the *Post's* story as symptomatic of a decline that "began with the ascension of publisher Arthur Sulzberger, Jr., and has quickened under executive editor Howell Raines. It's too bad the *New York Herald Tribune* isn't still around," he wrote.[50]

Hentoff's criticism of the *Times* was unduly severe. If the *Times* was not leading the way in attacking the government's war policies as it had done in the early days of Vietnam, that was because since September 11th the other major dailies—with the exception of the *Wall Street Journal,* which acted as an uncritical cheerleader for the administration—had matched the readiness of the *Times* to take up the cause of the Afghan

people, to advocate for the rights of terror suspects, to warn against threats
to the civil liberties of American citizens accomplished by executive order
and sometimes (as in the passage of the Patriot Act) with the collusion of
Congress, and to criticize the cloak of secrecy under which the administration sought to shield many of its actions from public scrutiny. Sometimes
other voices led the debate, but there was no breakaway front runner. The
Washington Post editorialized more often on the cases of the American captives, Lindh, Hamdi and Padilla, but the *Times* was in the vanguard as it
argued for the detainees—citizen and non-citizen alike—to be tried in
open court. Its editorials were as forceful and eloquent as any on this and
other aspects of the war on terrorism. The failure of the *Times,* when it
came, was a lapse, not a decline.

In the chaotic weeks and months after September 11th, the foundations
on which our confidence as Americans had rested for so long, especially
our sense of invulnerability in the homeland, was shaken as never before.
We wondered for a time if we would find our footing again. This sense of
uncertainty pervaded the press too, but even in that time of disruption the
press acquitted itself well. To review the news and editorial columns of the
mainstream and alternative press from late 2001 through the winter of
2003 is to find a sense of continuity where, at the time, it seemed there
was none. Scores of other publications large and small, as well as radio and
television outlets, web pages and blogs, informed the debate and called the
government to account for each perceived offense. Not in unison or with
equal fervor, but criticisms that ranged from mild to harsh and protests
from sober to shrill were written and published and spoken, and they
made their mark. As in every great contest between the press and the government at a time of crisis, the Founders' principles were marshaled, to be
laid not before the present King George, who was as deaf to entreaty as his
predecessor of the colonial period, but before the people, in the hope that
once again they would recognize the rights enumerated in the Constitution as essential safeguards against tyranny. And if the people seemed to
pay insufficient heed while the wounds inflicted by September 11th were
still raw, it was because, as the *Washington Post* later had occasion to write
in a retrospective critique of what it called President Bush's executive

"overreaching" since the September 11th attacks, "The American people do want Mr. Bush to keep them safe . . . and they may be slow to wake to infringements on their liberty. But they also understand that due process can be infringed only so much before the injury becomes irreparable."[51]

In the spring of 2003 the war in Iraq overshadowed these stories for a time, but by an irony that was neither intended nor welcomed by the Bush administration, it was the war in Iraq that would fling open Pandora's box once and for all, and bring the subject of torture into the glare of public scrutiny.

11

IRAQI FREEDOM

Iraq (2003–)

At the end of the 1991 Gulf War, the United Nations Security Council mandated on-site inspections of Iraq's biological and chemical weapons facilities by a U.N. Special Commission that became known as UNSCOM. A Security Council resolution required the elimination of Iraq's biological and chemical weapons capability and of any missiles with a range greater than one hundred fifty kilometers. It requested that the director general of the International Atomic Energy Agency undertake similar inspections with regard to Iraq's nuclear capability and provided that UNSCOM would assist the IAEA in this endeavor.

Iraq destroyed missiles and chemical weapons under U.N. supervision. The inspectors found evidence of a program to develop materials for nuclear weapons. By the end of 1992, the IAEA was confident it had rendered Iraq's nuclear program harmless,[1] but from the outset, the Iraqis blocked and delayed the inspectors' access to some sites, they concealed others, they moved equipment and materials frequently, they withheld documents, and they harassed, intimidated and threatened UNSCOM members. In an effort to overcome the Iraqi obstructions, UNSCOM established a remote monitoring system, with the Iraqis' knowledge and consent, that eventually recorded video and electronic signals at more than three hundred research and weapons facilities in Iraq. Beginning in 1996, the signals from the monitoring devices were transmitted over a system of microwave repeaters to UN-SCOM's headquarters in Baghdad. Intelligence gathered by the monitoring system was reported to the Security Council, but neither the Security Council nor UNSCOM knew that the monitoring and transmission system also contained hidden devices, covertly installed by American intelligence operatives working as UNSCOM technicians, that were capable of receiving Iraqi military communications unrelated to UNSCOM's mission. Intelligence from this system was conveyed only to the United States.

UNSCOM inspectors withdrew from Iraq in December 1998 when they received advance warning of planned U.S. and British air strikes on Iraqi military installations. They never returned. In March 1999, the *Boston Globe* and the *Washington Post*[2] exposed the clandestine American monitoring system, confirming Iraq's long-standing charges that the United States was using UN-SCOM as a cover for espionage. The revelation caused a diplomatic furor. The willingness of the United States to subvert the international inspection regimen drove a wedge between the Clinton administration and the U.N. Secretariat and so thoroughly discredited UNSCOM that the Security Council was forced to disband the old commission and form, in December 1999, the U.N. Monitoring Verification and Inspection Commission—UNMOVIC. Iraq rejected the resolution that created the new inspection group. The issue of resuming inspections remained at an impasse for almost three years, until September 2002, when President George W. Bush warned the United Nations that if the world organization did not seek out and destroy Iraq's weapons of mass destruction, the United States would do so without the U.N.'s approval. On September 16, Iraq announced that it would allow U.N. weapons inspectors to return, but delayed approving the terms under which UNMOVIC would operate. In December, the fourth anniversary of UNSCOM's withdrawal came and went with no U.N. inspectors in Iraq.

⌒

Within days of the September 11, 2001, terrorist attacks on the United States, speculation appeared in the press about the possibility that Iraq would become a target for American reprisals. President Bush's declaration on the evening of September 11th that "We will make no distinction between the terrorists who committed these acts and those who harbored them" opened, in the opinion of the *Washington Post,* "a broad array of potential targets," including Iraq, Iran, Syria, North Korea, Sudan, Yemen, and the most obvious, Afghanistan. The *Post* said "It is impossible to imagine the United States 'winning' this war in any meaningful sense while Saddam Hussein remains in power in Iraq."[3]

The climate of suspicion and distrust created by Iraq's persistent efforts to frustrate the U.N. weapons inspections was so pervasive that almost no one doubted that Iraq had revived its weapons programs after UNSCOM inspectors left the country at the end of 1998, but while there was virtual unanimity that Saddam Hussein posed a real danger to the Middle East, and perhaps beyond, some prominent newspapers argued against a precipitate attack on Iraq. The *Atlanta Journal-Constitution* advised on October 11, 2001, with air strikes under way in Afghanistan, that "the Bush administration should unequivocally disavow any imminent, unprovoked attack on another nation."[4]

In the third week of November, with the campaign in Afghanistan going better than the most optimistic predictions, *USA Today* reported that the Pentagon was "building a case for a massive bombing of Iraq as a new phase of President Bush's war against terrorism." Administration officials, "spearheaded by Deputy Defense Secretary Paul Wolfowitz," *USA Today* reported, "are now arguing privately that still-elusive evidence linking Iraqi leader Saddam Hussein's regime to the Sept. 11 terrorist attacks is not necessary to trigger a military strike."[5] On CNN, National Security Adviser Condoleezza Rice said, "We didn't need Sept. 11 to tell us that [Saddam Hussein] is a threat to our interests. We'll deal with that situation eventually."[6] In response to this saber-rattling, the *Atlanta Journal-Constitution* cautioned "The headiness of success can lure you into an expanded war." It pointed by way of example to General MacArthur's advance to the Yalu River in Korea, which led to the massive intervention by Red China.[7] The *Journal-Constitution*'s concern about Iraq grew stronger when it appeared that the coalition forces in Afghanistan were on the verge of victory: "If we use force to remove Saddam from power," the *Journal-Constitution* warned on December 9, "but turn an Islamic world simmering with anti-U.S. sentiment up to an angry boil by doing so, we have lost, and the repercussions will echo for decades."[8]

The *Wall Street Journal* had no qualms about returning to Iraq to take care of unfinished business, and the sooner the better: "President Bush has said he'll take the war to any country that harbors terrorists. But Saddam Hussein doesn't merely harbor them. He is the terrorist. The question now is whether the Bush Administration allows his reign of terror to continue, or saves the world from it once and for all."[9]

The *New York Times* couldn't seem to make up its mind. "The Bush administration would make a serious mistake by moving to wage war in Iraq," it cautioned. In the same editorial the *Times* conceded that "The world would be a safer place with Mr. Hussein's cruel dictatorship removed," but admitted it saw "no good short-term options for getting rid of him."[10] In January 2002, with the Taliban and al Qaeda apparently driven from Afghanistan, the *Times* expressed half-hearted reservations against targeting Iraq: "With no effective opposition movement inside Iraq and much of Europe and the Arab world strongly opposed to military action, this is not the time for Washington to wage war against Saddam Hussein."[11]

On June 1, 2002, in a graduation address to the cadets at West Point, President Bush articulated a doctrine of "preemptive action when necessary to defend our liberty and to defend our lives."[12] This radical departure from the containment strategy that had guided the American response to the Cold War threat from the Soviet Union became known as the Bush Doctrine, a term that had first been applied to the president's declaration on September 11th that the United States would target those who supported terrorists as well as the terrorists themselves.

On September 19, 2002, a week after he warned the United Nations to force Saddam Hussein to disarm, George W. Bush sent a draft resolution to Congress requesting authority to use military force against Iraq if Hussein did not submit to inspections and give up his weapons programs. On October 3, on the floor of the U.S. Senate, West Virginia's Robert Byrd summoned all his powers of oratory to oppose the resolution, which Byrd called "a product of presidential hubris" that was "breathtaking in its scope." He cited Abraham Lincoln, James Madison and the U.S. Constitution in support of the wisdom of investing the war-making power not in the executive branch but in the Congress. Byrd warned that the proposed resolution was "an unprecedented and unfounded interpretation of the President's authority under the Constitution of the United States, not to mention the fact that it stands the charter of the United Nations on its head."[13]

Unmoved, the House of Representatives passed the resolution by 296 to 133 on October 10, the Senate by 77 to 23 in the early morning hours of October 11, with thirty Democrats voting in the majority. The *New York Times* made no objection to the bill, nor did it criticize those who voted for it. "The desirable alternative to war," the *Times* meekly offered, "is to send U.N. arms investigators back into Iraq with no restrictions on their ability to search out and destroy Baghdad's illegal weapons programs. It needs to be fully explored."[14]

The *Los Angeles Times* was forthright in denouncing Bush's doctrine of preemptive war: "The resolution Congress passed early today authorizing the use of military force against Iraq gives too much power to this and, potentially, future presidents to attack nations unilaterally based on mere suspicions." The paper warned, "This could fundamentally change the nation's approach to foreign policy," and it cited John Quincy Adams' declaration that America "goes not abroad, in search of monsters to destroy." The paper argued for continuing that long-standing policy: "In two world wars and the Cold War, the United States could pride itself on acting defensively. America did not seek out evil; evil sought out America." But even as the *L.A. Times* urged that the United States should not abandon its guiding principles, it conceded: "Iraq must be disarmed."[15]

In the *Village Voice*, Richard Goldstein observed that "The Bush doctrine abrogates the major innovation of American foreign policy, which was to rely on our economic strength rather than our military power." He wondered, "How can anyone believe that the U.S., which gave chemical weapons to Saddam (in order to strengthen his position against Iran) and armed the fundamentalists in Afghanistan (in order to build a bulwark against the Soviets), is now able to manage a region embroiled in the consequences of its machinations?"[16]

On November 9, 2002, the U.N. Security Council unanimously passed a resolution demanding that Saddam Hussein account for Iraq's weapons of mass destruction and threatening "serious consequences" if he did not comply. To ward off a resolution authorizing military action, Iraq finally admitted the UNMOVIC inspectors. The team made its first inspections on November 28, as the United States and Britain deployed ground, air and naval forces to the Persian Gulf.

On January 27, 2003, UNMOVIC's chief inspector, Hans Blix, and Mohamed ElBaradei, the director general of the International Atomic Energy Agency, appeared before the Security Council to report on their progress. Blix reported that Iraq had "cooperated rather well" but "appears not to have come to a genuine acceptance, not even today, of the disarmament which was demanded of it."[17] ElBaradei's report was cautiously optimistic. "No prohibited nuclear activities have been identified," he said.[18]

The widespread reaction in the American press was to seize on the negative aspects of Blix's statements. The *Washington Post* headlined on January 28, "Report Faults Iraq on Arms Hunt" on its front page and opposed continued inspections in an editorial, "No More Second Chances."

That evening, in his State of the Union address, President Bush contradicted ElBaradei's findings: "The British government has learned that Saddam Hussein recently sought significant quantities of uranium from Africa," Bush said.[19] On February 5, Secretary of State Colin Powell appeared before the Security Council to make the case for war against Iraq. In his presentation, Powell declared that "Saddam Hussein and his regime are concealing their efforts to produce more weapons of mass destruction," and he said that Iraqi officials' denials of ties between al Qaeda and Iraq "are simply not credible."[20] Powell's appearance was extensively covered on television and produced overwhelmingly favorable reviews in newspapers that spanned the political spectrum. But the secretary did not convince everyone. Looking beyond the justifications for war, Sandra Mackey wrote in *USA Today* that "the real risks for the USA are not in war, but in the peace that follows." She warned, "If the Bush administration ignores the United Nations and invades Iraq unilaterally, the United States becomes the governing authority for a state that has never become a nation."[21]

After a second report to the Security Council by the U.N. weapons inspectors on February 14, in which Blix noted that "many proscribed weapons and items are not accounted for,"[22] the *New York Times* had no patience for further inspections or delays. The *Times* urged the Security Council to support a British resolution authorizing force against Iraq and declared: "A Council visibly moving toward authorizing force is the last remote hope of getting Iraq to disarm peacefully. . . . In the face of Baghdad's stonewalling, the Council needs to reunite and stand behind its firm

warnings of last fall. What's needed is not more time but an entirely different attitude from Iraq."[23]

The Bush administration continued to depict Iraq as deceptive and
defiant, but three weeks later, on March 7, in their third report to the Security Council, Blix and ElBaradei were united in optimism. Blix reported
that the Iraqis had improved their cooperation and he estimated that it
would take just months to complete the inspection process, not years. As
the *Washington Post* reported, "ElBaradei's report was even more damning
to the administration's position. . . . He said experts had concluded . . .
that the documents used to allege the connection between Iraq and Niger
[where Iraq had supposedly tried to buy uranium ore] were fabricated.
Overall, he concluded, there is no evidence that Iraq has revived a nuclear
weapons program."[24]

Faced with Blix and ElBaradei's positive reports, the *Times* performed
an about-face and called for continuing inspections as an alternative to
war: "We believe there is a better option involving long-running, stepped-
up weapons inspections. . . . If it comes down to a question of yes or no to
invasion without broad international support, our answer is no."[25]

The *Washington Post* was not convinced. Although some of its own reporters, notably Walter Pincus, had repeatedly emphasized in the pages of
the *Post* that there was scant evidence of a meaningful connection between
Iraq and al Qaeda or that Saddam Hussein still possessed weapons of mass
destruction, the *Post* remained resolute in its editorial position: "A regime
and an arsenal that have threatened and destabilized the Middle East for
two decades can be eliminated; prisoners can be released, ethnic minorities freed from brutal repression, war criminals brought to justice, and a
polity based on torture and murder replaced by one that respects basic political and human rights. That is the kind of cause that the United States
has always embraced; it is a cause worthy of the sacrifices that will now be
asked of American men and women in uniform."[26]

Operation Iraqi Freedom began in the early hours of March 20,
2003, Baghdad time, with coordinated air and ground assaults. Dan
Kennedy predicted in the *Boston Phoenix* that no good would come of it.
However glad the Iraqis might be to be rid of Saddam Hussein,
Kennedy wrote, they "will soon begin to resent us, then to hate us, then
to demand that we get our hands off their land and their government
and their oil and *get out.*" History, he said, "suggests that this war will

have unintended consequences. Just as the 1991 Gulf War led to the permanent US presence in Saudi Arabia that convinced the then un-known Osama bin Laden to declare *jihad* against the United States, so will this war create monsters that don't yet have a name."[27]

When the Arab-language television station al Jazeera broadcast video of dead and captured American troops in the first days of the war, Defense Secretary Donald Rumsfeld protested on CBS's *Face the Nation,* "The Geneva Convention indicates that it's not permitted to photograph and embarrass or humiliate prisoners of war." President Bush announced that the United States expected the captive troops "to be treated humanely, just like we'll treat any prisoners of theirs that we capture, humanely." In the *Boston Phoenix,* Richard Byrne questioned whether "an administration that disdains and even undermines institutions of international law" had the right to criticize al Jazeera, when "The treatment of detainees . . . at the US military base in Guantánamo Bay, Cuba . . . has raised even more profound questions of US adherence to the rules of war. . . . After all," Byrne wrote, "we are living in times when the traditional notion of a 'pris-oner of war' has been overturned by the Bush administration with mere semantics."[28]

On the battlefield, access for correspondents covering the new war in Iraq was dramatically improved over the 1991 Gulf War. The press-pool system from Desert Storm was a thing of the past. Reporters were now "embedded" with specific military units and under no obligation to share their stories. When the war began on March 20, there were more than five hundred reporters embedded with the troops.[29] In the thick of the ad-vance, with no military minders looking over their shoulders and equipped with easily portable satellite equipment that enabled them to re-port live from the field, the press corps—the great majority inexperienced in war and many reporting from overseas for the first time—filed un-counted hours of video of armored vehicles rolling across desert landscape, complete with breathless narration. The *Boston Phoenix's* Dan Kennedy judged the embedding policy "a plus" overall, but he observed that "cool field reports from the back of a jeep are no substitute for understand-ing."[30] ABC's Ted Koppel drew a distinction between "coverage" and jour-nalism, and characterized live coverage as "bad journalism." Journalism, Koppel said, meant "sifting the wheat from the chaff," giving the event you're reporting some kind of context, saying what it means.[31]

From this critical perspective, the coverage of Operation Iraqi Freedom, although more varied than that of Desert Storm, failed to show the true context of war. Once again, war was sanitized, with few images of dead or wounded troops or civilians. Television coverage favored video-game clips of smart bombs acquiring and destroying their targets, or night-vision views of vehicles on the move. CNN's Christiane Amanpour, who had criticized the press's self-censorship in the first Gulf War, later said of the second, "I think the press was muzzled and I think the press self-muzzled. I'm sorry to say but certainly television, and perhaps to a certain extent my station, was intimidated by the Administration and its foot soldiers on Fox News."[32]

Some veteran correspondents saw the Pentagon's "embedding" policy as a successful attempt to co-opt the press corps and manage the coverage by means more subtle than the censorship in Desert Storm. If this was the intent of the policy, it may have succeeded to some degree during the invasion, but it also brought scores of reporters to Baghdad, where they were on hand to report the first real controversy of the war. Looting broke out in the capital before Saddam's statue was toppled from its pedestal (with the help of U.S. Marines) on April 9, the day Baghdad was officially declared secure. At first the looters attacked symbols of the regime—Saddam's statues and portraits, his offices and residences and those of his underlings—but the looting quickly became more wide ranging, turning into a mad scramble for anything that wasn't bolted down, and much that was. On April 12, the *New York Times* reported that the looters had moved on "to stores, warehouses and even hospitals. . . . Frightened citizens have barricaded themselves in their homes in some places, or have begun shooting suspected robbers." The *Times* accused Defense Secretary Donald Rumsfeld of being "stunningly off message" when he responded to the images on American television by saying, "Freedom's untidy. And free people are free to commit mistakes, and to commit crimes." From the beginning, the *Times* said, the "chief concern" about the war plan for Iraq was not "the Pentagon's ability to prevail on the battlefield, but the Bush administration's ability to plan for the day after victory. So far, nothing has happened to alleviate that concern."[33]

Americans were shocked as they watched on television while the National Museum of Antiquities in Baghdad was stripped bare by looters. The *Boston Globe* found the images appalling: "Most horrific were lootings at

Iraqi hospitals, where bands of thieves stole baby incubators, medicines, food, and water." The *Globe* was unforgiving in fixing the blame: "Such crimes should have been prevented or at least halted in the early stages by US troops. As an occupying power, the United States has an obligation under the Geneva Convention's laws of war to ensure public order and protect the civilian population." The *Globe* scolded Donald Rumsfeld for his callous remarks and declared, "Liberators do not allow babies to die and they do not stand by for two days while thieves carry away the heritage of humanity."[34]

The *Washington Post* drew a larger lesson from the pandemonium. The looting, it said, "vividly demonstrated a truth that the Bush administration has been slow to accept: that the United States cannot manage postwar Iraq on its own."[35]

The high visibility of the failure to protect Iraq's institutions and to restore order raised questions about whether the United States had enough manpower in Iraq. Donald Rumsfeld had marshaled 100,000 troops for the invasion, one-fifth of the half million that President George H. W. Bush had deployed to the Persian Gulf in 1990–91 to drive Saddam Hussein's army out of Kuwait—but not to garrison Iraq. Coming after Baghdad was declared "secure," the looting, and statements to the press by American officers that they didn't have enough troops to police all of Baghdad, let alone the rest of the country, reinforced the perception that the invasion force was stretched thin.

As the looting played itself out, Iraqis stripped vital equipment from power plants and oil fields, destroyed civil records, and moved on, in the last phase, to the Iraqi army's huge weapons depots, which were mostly unguarded, despite the best efforts of some in the American forces.[36]

Seymour Hersh reported in the April 7 *New Yorker* that "several senior war planners" at the Pentagon were angry with Donald Rumsfeld and his civilian advisers because they "had insisted on micro-managing the war's operational details." The planners' chief complaint was that Rumsfeld had repeatedly rejected the Pentagon's war plans for Iraq, insisting "that the number of ground troops be sharply reduced" in keeping with his vision of a leaner and meaner military. An early Pentagon plan, Hersh related, called for "a wide range of forces from the different armed services, including four or more Army divisions." Rumsfeld had rejected the plan, according to Hersh's informants, insisting "that a smaller, faster-moving attack force, combined with overwhelming air power, would suffice."[37]

In the previous issue of the *New Yorker,* when the war was less than two weeks old, Hersh had accused the Bush administration of using dubious intelligence to build congressional support for the war-powers resolution. Hersh reported that CIA Director George Tenet and Secretary of State Colin Powell had met in secret session with the Senate Foreign Relations Committee in September of 2002 to brief the senators on a CIA report that Iraq had attempted to buy large quantities of "yellow-cake" uranium ore from Niger between 1999 and 2001. "The testimony from Tenet and Powell helped to mollify the Democrats," Hersh wrote, "and two weeks later the [war-powers] resolution passed overwhelmingly, giving the President a congressional mandate for a military assault on Iraq." When the White House finally released to the International Atomic Energy Agency documents to back up the claim—after George W. Bush had repeated the story of Iraq's purported effort to acquire uranium during his State of the Union message in January 2003—it took the IAEA's Iraq Nuclear Verification Office, Hersh recounted, "only a few hours to determine that the documents were fake." The errors in the documents were so glaring that one senior IAEA official told Hersh, "I cannot imagine that they came from a serious intelligence agency." The mistakes, the official said, "could be spotted by someone using Google on the Internet."[38]

In the May 12 *New Yorker,* Hersh examined in more detail how the administration had assembled and evaluated intelligence before the Iraq war began. After September 11th, Hersh reported, Deputy Secretary of Defense Paul Wolfowitz had brought together "a small cluster of policy advisers and analysts" and created an "Office of Special Plans" within the Pentagon. Within a year Wolfowitz's group rivaled the CIA and the Pentagon's own Defense Intelligence Agency "as President Bush's main source of intelligence regarding Iraq's possible possession of weapons of mass destruction and connection with Al Qaeda," Hersh reported. A Pentagon adviser who worked for one of the members of the new group told Hersh that the office "was created to find evidence of what Wolfowitz and his boss, Defense Secretary Donald Rumsfeld, believed to be true—that Saddam Hussein had close ties to Al Qaeda and that Iraq had an enormous arsenal of chemical, biological, and possibly even nuclear weapons that threatened the region and, potentially, the United States." This accusation was supported by "a former Bush administration intelligence official" who told Hersh that he left his job because the White House seemed to him to be "using the intelligence from the C.I.A. and the other agencies only when it fit their agenda. . . . If it doesn't fit their theory, they don't want to hear it."[39]

In mid-June 2003, Philip Gourevitch, another regular contributor to the *New Yorker,* accused the Bush administration of using the supposed threat posed by Saddam's weapons of mass destruction as "a pretext for a campaign whose larger motives and purposes the Administration has never seen fit to articulate to the public." With no prohibited weapons yet found in Iraq, Gourevitch wrote that the "charges now circulating that Bush's war cabinet depended on false, or, worse, falsified intelligence to exaggerate the threat of those weapons in the first place is much more than a technicality."[40]

By early July, roadside bombs and other attacks on American forces were becoming more common. Some thirty American personnel had died since May 1,[41] when President Bush declared that "major combat operations in Iraq have ended," and American troop strength in Iraq had been raised to 147,000.[42] General John Abizaid, who had recently replaced the invasion commander, General Tommy Franks, as commander of the forces in Iraq, characterized the attacks against his troops as "a classical guerrilla-type campaign,"[43] contradicting his civilian boss, Donald Rumsfeld, who had said only recently that the attacks on coalition troops were too random to qualify as organized resistance. Rumsfeld and the White House tried to depict the insurgents as foreign Islamic terrorists—often suggested to be al Qaeda jihadists—joining with a few "holdouts" or "remnants" of Saddam Hussein's Baathist regime. These efforts to assert an al Qaeda connection in Iraq that still was not proven fueled ongoing investigations by the press into the administration's prewar allegations of such a relationship and the other justifications it had employed to make the case for war.

On July 6, 2003, the *New York Times* published an op-ed piece by Joseph C. Wilson, a former ambassador and foreign-service officer with extensive experience in Africa. "Based on my experience with the administration in the months leading up to the war," Wilson wrote, "I have little choice but to conclude that some of the intelligence related to Iraq's nuclear weapons program was twisted to exaggerate the Iraqi threat." He revealed that he was the "unnamed former envoy" mentioned in some news stories who went to Niger early in 2002 to investigate the allegations that Iraq had tried to buy uranium ore from that country. Wilson had concluded that "it was highly doubtful that any such transaction had ever taken place." On his return to the United States, in March 2002, Wilson wrote in the *Times,* he had briefed the CIA and the State Department on his trip, and if his information was ignored "because it did not fit certain preconceptions about Iraq, then a legitimate argument can be made that we went to war under false pretenses."[44]

There was surprisingly little reaction to Wilson's piece at first. It became the subject of more attention after the syndicated columnist Robert Novak reported, on July 14, information received from unnamed officials high in the Bush administration that Wilson's wife, Valerie Plame Wilson, was a CIA agent, and that she had been involved in arranging Wilson's mission to Niger. In the *New York Times,* Paul Krugman pointed out that "if [Novak's sources'] characterization of Mr. Wilson's wife is true (he refuses to confirm or deny it), Bush administration officials have exposed the identity of a covert operative. That happens to be a criminal act; it's also definitely unpatriotic."[45]

Dan Kennedy saw the Niger controversy as a symptom of a larger problem. "What matters is that since September 11, 2001, the Bush administration has engaged in a systematic campaign of deception aimed at building support for war in Congress, with the public, and among US allies," Kennedy wrote in the July 25 *Boston Phoenix.* Referring to a recent address to Congress by British Prime Minister Tony Blair, in which Blair had said removing Saddam Hussein from power was worth the effort even if no weapons of mass destruction were found, Kennedy wrote, "Unlike Bush, Blair is eloquent and persuasive. But neither the British people nor the American people were told they were going to war to end Saddam's horrendous human-rights abuses. They went to war because they were told that if they didn't, they were in imminent danger of being infected, gassed, or nuked. It wasn't true."[46]

In a commentary for the *Wall Street Journal,* which had backed the war since long before the invasion, Albert R. Hunt wrote, "The phony Iraq-Niger deal may be the smoking gun in what was a pervasive pattern of exaggeration and distortion to justify the war against the Iraqi dictator. . . . Yet Congress, under pressure from the White House, is abdicating its responsibility to investigate why the public was misled on such a

momentous matter."[47] (The *Journal* stuck to its editorial support for
Bush's policies and tried to discredit Joseph Wilson for "politicizing" the
Niger story.[48])

David Remnick, the editor of the *New Yorker,* wrote in a commentary
for the magazine, "it's impossible to be indifferent to the prospect that intelligence has been manipulated, forged, or bullied into shape. . . . The
Administration evidently calculates that its popularity is such that no one
much cares about the petty questions of means and ends. The Administration is wrong."[49]

Since September 11th, the *New Yorker* had been a pacesetter in guiding press scrutiny of the Bush administration's management of the war on
terrorism. With seventeen articles written under the "Annals of National
Security" banner between 9/11 and the end of July 2003, Seymour Hersh
was at the forefront of this effort. (Among other important contributors at
the *New Yorker* were Jane Mayer, Jon Lee Anderson, George Packer,
Nicholas Lemann, Hendrik Hertzberg, and Remnick himself, whose editorial guidance coordinated the effort.) In October 2003, Hersh accused
the Bush administration of corrupting the established procedures of the
U.S. intelligence services. Even before September 11th, Hersh charged,
the White House had begun bypassing "the government's customary procedures for vetting intelligence" by experienced analysts in the CIA and
other agencies in order to "stovepipe" raw intelligence to top administration officials. Among the unevaluated materials passed along by this
means, according to those Hersh interviewed, were accounts by Iraqi exiles and defectors that became the basis for administration policies that
continued even after the CIA and other sources provided conflicting information that contradicted the stovepiped accounts. Hersh wrote that by
March 2002, President Bush had decided, "in his own mind, to go to
war," and that this decision "had a devastating effect on the continuing
struggle against terrorism. . . . The Bush Administration took many intelligence operations that had been aimed at Al Qaeda and other terrorist
groups around the world and redirected them to the Persian Gulf."[50]

After the March 2003 invasion, the United States, Britain and Australia had formed the Iraq Survey Group to search Iraq for weapons of
mass destruction. The group's director, David A. Kay, was an American.
Kay worked on behalf of and with the support of the CIA and the Defense Intelligence Agency. He reported to the American government, as

Survey Group members from other nations reported to their own governments. On January 23, 2004, Kay resigned his position to protest the decision by the White House and the Pentagon to shift intelligence resources in Iraq away from the search for weapons and toward counterinsurgency efforts. Kay had believed that Saddam Hussein was concealing weapons and he had supported the war, but more than eight months of searching had produced no WMD. "It turns out that we were all wrong," Kay testified before the Senate Armed Services Committee, "and that is most disturbing."[51] Although the Survey Group's official report was not issued for another nine months, Kay's testimony put the nail in the coffin of the Bush administration's claims that Iraq had weapons of mass destruction. The *New Yorker* warned, prophetically, that the CIA should not be made a scapegoat. "Intelligence, by its very nature, is usually uncertain and often wrong," John Cassidy wrote in a comment on Kay's testimony. "It should always be treated with skepticism and caution, two attributes that were, and are, conspicuously missing from the Bush White House."[52]

The next blow to the administration's credibility came in March 2004, on the first anniversary of the invasion, when Richard A. Clarke, the government's counterterrorism "czar" under Presidents Clinton and George W. Bush, testified before the bipartisan 9/11 Commission that had been created by an act of Congress in late 2002 to look into "the circumstances surrounding" the attacks. Clarke told the commission that the Bush administration had been less diligent than the Clinton team in pursuing terrorists before September 11th, and had sought to blame Iraq immediately after the attacks. Clarke testified that Bush had ordered him, on September 12, to "see if Saddam did this, see if he's linked in any way." Clarke told the commission that in his opinion, "by invading Iraq the president of the United States has greatly undermined the war on terrorism."[53]

Clarke had expressed the same criticisms in his recently published book *Against All Enemies,* and White House minions had been dispatched in all directions to discredit him. "The White House's schoolyard name-calling," the *Times* scolded, "does no one any good, least of all Mr. Bush, who is made to appear far more interested in undermining Mr. Clarke's credibility than in addressing the heart of his critique."[54] The *Chicago Tribune* supported the *Times* by name (Robert McCormick must have been spinning in his grave like a rotary press), and declared, "No matter how controversial his book, Clarke has high standing as an anti-terrorism expert. He isn't the issue. The questions he raises about the Bush administration's approach to terror are. The administration must answer them with more than bluster or risk losing Americans' confidence on this matter altogether."[55]

At this time, CBS News and Seymour Hersh were independently pursuing a story in Iraq that would shake American's confidence in the administration's conduct of the war more than any revelation about prewar intelligence. CBS was prepared to air its report on the abuse of prisoners at the infamous Abu Ghraib prison outside Baghdad in the second week of April 2004, but the network delayed airing it for two weeks at the request of General Richard Myers, chairman of the Joint Chiefs of Staff, who feared the news would worsen an already bad situation in the Iraqi city of Fallujah, then dominated by insurgents and under attack by U.S. Marines.[56] Hersh's article was scheduled for the May 10 issue of the *New Yorker*. Possibly because CBS learned of its impending publication, the network ran the Abu Ghraib story on *60 Minutes II* on April 28.

The controversy ignited by the broadcast, which included the appalling photographs taken by American troops at Abu Ghraib, probably heightened interest in Hersh's *New Yorker* account, which detailed the abuse and its origins in far more detail, but in pages of text with just two photographs. (The photos were appalling not least because American soldiers were so obviously enjoying the indecencies inflicted on the prisoners, and because they thought it appropriate to photograph the proceedings.) Hersh reported that prisoners were loosened up by rough treatment at the hands of military police before they were interrogated by intelligence officers, and he noted that a report on the military prisons in Iraq written by the Army's provost marshal traced this practice back to Afghanistan (as Dana Priest and Barton Gellman had reported in the *Washington Post* in December 2002). The *New Yorker* had obtained a copy of an internal Army report "not meant for public release," prepared by Major General Antonio M. Taguba, who had investigated conditions at Abu Ghraib earlier in the year. Taguba's report, in Hersh's words, revealed a picture "in which Army regulations and the Geneva Conventions were routinely violated, and in which much of the day-to-day management of the prisoners was abdicated to Army military-intelligence units and civilian contract employees. Interrogating prisoners and getting intelligence, including by intimidation and torture, was the priority." As Hersh reported Taguba's findings, "A lack of proper screening also meant that many innocent Iraqis were wrongly being detained—indefinitely, it seemed, in some cases."[57]

Although Hersh and some others in the press used "torture" to describe the abuses at Abu Ghraib, Donald Rumsfeld, in a press conference, quibbled that "what has been charged thus far is abuse, which I believe technically is different from torture."[58] Rumsfeld and President Bush both professed to be shocked by the photographs and tried to paint the abuses as the actions of a few bad apples who "did not reflect the conduct of the military as a whole," as Hersh reported the administration's reaction. "Taguba's report, however," Hersh wrote, "amounts to an unsparing study of collective wrongdoing and the failure of Army leadership at the highest levels."[59]

The *New York Times* reminded its readers in its May 3 edition that it was the terrorists' goal to goad the western democracies "into demonstrating that their worst anti-American propaganda was true. Abu Ghraib was an enormous victory for them, and it is unlikely that any response by the Bush administration will wipe its stain from the minds of Arabs."[60] On May 7, the *Times* charged that Donald Rumsfeld "has morphed over the last two years, from a man of supreme confidence to arrogance, then to almost willful blindness." In the *Times*'s editorial view, there could be only one remedy: "This page has argued that the United States, having toppled Saddam Hussein, has an obligation to do everything it can to usher in a stable Iraqi government. But the country is not obliged to continue struggling through this quagmire with the secretary of defense who took us into the swamp. . . . It is long past time for a new team and new thinking at the Department of Defense."[61] (The *Times* was among the first to charge that the Bush administration had accomplished the difficult task of creating a quagmire in a desert.)

Seymour Hersh followed his May 10 *New Yorker* piece on Abu Ghraib with two more, published in succeeding weeks, in which he marshaled evidence to show that the interrogation practices at Abu Ghraib had been imposed from high in the chain of command, and that they had originated in Afghanistan and at Guantánamo.[62] When Hersh's May 24 article hit the stands, David Carr wrote in the *Times* that Hersh had "helped set the political agenda by reporting that once again American soldiers in the midst of a war . . . have committed atrocious acts."[63] Carr neglected to mention that Hersh had traced the responsibility for the atrocious acts committed by enlisted soldiers at Abu Ghraib through the military and civilian chains of command until it arrived at the very top. In the summer of 2004, Hersh's allegations were supported by the conclusions of two reports on the origins of detainee abuse at Abu Ghraib, the first issued by an independent group chaired by former Secretary of Defense James Schlesinger and cosigned by former Secretary of Defense Harold Brown, and the second an official Army report. In the *Washington Post,* James Diehl wrote that there was no mistaking where the responsibility lay: "The causal chain is all there: from Bush's February 2002 decision [about the limits on applying the Geneva Conventions] to Rumsfeld's December 2002 authorization of nudity, stress positions and dogs; to the adoption of those methods in Afghanistan and their sanction in Iraq by a commander looking back to Bush's decision; and finally, to their use on detainees by soldiers who reasonably believed they were executing official policy."[64]

With the revelations from Abu Ghraib, one of the monsters Dan Kennedy had predicted at the start of the invasion now stood revealed.

Each unforeseen consequence of the war—the looting, the insurgency, the abuses at Abu Ghraib—called into question once more the rationale for the invasion and the prewar intelligence that had been used to justify it. On May 26, 2004, the editors of the *New York Times,* after first patting themselves on the back for "an enormous amount of journalism that we are proud of," acknowledged that in covering the "decisions that led the United States into Iraq" there were instances when the *Times*'s coverage "was not as rigorous as it should have been." But in the act of contrition, the editors stumbled. While it was still possible that prohibited weapons might be found in Iraq, they wrote, "in this case it looks as if we, along with the administration, were taken in." By portraying the Bush administration as gullible rather than culpable, the *Times* turned a blind eye to the evidence, compiled by Seymour Hersh and other reporters, that the administration had created the very conditions in which it perverted bad intelligence to its own uses. For a more critical evaluation of the White House's responsibility, the editors of the *Times* could have found in their own pages one that columnist Frank Rich had written just a few weeks earlier: "The demons that keep rising up from the past to grab Mr. Bush are the fictional W.M.D. he wielded to take us into Iraq. They stalk him as relentlessly as Banquo's ghost did Macbeth. From that original sin, all else flows."[65]

In the *Boston Phoenix,* Dan Kennedy expressed the view that even if the *Times* and the rest of the mainstream media had done a better job, "the case for Iraq's weapons capabilities and terrorist ties couldn't have been absolutely disproven any more than it could have been proven. The media didn't fail because they were unsuccessful in stopping the war," Kennedy wrote. "Rather, they failed because, in all too many instances, they parroted the White House's rationale for war rather than subjecting it to rigorous, skeptical analysis. That is to say, they failed because they forgot what journalism is for."[66]

On the question of prewar intelligence and the administration's justifications for war in Iraq, the coverage by many—perhaps a majority—of the major dailies and news magazines in 2002–03, like that of the *Times,* was not as rigorous as it should have been. But from early in the war there was a gradual increase in critical journalism for the simple reason that things did not go well after the initial invasion. With each bad turn of events the critical impulse in the press gained momentum until the majority had adopted the attitude of the skeptical minority that had questioned the administration's motives during the runup to war. By the summer of 2004, every aspect of the war in Iraq was the subject of continuing debate and criticism in the press. Scrutiny of the government's war policy was no longer in question. What remained to be seen was whether public opinion would follow.

In November 2004, despite polls that showed a steady erosion of support for the war, despite the manifestly inadequate planning for the occupation, despite ongoing questions about prewar intelligence, despite the rising insurgency in Iraq and the failure to kill or capture Osama bin Laden, George W. Bush won a second term in the White House. In the face of many indications to the contrary, Bush regarded the returns as a validation of his policies in Iraq. Asked shortly before his second inaugural by a *Washington Post* reporter why no one had been held accountable for the "mistakes or misjudgments" in the war, Bush replied, infamously, "We had an accountability moment, and that's called the 2004 elections."[67]

It was not until November 2006 that the voters called Bush to account for Iraq. In the meantime, the *Times* of London published the Downing Street Memo, a secret British government memorandum that documented the view held by the head of British intelligence, following consultations in Washington in July of 2002, that President Bush had already decided on war with Iraq by that time, and that within the U.S. government, "the intelligence and facts were being fixed around the policy." The memo also recorded that "There was little discussion in Washington of the aftermath after military action." In its key sentences, the memo confirmed that the decision to go to war in Iraq was not based on intelligence, but that the intelligence was used to support the decision.

On March 20, 2006, on the third anniversary of the invasion, former National Security Adviser Zbigniew Brzezinski said on PBS's *News Hour with Jim Lehrer* that he believed the benefits to the United States of the Iraq war had been very few, beyond the removal of Saddam Hussein: "we have undermined our international legitimacy," Brzezinski said. "That's a very high cost to a superpower. We have destroyed our credibility; no one believes anything the president says anymore. We have tarnished our morality with Abu Ghraib and Guantánamo. These are phenomenal costs."

George W. Bush was beyond recall in the November 2006 elections, and so Donald Rumsfeld was made the sacrificial lamb in recognition of the voters' displeasure. Even with Rumsfeld gone, the *New York Times* was not sanguine about the prospect for an honest reassessment of the war. "We're still waiting for a sign that Mr. Bush has grasped the steady unraveling of his Iraq strategy as anything beyond a political problem."[68]

⌁

In the second Iraq war, as in Vietnam, the press contributed to a shift in public opinion from supporting the war to opposing it. As in Vietnam, the press was slow to question the wisdom of the political decisions that led to war, but it was dogged in its persistence, once fixed on the failings of the policy, as if to atone for its sins. There is no prospect that the media will turn away from Iraq so long as the United States remains militarily engaged there, but since the midterm elections in November 2006, serious questions have been raised about the overall condition of the U.S. armed forces that the press has yet fully to explore. Each element of the story has been reported—the strain of repeated deployments on the troops, over-reliance on the National Guard, the difficulty of meeting military recruitment goals, the fact that the United States has never been involved in a war this long without a military draft to meet the need for manpower and increased taxes to pay for it, and the shameful fact that in this war, which is longer than U.S. forces were engaged in World War II, no sacrifices have been asked of anyone but the troops and their families—but the implication of all these elements taken together is virtually never considered, even when it's implicit in the day's top stories.

In spite of repeated accusations that the American force in Iraq was too small to stabilize the country, Donald Rumsfeld never authorized raising the number of troops significantly above the mid-2003 level. After Rumsfeld's departure, a "surge" of additional troops was authorized with the goal of pacifying Baghdad. Military leaders cautioned that such an increase could not be maintained indefinitely because the armed forces did not have the resources to sustain it. The clear implication was that beyond the surge in Iraq the United States could only sustain its commitments in Iraq and in Afghanistan at the pre-surge levels. Top-ranking military officers have sounded alarms about the extent of the problem. In April 2007, retired Marine Corps General James J. Jones, a former commander of NATO, conceded on *Charlie Rose* that American ground forces are "at the breaking point," and he stated that the service chiefs are "seeking to increase their rotation base," that is, to increase the strength of the armed forces.[69] Retired Army General William Odom, a former director of the National Security Agency and head of Army intelligence, has said on several occasions that in his opinion the Iraq war is "the greatest strategic disaster in U.S. history," and that as a result of the American engagement there, "We've destroyed our ground army." In Odom's view, it will take years, and a great deal of money, to restore it to an adequate state of readiness.[70]

These views have been reported, but at this writing the condition of America's armed forces, beyond how it affects the troops in Iraq, has not become part of the public debate. A cover story in the April 5, 2007, issue of *Time* magazine, "America's Broken-Down Army," by Mark Thompson, may have signaled that the subject is rising in prominence, but that is by no means certain.

Once again we have committed our ground forces on the land mass of Asia, and we are suffering the consequences. The picture that active and retired American officers paint of those forces' status is deeply disturbing in its implications not only for American troops in Iraq and Afghanistan, but for the nation's ability to respond to other threats to its security in both the short and the long term. As much as the failure to put enough troops into Iraq in 2003 to establish and maintain order, the present condition of the military as a whole is a consequence of the Bush administration's decision to invade a country that had no proven connection to the terrorist attacks of September 11, 2001. This outcome deserves more attention from the press. The failure of that attention would be a lapse potentially as serious as the failure to question the White House's reasons for going to war in the first place.

Beyond Iraq, the war on terrorism remains. It will continue after the last American troops are withdrawn from Iraq, and it will require, as it has required since September 11th, attention to the long-term strategic posture of the United States, if we are to be ready to meet what further threats and challenges that conflict may pose. On the part of the press, the larger struggle demands the kind of thinking that moves a journalist to walk the streets late at night, to ponder long and hard, and then to sit down and write beyond the day's headlines, as Walter Lippmann wrote a week into the Korean War, "It should be, it seems to me, a cardinal rule of U.S. policy that . . . we shall retain mobility and freedom for our own military forces. We must remember that our power is on the sea and in the air, and that we must not commit our meager infantry forces on distant beachheads, thus engaging large elements of our power in theaters that are not of our own choosing and where no decision can ever be had."[71]

12

THE LONG WAR

The War on Terrorism (2004–)

In 2004, with the revelations of prisoner abuse at Abu Ghraib and the appearance of al Qaeda jihadists in Iraq—where they had not been welcome before the war—the Iraq conflict reconnected with the wider war on terrorism in ways that no one—least of all those who planned the invasion of Iraq—had foreseen. In the view of Lawrence Wright, who has written on terrorism for the *New Yorker,* al Qaeda was "moribund" after it was driven from Afghanistan by the coalition invasion in 2001, but was revived by the war in Iraq, which Wright sees as the center of the group's anti-Western efforts since 2003.[1]

The press drew the connections immediately between Abu Ghraib and U.S. anti-terrorist efforts elsewhere. In the second week of the scandal, the *Washington Post* published three front-page articles about the locations of terrorist suspects held by the United States and the policies that governed their treatment. The primary reporter on each of the articles was Dana Priest, the *Post*'s national-security correspondent, who had revealed (with Barton Gellman) in December 2002 the existence of the government's "extraordinary rendition" program, and of a network of overseas detention centers for terrorist suspects. On May 9, 2004, Priest and Joe

Stephens reported that a classified list of "about 20 techniques" for inter-rogating prisoners had been "approved at the highest levels of the Penta-gon and the Justice Department," in the spring of 2003, "and represents the first publicly known documentation of an official policy permitting interrogators to use physically and psychologically stressful methods dur-ing questioning." On May 11, Priest and Stephens revealed that three of the government detention facilities were in Kabul, Afghanistan, at an American air base in Qatar, and in Iraq at a "huge hangar near the runway at Baghdad International Airport." Abu Ghraib, Priest and Stephens wrote, was "just the largest and suddenly most notorious in a worldwide constellation of detention centers—many of them secret and all off-limits to public scrutiny." Based on Pentagon figures and the opinions of "intel-ligence experts," Priest and Stephens estimated that "more than 9,000 per-sons" were being held overseas by the United States, most under military control. In the May 13 *Post*, Priest and Dan Morgan reported on justifica-tions for the military's interrogation techniques that had been offered the day before by Donald Rumsfeld and General Richard B. Myers, the chair-man of the Joint Chiefs of Staff, before a Senate committee, and the ob-jections of several governmental and nongovernmental figures to the officials' reasoning. Kenneth Roth, the director of Human Rights Watch, characterized interrogation techniques requiring special approval as "bla-tantly illegal," Priest and Morgan reported. As they recounted the view of retired Rear Admiral John Hutson, the Navy's judge advocate general from 1997 to 2000, "the Pentagon was trying to draw lines within the gray area between torture and benign treatment. 'I fundamentally disagree with where they drew the lines,' Hutson said."[2]

Seymour Hersh reported in the May 24 *New Yorker,* in his third article on the origins of the abuses at Abu Ghraib, that interrogation practices developed before the invasion of Iraq for Afghanistan and Guantánamo had so alarmed several "senior military legal officers from the Judge Advo-cate General's (JAG) Corps" that they had called on Scott Horton, the chairman of the New York City Bar Association's Committee on Human Rights, to express their concern about Defense Secretary Donald Rums-feld's "apparent disregard for the requirements of the Geneva conventions while carrying out the war on terror." The JAG officers were troubled by the use of civilian contractors in interrogations and the "atmosphere of legal ambiguity being created as a result of a policy decision at the highest levels in the Pentagon." The officers asked Horton to "challenge the Bush Administration about its standards for detentions and interrogations," Hersh reported. "They told him that, with the war on terror, a fifty-year history of exemplary application of the Geneva Conventions had come to an end."[3]

In the Sunday *New York Times Magazine* the same week, Susan Sontag scorned Rumsfeld's semantic hair-splitting over what constituted "abuse" or "torture," and declared, "To refuse to call what took place at Abu Ghraib—and what has taken place elsewhere in Iraq and in Afghanistan and at Guantánamo Bay—by its true name, torture, is as outrageous as the refusal to call the Rwandan genocide a genocide." Sontag rebuked those who sought to justify stretching the bounds of traditional American morality in the face of the new and terrible threat to international order by citing the 1984 International Convention Against Torture, to which the United States was (and is) a signatory: "No exceptional circumstances whatsoever, whether a state of war or a threat of war, internal political instability or any other public emergency, may be invoked as a justification of torture." Sontag wrote, "The notion that apologies or professions of 'disgust' by the president and the secretary of defense are a sufficient response" to the controversy over the treatment of detainees "is an insult to one's historical and moral sense. The torture of prisoners is not an aberration. It is a direct consequence of the with-us-or-against-us doctrines of world struggle with which the Bush administration has sought to change, change radically, the international stance of the United States and to recast many domestic institutions and prerogatives."[4]

A reporter for the *Wall Street Journal,* Jess Bravin, broke the news on June 7 that early in 2003 the Pentagon had prepared a classified report on interrogation methods for Secretary Rumsfeld "after commanders at Guantánamo Bay, Cuba, complained in late 2002 that with conventional methods they weren't getting enough information from prisoners." Bravin reported that in the opinion of a military lawyer who helped to prepare the report, the "political appointees heading the working group sought to assign to the president virtually unlimited authority on matters of torture—to assert 'presidential power at its absolute apex.'"[5]

On June 8, in the *Washington Post,* Dana Priest traced the rationalizations for torture back to August of 2002, when "the Justice Department advised the White House that torturing al Qaeda terrorists in captivity abroad 'may be justified,' and that international laws against torture 'may be unconstitutional if applied to interrogations' conducted in President Bush's war on terrorism, according to a newly obtained memo." The memo, prepared by the Justice Department's Office of Legal Counsel, "defined torture in a much narrower way, for example, than does the U.S. Army," Priest reported. As the memo defined it, "moderate or fleeting pain does not necessarily constitute torture." Quoting a phrase that would become notorious, Priest related, "Torture, the memo says, 'must be equivalent in intensity to the pain accompanying serious physical injury, such as organ failure, impairment of bodily function, or even death.'"[6]

The *New York Times* condemned the repeated denials of torture by administration officials up to and including the president, and declared, "Each new revelation makes it more clear that the inhumanity at Abu Ghraib grew out of a morally dubious culture of legal expediency and a disregard for normal behavior fostered at the top of this administration."[7] The *Washington Post* took the administration to task for refusing to release the list of interrogation techniques it had approved, and said, "thanks again to an independent press, we have begun to learn the deeply disturbing truth about the legal opinions that the Pentagon and the Justice Department seek to keep secret. According to copies leaked to several newspapers, they lay out a shocking and immoral set of justifications for torture." The *Post* stated its view that "There is no justification, legal or moral, for the judgments made by Mr. Bush's political appointees at the Justice and Defense departments. . . . The news that serving U.S. officials have officially endorsed principles once advanced by [Chilean dictator] Augusto Pinochet brings shame on American democracy." Before the Bush administration took office, the *Post* informed its readers, "the Army's interrogation procedures . . . established this simple and sensible test: No technique should be used that, if used by an enemy on an American, would be regarded as a violation of U.S. or international law."[8] (Rosa Brooks later suggested in the *Los Angeles Times* another yardstick, even simpler: "If in doubt, take any of the 'alternative' methods that Bush wants to use on U.S. detainees and imagine someone using those methods on your son or daughter."[9])

While the debate about the treatment of detainees continued, the Supreme Court ruled against the government in two landmark cases regarding their legal standing. On June 28, 2004, the Court ruled 6 to 3 in favor of a group of Guantánamo detainees who had sued for the right to challenge their imprisonment and announced in an 8 to 1 decision that the imprisonment of Yaser Esam Hamdi, the American citizen who had been captured in Afghanistan in 2001 and held since then without being charged or accorded the right to consult his attorney, "had either been invalid from the beginning or had become so, for constitutional or statutory reasons," as the *Times* reported the decision.[10] The *Atlanta Journal-Constitution* considered the rulings "a major victory for those who believe the U.S. Constitution guarantee of due process applies all the time, during war and peace."[11] The *Boston Globe* wrote that in its decisions, "the Supreme Court yesterday kept the Bill of Rights from being a collateral victim of the war on terror."[12] The *Christian Science Monitor* judged the court's rulings not only a vindication for the right of an accused person to be brought before a court of law, but "also a victory in the war on terror itself which, after all, is a campaign to assert such liberties against those who would deny them wholesale by force."[13]

The resolution of the Hamdi case was an anticlimax. In October 2004, the government released Yaser Hamdi to Saudi Arabia on the condition that he give up his U.S. citizenship and promise not to sue the government over his captivity. In a letter to the *Times,* a law professor from the University of Houston cited a case in which "the Supreme Court made it clear that the government cannot coerce someone to surrender citizenship. By trying to do precisely that, the United States has continued to act lawlessly toward Mr. Hamdi."[14] The *Washington Post* noted that Hamdi's release "means that the government never had to explain why he was detained in the first place."[15]

After Abu Ghraib, the question of whether the United States was torturing prisoners would not go away. In February 2005, Jane Mayer reported in the *New Yorker* that the U.S.'s program of extraordinary rendition, which began in the 1990s under the Clinton administration, was dramatically expanded after September 11, 2001. She also reported that terror suspects not rendered to third parties were secretly transported and held by the CIA in Thailand, Qatar, and Afghanistan, "among other countries," in violation of the Geneva Conventions' requirement that soldiers and civilians captured in war be promptly registered "so that their treatment can be monitored." The portrait of the administration's antiterrorism strategy that Mayer drew in the article was one in which the ends justified the means.[16]

Many of Mayer's sources for the article were military and civilian intelligence professionals who opposed, for reasons that were as often hardheaded and practical as idealistic, both the rendition program and the harsh treatment of suspects. One former CIA official, evidently moved by moral outrage, described the post-9/11 program as "an abomination." Other informants told Mayer that "Years of experience in interrogation have led them to doubt the effectiveness of physical coercion as a means of extracting reliable information," she reported, and that "By holding detainees indefinitely, without counsel, without charges of wrongdoing, and under circumstances that could, in legal parlance, 'shock the conscience' of a court, the Administration has jeopardized its chances of convicting hundreds of suspected terrorists, or even of using them as witnesses in almost any court in the world." Mayer's sources told her that long-established interrogation methods "aimed at forging relationships with detainees" fell out of favor after September 11th, despite the fact that this style of interrogation "had yielded major successes," including in the case of the American embassies bombed in Africa in 1998, which resulted in the conviction of four al Qaeda operatives and "created an invaluable public record about Al Qaeda." One former FBI agent with extensive experience in antiterrorism cases told Mayer, "Due process made detainees more compliant, not less." A former officer of MI5, the British intelligence agency, told her that the British government's experience with suspected Irish Republican Army members who were subjected to "forceful interrogations" convinced the government in the end that "detainees aren't valuable." The former MI5 officer hoped the United States would not do what the British had done in the 1970s, "detaining people and violating their civil liberties," because "It did nothing but exacerbate the situation. Most of those interned went back to terrorism. You'll end up radicalizing the entire population."[17]

In an article in July 2005, Mayer recounted an interview with a "military-intelligence officer who was familiar with practices at Guantánamo" that questioned the administration's designation of the detainees as "enemy combatants" without giving them a chance to challenge the reasons for their detention. The officer, Mayer reported, told her that during 2002 and 2003, the pressure on interrogators to get information from the detainees was "intense," and that "At the time, we didn't even understand what Al Qaeda *was*. We thought the detainees were all masterminds. It wasn't the case. Most of them were just dirt farmers in Afghanistan."[18]

At the *Washington Post,* Dana Priest concentrated on the treatment and status of detainees in stories on long-term planning by the administration for indefinitely imprisoning suspected terrorists, the death of a detainee in Afghanistan that was ruled a homicide, and accounts by suspects who claimed they had been tortured after the CIA handed them over to other countries, among other aspects of the controversy. On November 2, 2005, Priest disclosed new information about the scope of the CIA's secret network of prisons. She revealed that the agency had been "hiding and interrogating some of its most important al Qaeda captives at a Soviet-era compound in Eastern Europe." Priest also named "Thailand, Afghanistan and several democracies in Eastern Europe" as hosts to the secret facilities, and she reported that one was concealed within the larger prison complex at Guantánamo Bay in Cuba. Priest reported that more than one hundred suspects were then in the CIA program, which had originally been conceived "to hide and interrogate the two dozen or so al Qaeda leaders believed to be directly responsible for the Sept. 11 attacks, or who posed an imminent threat, or had knowledge of the larger al Qaeda network." The program, she wrote, "has been increasingly debated within the CIA, where considerable concern lingers about the legality, morality and practicality of holding even unrepentant terrorists in such isolation and secrecy, perhaps for the duration of their lives. Mid-level and senior CIA officers began arguing two years ago that the system was unsustainable and diverted the agency from its unique espionage mission." Priest quoted "a senior CIA officer" who had protested the program from the beginning: "I kept saying, where's the help? We've got to bring in some help. We can't be jailers—our job is to find Osama." Another informant, whom Priest identified only as "an intelligence official," described the system as "just a horrible burden."[19]

In an editorial, the *Post* declared, "This shameful situation is the direct result of Mr. Bush's decision in February 2002 to set aside the Geneva Conventions as well as standing U.S. regulations for the handling of detainees."[20]

The *Times* also placed the blame on President Bush for "needlessly scrapping the Geneva Conventions and American law" over the objections of military lawyers. The paper rebuked the "rigid ideologues" in the administration who had justified that decision by claiming that the conventions' definitions of torture were "too vague." "Which part of no murder, torture, mutilation, cruelty or humiliation do they not understand?" the *Times* demanded. "The restrictions are a problem only if you want to do such abhorrent things and pretend they are legal."[21] When the Republican leadership in Congress demanded an investigation into Priest's sources for her November 2 article, the *Times* charged that "These same leaders have spent 18 months crushing any serious look at the actual abuse of prisoners at those camps, and at camps run by the American military." In a reference to Valerie Plame Wilson, the *Times* pointed out that for more than two years, the Republican leaders "have expressed no interest in whether the White House leaked the name of a covert C.I.A. operative to punish a critic of the Iraq war." The paper refuted charges that Priest's article "damaged America's image, harmed national security and jeopardized American soldiers and agents" and it condemned the attempts by the administration and its supporters to blame the messenger: "The truth is that the damage is caused by the administration's underlying acts and policies, not by the news media's disclosures, which serve only to hold officials accountable for their actions."[22]

The next disclosure made headlines around the world and prompted outrage on editorial pages across America. On December 16, 2005, the *Times* reported that early in 2002 President Bush had authorized the National Security Agency to intercept telephone calls and e-mails between U.S. citizens and foreign countries without first obtaining warrants from special secret courts set up under the Foreign Intelligence Surveillance Act (FISA) of 1978. The account, by James Risen and Eric Lichtblau, reported that the Bush administration had asked the *Times* not to print the story and that the paper had delayed publishing it for almost a year "to conduct additional reporting." The *Times* then printed the story without the administration's blessing, Risen and Lichtblau related, although it did withhold some information "that administration officials argued could be useful to terrorists."[23]

The *Los Angeles Times* called Bush's action "one of the more egregious cases of governmental overreach in the aftermath of 9/11," and suggested that "the latest revelations may serve as a timely reminder of why the American constitutional system requires the judiciary—the third branch of government—to review the actions of the executive branch when necessary to protect the people's liberty."[24] The *Washington Post* declared that President Bush, by ignoring FISA's requirements, "shows a profound disregard for Congress and the laws it passes."[25] The *Boston Globe* wrote, "No president should be allowed to create a law-free zone in which government agencies spy on people in this country without legal authorization from Congress and warrants from a court."[26] The title of an editorial in *USA Today* neatly summed up the paper's position: "Want to snoop in America? Get a court order."[27] (As did the *Wall Street Journal's* editorial, "Thank you for wiretapping."[28]) The *Denver Post* pointed out, as others had done on many occasions since September 11th, "If we give up our liberties in the name of antiterrorism, the terrorists have already won."[29]

Perhaps not since the Civil War had constitutional principles been invoked so often by the press as they were in the fifth year of war on terrorism, as the debate returned again and again to questions about the limits of presidential power. A few days after the *Times* broke the story of the NSA's warrantless wiretapping, when Vice President Cheney said that those who accused President Bush of abusing his power were growing complacent over the terrorist threat, the *Washington Post* responded, "If there were an attack tomorrow, would we still be complaining the day after about torture, or secret detentions, or spying on Americans? Fair to ask; and the answer is yes, we would be complaining, and not just because of the damage done to core American values and traditions. It's also become clear, since the attacks, that the president's overreaching has damaged U.S. standing in the war that he and Mr. Cheney rightly cite as their priority."[30]

The *Times* saw Dick Cheney as the Svengali behind the quest for expanded executive power. In a December 23 editorial, "Mr. Cheney's Imperial Presidency," the paper charged that "Virtually from the time he chose himself to be Mr. Bush's running mate in 2000, Dick Cheney has spearheaded an extraordinary expansion of the powers of the presidency—from writing energy policy behind closed doors with oil executives to abrogating longstanding treaties and using the 9/11 attacks as a pretext to invade Iraq, scrap the Geneva Conventions and spy on American citizens."[31]

Peter S. Canellos ventured in the *Boston Globe*, "Bush's refusal to submit to the [FISA] warrant process seems deliberately provocative, intended to send the message that the president doesn't have to follow Congress's laws dealing with national security."[32]

Some thought the president's disregard for the laws of the land had risen to the level of high crimes and misdemeanors. For some time there had been calls to "Impeach Bush" at public protests and in letters to the editor, on bumper stickers and weblogs, but few serious proposals in the press. On December 18, 2005, two days after the *Times* broke the story of the NSA's wiretapping program, Michigan Congressman John Conyers, the ranking Democrat on the House Judiciary Committee, introduced a resolution inviting the committee "to investigate the Administration's intent to go to war before congressional authorization, manipulation of pre-war intelligence, encouraging and countenancing torture, retaliating against critics, and to make recommendations regarding grounds for possible impeachment."[33] Asked in a television interview why he took the trouble to introduce a resolution that would go nowhere in the Republican-controlled Congress, Conyers replied that he didn't want history to think that Americans were unaware of the magnitude of this president's offenses; he wanted it on the record that at least one member of Congress believed they were worthy of impeachment.[34]

The press took virtually no notice of Conyers' action, but there were others who shared his view of Bush's responsibility. In January 2006, former Congresswoman Elizabeth Holtzman wrote in *The Nation,* "Finally it has started. People have begun to speak of impeaching President George W. Bush—not in hushed whispers but openly, in newspapers, on the Internet, in ordinary conversations and even in Congress. As a former member of Congress who sat on the House Judiciary Committee during the impeachment proceedings against President Richard Nixon, I believe they are right to do so." Holtzman found Bush's argument that as commander in chief he had the authority to violate any law in the interests of national security "highly dangerous in its sweep and implications." She pointed out that "the Supreme Court has never upheld the President's right to do this in the area of wiretapping, nor has it ever granted the President a 'monopoly over war-powers' or recognized him as 'Commander in Chief of the country' as opposed to Commander in Chief of the Army and Navy."[35]

Holtzman's case for impeachment was supported by the veteran journalist Lewis Lapham in the March 2006 issue of *Harper's Magazine.* Lapham, a former reporter and the editor of *Harper's* for the better part of thirty years, approached the fervor of the patriot printers of the American Revolution in denouncing Bush's justification for his authorization of the NSA wiretapping program. Lapham cited the president's protestations that "We're at war," and that "we must protect America's secrets," and he rebutted Bush's contentions: "No, the country isn't at war, and it's not America's secrets that the President seeks to protect. The country is threatened by free-booting terrorists unaligned with a foreign government or enemy army; the secrets are those of the Bush Administration, chief among them its determination to replace a democratic republic with something more safely totalitarian. The fiction of permanent war allows it to seize, in the name of national security, the instruments of tyranny."[36]

The administration threatened reprisals against those who leaked the NSA wiretapping story to the *Times,* and possibly against the newspaper itself, but the Pulitzer Prize Board took a different view of the recent contention between the administration and the press. Among the Pulitzers announced on April 17, 2006, were awards to Dana Priest, of the *Washington Post,* "for her persistent, painstaking reports on secret 'black site' prisons and other controversial features of the government's counterterrorism campaign,"[37] and to James Risen and Eric Lichtblau of the *New York Times* "for their carefully sourced stories on secret domestic eavesdropping that stirred a national debate on the boundary line between fighting terrorism and protecting civil liberty."[38] The *Washington Post* found it striking that "the Pulitzer board honored two reports—on the secret prisons and domestic surveillance—that President Bush personally urged the editors not to publish."[39]

The *Boston Globe* reminded its readers that President Bush himself had leaked information about Saddam Hussein's nuclear program (the alleged attempt to buy uranium ore), and had defended his right to declassify information whenever he saw fit. "The main point is," the *Globe* wrote, "the *Post* and *Times* stories were true, while the Bush leak was at best highly misleading, with a significant part being outright fiction."[40]

On April 30, 2006, the *Globe* broke a story of its own that had serious implications for the constitutional separation of powers. *Globe* reporter Charlie Savage revealed that President Bush "has quietly claimed the authority to disobey more than 750 laws enacted since he took office, asserting that he has the power to set aside any statute passed by Congress when

it conflicts with his interpretation of the Constitution." When signing
bills passed by Congress, Savage reported, "after the media and the lawmakers have left the White House, Bush quietly files 'signing statements'—official documents in which a president lays out his legal
interpretation of a bill for the federal bureaucracy to follow when implementing the new law." The practice originated in the Reagan administration, Savage reported, but George W. Bush had used it far more
extensively than any of his predecessors. It had attracted little notice until
Bush challenged two recent laws, "a torture ban and a requirement that he
give detailed reports to Congress about how he is using the Patriot Act."
Savage reported that "Legal scholars say the scope and aggression of Bush's
assertions that he can bypass laws represent a concerted effort to expand
his power at the expense of Congress, upsetting the balance between the
branches of government."[41]

The *Times* observed, "One of the abiding curiosities of the Bush administration is that after more than five years in office, the president has
yet to issue a veto." In the *Globe*'s revelation of Bush's signing statements,
the *Times* found the explanation: "President Bush doesn't bother with ve-
toes; he simply declares his intention not to enforce anything he dis-
likes." The *Times* noted, as Savage had reported, that the idea for
presidential signing statements had first been proposed by Ronald Reagan's attorney general, Edwin Meese III. "He was helped by a young
lawyer who was a true believer in the unitary presidency, a euphemism
for an autocratic executive branch that ignores Congress and the courts,"
the *Times* wrote. "Unhappily, that lawyer, Samuel Alito Jr., is now on the
Supreme Court."[42]

Boston Globe columnist Scott Lehigh, looking beyond the newest
claim of presidential power to other recent exercises, noted that Senator
Arlen Specter, the chairman of the Senate Judiciary Committee, had proposed a week before the *Globe* broke the story of Bush's signing statements
that the secret FISA court should rule on the constitutionality of the NSA
wiretapping programs. "It speaks volumes about the attitude of the White
House," Lehigh commented, "that a member of the president's own party
would have to make such a move to protect bedrock constitutional principles. Yet it will probably take something much more dramatic than
Specter's tentative threat to remind George W. Bush that he's president,
not king."[43]

Less than two weeks after the *Globe*'s story on presidential signing statements, *USA Today* revealed, on May 11, that in addition to monitoring the overseas communications of American citizens, the National Security Agency "has been secretly collecting the phone call records of tens of millions of Americans," with the help of several of the nation's largest telecommunications companies. The program, the newspaper reported, "reaches into homes and businesses across the nation by amassing information about the calls of ordinary Americans—most of whom aren't suspected of any crime." The NSA didn't actually listen to calls under the program, *USA Today*'s sources told the paper, "But the spy agency is using the data to analyze calling patterns in an effort to detect terrorist activity."[44] In *USA Today*'s editorial opinion, "Creating a huge, secret database of Americans' phone records does far more than threaten terrorists. It is a deeply troubling act that undermines U.S. freedoms and threatens us all."[45]

The *Times* found the scope of the data mining program "breathtaking" and warned that the September 11th attacks "did not give the president the limitless power he now claims to intrude on the private communications of the American people."[46]

On June 23, 2006, several news agencies revealed that the government had been monitoring, since shortly after September 11th, "a vast international database," as the *Times* reported the story, recorded banking transactions involving moving funds in and out of the United States, as well as between parties overseas.[47] *USA Today* warned, "Support for fighting the war on terrorism aggressively is broad. So, too, is resistance to needless invasions of privacy, secret government and executive arrogance."[48]

Press reports revealed that the Bush administration had asked both the *New York Times* and the *Los Angeles Times* not to publish the story. The president accused the *New York Times* of a "disgraceful" breach of national security. Representative Peter King of New York and Senator Jim Bunning of Kentucky went so far as to accuse the *Times* of "treason." On July 2, the Sunday of a long Fourth of July weekend, *Times* columnist Frank Rich lambasted the attacks and declared that "story of how [the government] vilified *The Times* is more damning than anything in the article that caused the uproar." Of the accusations of "treason" and charges that those at the *Times* had "blood on their hands," Rich wrote, "Such ravings make it hard not to think of the official assault on *The Times* and

The Washington Post over the Pentagon Papers. . . . The assault on a free press during our own wartime should be recognized for what it is: another desperate ploy by officials trying to hide their own lethal mistakes in the shadows. It's the antithesis of everything we celebrate with the blazing lights of Independence Day."[49]

Rich's commentary may have received less notice than it perhaps deserved because it was published just three days after a Supreme Court decision that delivered an uppercut to the administration's plans for trying suspected terrorists before military commissions. The case had been brought on behalf of Salim Ahmed Hamdan, a Yemeni who had been Osama bin Laden's driver and mechanic in Afghanistan. Hamdan had been captured by Afghan warlords near the Pakistan border in November 2001 and was handed over to the Americans for a $5,000 reward. Since May 2002, Hamdan had been imprisoned at Guantánamo Bay. His government-appointed attorney, Navy Lieutenant Commander Charles Swift, maintained that Hamdan, who had little education, was scarcely aware of the larger implications of bin Laden's activities. On Hamdan's behalf, Swift had sued to have the military tribunals ordered by President Bush declared illegal.[50]

On June 29, the Supreme Court agreed with Swift. "Brushing aside administration pleas not to second-guess the commander in chief during wartime," the *Washington Post* reported the Court's decision, "a five-justice majority ruled that the commissions, which were outlined by Bush in a military order on Nov. 13, 2001, were neither authorized by federal law nor required by military necessity, and ran afoul of the Geneva Conventions."[51] The *New York Times* hailed the decision as "the latest in a series of rebukes for the administration," and declared that it "is far more than a narrow ruling on the issue of military courts. It is an important and welcome reaffirmation that even in times of war, the law is what the Constitution, the statute books and the Geneva Conventions say it is—not what the president wants it to be. . . . The message of this ruling is that the executive branch cannot continue in its remarkable insistence that because there is a war on terror, it no longer needs to follow established procedures that would subject it to scrutiny by another branch of government."[52] The *Boston Globe* recommended that "Bush should do what he should have done in 2002: Try suspects fairly in courts, military or civilian, that would show that justice has not fallen victim to terrorism in the United States."[53]

The Bush administration went to great lengths to keep its secret programs, and terrorist suspects, hidden from public view. Even more rare
than glimpses of individual detainees like Hamdan were profiles of the
unelected bureaucrats who planned the secret and not-so-secret programs
that caught up Hamdan, Lindh, Padilla, Hamdi and thousands of others.
Fresh on the newsstands when the Supreme Court delivered its ruling in
Hamdan v. Rumsfeld was Jane Mayer's latest article for the *New Yorker,* in
which she probed the administration's veils of secrecy to explore the origins of the extraordinary claims of executive power made by the Bush
White House. Mayer laid responsibility for many of those claims at the
door of David S. Addington, Vice President Cheney's chief of staff and
longtime legal adviser. Even before September 11th, Mayer reported, Cheney and Addington had been laying the groundwork for reasserting
presidential power, which Cheney saw as having been eroded by Vietnam
and Watergate. Their strategy was based "on a reading of the Constitution that few legal scholars share," Mayer wrote, "namely that the President, as Commander-in-Chief, has the authority to disregard virtually all
previous legal boundaries, if national security demands it." Mayer's
sources told her that Addington was the guiding force behind authorizing military commissions to try terrorists, a January 2002 legal memorandum dismissing the Geneva Conventions as "obsolete" and "quaint,"
and the memos from the Department of Justice's Office of Legal Counsel
asserting the president's "inherent constitutional authority to take whatever military action he deemed necessary," as well as those justifying torture. "According to the *Boston Globe,*" Mayer noted, "Addington has been
the 'leading architect'" of President Bush's signing statements. Her
sources told her that Addington had also been instrumental in keeping
the new antiterrorism programs secret, in many cases, even from some of
the officials whose responsibility covered the areas in which the programs
operated. Mayer reported that high-ranking officers of the judge advocate general's office were excluded from drafting the plan to try suspected
terrorists before military commissions, and that a Pentagon lawyer whose
job was to supervise legal advisers to the National Security Agency knew
nothing of the NSA's warrantless wiretapping program until he read
about it in the *Times.*[54]

Mayer ascribed the extent of Addington's influence in part to the remarkable fact that in the Bush administration's first term neither the

president nor the vice president, the secretaries of state and defense, nor the national security adviser, were lawyers. As Mayer reported the view of Bruce Fein, "a Republican legal activist" and former associate deputy attorney general in the Reagan Justice Department, "It's frightening. No one knows the Constitution—certainly not Cheney."[55] Among those Mayer interviewed who condemned Addington's influence was Scott Horton, the New York Bar Association lawyer whom the JAG officers had visited in 2003 to protest Donald Rumsfeld's rules for interrogating detainees. Horton's view, as he related it to Mayer, was that Addington and the administration's top lawyers had tried to "overturn two centuries of jurisprudence defining the limits of the executive branch. They've made war a matter of dictatorial power." Mayer reported that the Pulitzer-prize-winning historian Arthur Schlesinger, Jr., considered Bush to be "even more grandiose than Nixon," and said of the administration's justifications of torture, "No position taken has done more damage to the American reputation in the world—ever."[56]

A close associate of former Secretary of State Colin Powell told Mayer that after Powell left the Bush administration he summed up Addington in a single damning sentence: "He doesn't care about the Constitution."[57]

The White House experienced another legal setback in August 2006, when the U.S. District Court in Detroit ruled, as the *Times* reported the decision, "that the National Security Agency's program to wiretap the international communications of some Americans without a court warrant violated the Constitution."[58] In the final days of September, however, President Bush won what the *Times* called "a signal victory, shoring up with legislation his determined conduct of the campaign against terrorism in the face of challenges from critics and the courts."[59] In hasty proceedings that reminded some observers of those that produced the Patriot Act in October 2001, the Republican-controlled Congress passed the Military Commissions Act of 2006, which in addition to authorizing the commissions denied detainees the right to file writs of habeas corpus challenging their imprisonment, before recessing for a final spate of campaigning for the midterm elections. In the opinion of Yale Law School Dean Harold Koh, reported in the *Washington Post*, "the image of Congress rushing to strip jurisdiction from the courts in response to a politically created emergency is really quite shocking, and it's not clear that most of the members understand what they've done."[60]

After the election, the *Washington Post* took congressional Democrats to task for making "only a token effort to stop passage of deeply flawed Bush administration legislation. . . . First they hid behind a group of Republican moderates who tried to modify the law's worst aspects; when that resulted in a bad compromise, they gave up serious opposition rather than risk being accused of being weak on terrorism in the run-up to an election." In the new Congress, the *Post* counseled, "the Democrats now have a second chance to temper the administration's excesses and to insist on accountability for past crimes. It ought to be at the top of their agenda."[61] In the opinion of the *New York Times,* the new law, taken as a whole, "will give the president more power over terrorism suspects than he had before the Supreme Court decision this summer in Hamdan v. Rumsfeld that undercut more than four years of White House policy."[62]

Beginning in 2004, General John Abizaid, the commander of Centcom, sometimes referred to the war on terrorism as "the long war." This was not an attempt to rebrand the conflict for political purposes, as in 2005, when Donald Rumsfeld's effort to substitute "the global struggle against violent extremism" for "the War on Terror" was met with derision and sank without a trace. Rather, "the long war" reflects the judgment within the high command of the United States military that it will be engaged against terrorists and extremists for a very long time to come. In an editorial published on June 28, 2006, the *New York Times* expressed the same conviction: "The country is in this for the long haul, and the fight has to be coupled with a commitment to individual liberties that define America's side in the battle."[63]

If the war on terrorism lasts for a generation or more, the struggle to safeguard bedrock American principles will be longer. The Founders thought it might be the legislature that posed the greatest threat to constitutional liberties, but history has shown that the impulses that upset the balance of powers have come most often from the executive, especially in times of war, when presidents have sought to arrogate power to themselves at the expense of the legislative and judicial branches.

Neither the *New York Times* nor any other journal, among those that take seriously their responsibility to guard the liberties of the citizens and the well-being of the nation against government encroachment, need apologize for its reporting of executive excesses or congressional sins in the war on terrorism. There has been no general reluctance to examine and criticize the government's conduct of this war as there was in scrutinizing the intelligence used, and misused, to justify making war on Iraq. Since September 11, 2001, the press has described a pattern of deception and overreaching by the executive branch, often abetted by a compliant Congress, that may be more dangerous to the republic in the long term than the Iraq conflict or the war on terrorism.

Why is it then that we could see so clearly in the results of the 2006 midterm election a rebuke to the government's war policy in Iraq and no similar judgment against the abuses of essential liberties in the war on terrorism? One answer is that it has always been easier to arouse people against the costs of a war that they can see and feel—the numbers of dead and wounded reported every week, the fear and carnage on television—than to energize opposition with editorials about checks and balances, the separation of powers, and other constitutional principles imperiled by executive encroachment or legislative neglect. Another is that with the great majority of the public dependent on television for news, and with the influence of network news diluted by the proliferation of channels and a diminished corporate commitment to news throughout the electronic media, even when outspoken commentators—Bill Moyers, for instance, and Keith Olbermann—criticize the government with something like the zeal of their Revolutionary predecessors, those protests reach only a tiny fraction of the viewing audience. In today's media environment, no single voice can have anything remotely like the influence of Walter Cronkite in the Vietnam War.

But the ability to muster majority opinion is not the only measure of whether the free press is doing its job. The influence of the print journals, and authoritative voices in the electronic media, are enough to keep important issues on the table and to reach some portion of the public. It's safe to say that the controversies and commentaries in the media about the White House's conduct of the war on terrorism contributed, at the very least, to the deepening distrust of the Bush administration and its supporters in Congress that was manifested in the 2006 election results.

The benefits of a free press are not cumulative; they must be constantly renewed. So long as the war in Iraq and the wider war on terrorism continue, the press must not give in to the temptation to follow only the hot war in the Middle East at the expense of the less dramatic struggle in Afghanistan and the efforts to restore the constitutional safeguards and the balance of powers that have been threatened here at home since September 11th.

In its best moments, the press invokes the founding principles of the republic because they are the touchstones of who we are as a people and who we want to be. When our principles are betrayed by our leaders, or when we betray them ourselves—by electing an oppressive or incompetent government, by keeping silent when we should protest—we depend on the press to ask: Is this who we are, and who we want to be?

There is a limit to what we can ask. It is the job of the press to sound the alarm, not to cure all the ills of government or vanquish every threat to liberty. For that, the Founders depended on the people.

On his retirement from CBS News in 1977, the veteran journalist Eric Sevareid closed his next-to-last commentary for the *CBS Evening News* by looking into the camera and imparting the most important lesson he had learned in a long life on the front lines of the press: "Democracy is not a free ride; it demands more from each of us than any other arrangement."[64]

NOTES

It is customary not to cite page numbers for newspapers published since printing technology made it possible to print several editions in a single day, because articles often appeared on different pages in different editions. In general I have kept to this guideline, but in citing important stories that I judged likely to remain on the front pages of all editions, I have often indicated that these were page one stories. In citing articles published in the sections of Sunday editions that are printed a day or more ahead of time, I have felt that it is safe to cite a section and page number. I have also given page references for citations from weekly papers such as the *Village Voice* and the *Boston Phoenix.*

J.B.C.

INTRODUCTION

1. "Centinel" Number 1 (October 5, 1787), in *The Anti-Federalist Papers and the Constitutional Convention Debates,* Ralph Ketcham, ed. (New York: New American Library, 2003.) 236.
2. James Madison, *Address of the General Assembly to the People of the Commonwealth of Virginia, 23 Jan. 1799;* Writings 6:333–336, in *The Writings of James Madison,* Gaillard Hunt, ed., 9 vols. (New York: G. P. Putnam's Sons, 1900–1910). Vol. 5, Amendment I (Speech and Press), Document 21. From the University of Chicago Press website, http://press-pubs.uchicago.edu/founders/documents/amendI_speechs21.html.
3. *New York Times,* May 28, 2004, Ginna Gracey, Dover, Mass., letter to the editor.

CHAPTER 1

1. Executive power in the British government was not yet formally vested in the king's first minister. In the American colonial press, as well as in English newspapers, the government, apart from the king, was often referred to simply as "the ministry."
2. Benjamin Franklin Thomas, *Memoir of Isaiah Thomas* (Albany: Munsell, Printer, 1874), 49, attributed to Isaiah Thomas. (B. F. Thomas was Isaiah Thomas's grandson.)
3. Thomas, *Memoir,* 50. Thomas places Isaiah at Lexington, and says: "As one of the minute men, he engages in the fight which was the beginning of the end." (Massachusetts Spy [hereafter *MassSpy*], May 3, 1775.)
4. Thomas, *Memoir,* 51; the author cites "the journal of the Committee of Safety."
5. *MassSpy,* May 3, 1775, "Worcester, May 3."
6. Richard C. Steele, *Isaiah Thomas* (Worcester: Worcester Telegram & Gazette and Worcester Historical Museum, 1981), 11.
7. There was no Whig political party at this time, either in England or America. In the American colonies, the term was applied to those who had a rebellious attitude toward the British monarchy, as "Tory" was applied to those who supported the Crown.
8. *MassSpy,* Aug. 11, 1770.
9. Thomas, *Memoir,* 30.

10. Isaiah Thomas, *The History of Printing in America,* Marcus A. McCorison, ed. (Barre, Mass., 1970), 266–267; in Bernard Bailyn and John B. Hench, eds., *The Press & the American Revolution* (Worcester: American Antiquarian Society, 1980), 5.

11. Stephen Botein, "Printers and the American Revolution," in Bailyn and Hench, *The Press & the American Revolution,* 45, apparently citing Clifford K. Shipton, *Isaiah Thomas: Printer, Patriot, and Philanthropist, 1749–1831* (Rochester, N.Y. 1948). Botein mentions Thomas considering a move to the West Indies in 1772 (44).

12. *MassSpy,* May 2, 1771, "For the Massachusetts Spy," 2.

13. *MassSpy,* June 27, 1771.

14. *MassSpy,* Nov. 14, 1771, "For the Massachusetts Spy," 1, col. 3.

15. Thomas, *Memoir,* 34–35.

16. Ibid., 36–38, relates the attempted legal actions against Isaiah Thomas and the dismissal of Joseph Greenleaf.

17. Marcus A. McCorison, foreword, in Bailyn and Hench, *The Press & the American Revolution,* 5; Thomas, *Memoir,* 29.

18. *MassSpy,* Oct. 8, 1772, 1, col. 3.

19. *Boston Gazette,* May 16, 1774, "From the Public Advertiser of March 30."

20. Thomas, *Memoir,* 49; Marcus A. McCorison, foreword, in Bailyn and Hench, *The Press & the American Revolution,* 7.

21. *Boston Evening Post,* Sept. 19, 1774, in Thomas, *Memoir,* 41.

22. Thomas, *Memoir,* 49.

23. *MassSpy,* May 3, 1775.

24. *MassSpy,* May 17, 1775, letter dated "London, January 30, 1775," under "New York, May 10," column head.

25. *MassSpy,* May 17, 1775, "The following Extracts from several intercepted letters of the soldiery in Boston," 4.

26. Ibid.

27. *MassSpy,* May 17, 1775.

28. *MassSpy,* May 3, 1775, "Worcester, May 3."

29. *MassSpy,* July 26, 1775, "Worcester, July 26."

30. James Russell Wiggins, "Afterword: The Legacy of the Press in the American Revolution," in Bailyn and Hench, *The Press & the American Revolution,* 370–371.

31. Thomas, *Memoir,* 55.

32. Steele, *Isaiah Thomas,* 21–22; Thomas, *Memoir,* 55.

33. Thomas, *Memoir,* 55.

34. *MassSpy,* Nov. 8, 1781, "Worcester, November 8."

35. In Thomas, *Memoir,* 59.

36. In Thomas, *Memoir,* 64–65.

CHAPTER 2

1. By the 1820s, Jeffersonian Republicans had divided into two factions, the Democratic Republicans, who gathered around Andrew Jackson and became simply "Democrats" after his election in 1828, and the National Republicans, who then became the "Whig" party, to evoke the philosophy of the patriots of the Revolutionary period.

2. *New York Tribune* (hereafter *NYTribune*), May 13, 1846, "The President's Message," 1.

3. *NYTribune,* May 13, 1846, editorial, "What Means This War?"

4. Mexico City was not yet called by that name; in the American press it was referred to as the City of Mexico or, as here, simply as Mexico, with the meaning evident from the context.

5. *New York Herald* (hereafter, *NYHerald*), May 18, 1846, editorial presented as a news column, "News from the Rio Grande—Invasion of Mexico."

6. Bennett increased the force; Congress had authorized President Polk to raise 50,000.

7. *NYHerald,* May 18, 1846, editorial, "The News from the Rio Grande—Invasion of Mexico."

8. Taylor was criticized in the press for these actions, but they were consistent with his orders to "take Matamoras or any other Spanish Post West of [the Rio Grande], but not penetrate any great distance into the interior of the Mexican Territory." (James K. Polk, *The Diary of James K. Polk During His Presidency, 1845 to 1849* [Chicago: A.C. McClurg & Co., 1910], 1: 8–9.)

9. Polk, *Diary,* 1: 252, 287, 453–54.

10. *NYHerald,* June 13, 1846, editorial, "The Oregon Question—Its Position."

11. *NYTribune,* June 15, 1846, "Peace with England Secured!" 1.

12. *NYTribune,* Aug. 14, 1846, editorial, "Remember Annexation!"

13. Communications with California depended entirely on letters and dispatches carried by sea and overland across Mexico, Nicaragua, or the isthmus of Panama. Delays of three or four months were common.

14. Polk, *Diary,* 1: 437–39.

15. John Bidwell, "Pioneer of '41," *The Century Illustrated Monthly Magazine,* XLI, no. 4 (February, 1891); from http://www.sfmuseum.org/hist6/fremont.html, a web page of the Virtual Museum of the City of San Francisco.

16. American newspapers employed "Monterrey" and "Monterey" interchangeably for the city south of the Rio Grande, sometimes causing confusion with Monterey on the coast of California.

17. Polk, *Diary,* 2: 245, 248.

18. *New Orleans Delta,* March 23, 1847, article reprinted in the *Hartford Courant,* April 3, 1847, "From the New Orleans Delta, March 23rd," gives the strength of Santa Anna's army at 17,000, Taylor's at "4 to 5,000 mostly volunteers," and says, "Every volunteer colonel but one, was killed or wounded." An undated article from the *Washington Union,* reprinted in the *Hartford Courant* of April 10, 1847, "From the Camp," numbers Santa Anna's force at 20,000.

19. *NYTribune,* March 25, 1847, editorial column, 2.

20. Polk, *Diary,* 2: 465.

21. *NYTribune,* April 12, 1847, editorial, "Capture of Vera Cruz"; Polk, *Diary,* 2: 464, says 36 killed.

22. *NYTribune,* April 12, 1847, editorial, "Capture of Vera Cruz."

23. *NYHerald,* Sept. 16, 1847, editorial, "The News from Mexico."

24. *NYTribune,* Sept. 18, 1847, editorial, 2.

25. *NYTribune,* Oct. 2, 1847, editorial, "The News from Mexico."

26. *NYHerald,* Oct. 8, 1847, editorial, "Our Relations with Mexico—The Destiny of the Two Republics."

27. Ibid.

28. *NYTribune,* Oct. 9, 1847, untitled editorial comment, col. 2, editorial page, following reprint of *NYHerald* Oct. 8 editorial.

29. *NYHerald,* Feb. 23, 1848, editorial.

30. *NYTribune,* Feb. 22, 1848, editorial, "Peace with Mexico."

31. Polk, *Diary,* 3: 346–350.

32. *NYHerald,* Mar. 12, 1848, editorial, "The Treaty Ratified—Peace with Mexico at Last."

33. *NYTribune,* Mar. 17, 1848, editorial.

34. *NYTribune,* Oct. 4, 1847, editorial, "The Mexican News."

CHAPTER 3

1. *New York Daily News* (hereafter *DNews*) March 5, 1861, editorial, "The Inaugural." (The nineteenth-century *Daily News* was not the lineal antecedent of the twentieth-century New York tabloid.) The references to "the code" and "the field" are to the code duello, which governed duels, and to the field of honor where they were fought.

2. *New York Tribune* (hereafter *NYTribune*), Apr. 13, 1861, editorial, "War Begun!"

3. *DNews,* Apr. 13, 1861, editorial "The War Commenced." Wood misquoted Hamlet, who said " . . . rough-hew them how we will" (V, ii).

4. *NYTribune,* Jan. 8, 1861, editorial, "The Mayor's Message."

5. *DNews,* Apr. 15, 1861, first editorial column, "Highly Important from Washington."

6. *DNews,* Apr. 15, 1861, editorial, "Support the President?—Never!"

7. *DNews,* June 22, 1861, editorial, "Pause Before the Battle."

8. *DNews,* July 22, 1861, "The Great War," 1.

9. *DNews,* July 23, 1861, editorial, "The Beginning of the End."

10. Brayton Harris, *Blue & Gray in Black & White, Newspapers in the Civil War* (Washington, D.C.: Brassey's, 1999), 98–102. Harris's work informs some of the background on the Civil War press in this chapter, as does this web page with text by Harris: http://www.civil-war-newspapers.com/WARCORRESPONDENT.asp.

11. *DNews,* Aug. 14, 1861, editorial, "Beware!"

12. *DNews,* August 16, 1861, "Abstract of News," editorial page. The "Conspiracy law" Wood refers to was a law against "seditious conspiracy" first passed in 1859, intended to prevent the Southern states from conspiring to secede, later augmented after the war began by amendments and by further laws that were used to prosecute the enemies of the Union.

13. *DNews,* Aug. 16, 1861, editorial, "Victims of Presidential Tyranny." Wood does not name the fort in this editorial, but does in a later editorial.

14. *DNews,* Aug.17, 1861, editorial, "Presentment of the Daily News by the Grand Jury of the U. S. Circuit Court."

15. *DNews,* Aug. 23, 1861, editorial, "The Government and the Daily News."

16. *NYTribune,* Aug. 22, 1861, editorial, "Attacks on the Administration."

17. *NYTribune,* Aug. 22, 1861, editorial, "The Carnival of Treason."

18. *NYTribune,* Aug. 23, 1861, editorial, "Freedom of Speech."

19. *NYTribune,* Aug. 30, 1861, editorial, "The Liberty of the Press."

20. *DNews,* Aug. 27, 1861, editorial, "Another Step."

21. *NYTribune,* Aug. 30, 1861, editorial, "The Liberty of the Press."

22. *DNews,* Aug. 31, 1861, editorial, "The Real Mischief-Makers."

23. *DNews,* Sept. 3, 1861, editorial, "The Crusade of the Press Against the Press."

24. *DNews,* Aug. 28, 1861, editorial, "Opposition to Misgovernment."

25. *DNews,* Sept. 9, 1861, editorial, "The Sovereignty of the Individual."

26. *DNews,* Sept. 10, 1861, editorial, "Constitutional Securities." Wood names the fort in this editorial, printing it as "La Fayette."

27. *DNews,* Sept. 5, 1861, editorial, "Governmental Restraints."

28. *DNews,* Sept. 14, 1861, "To the Public," editorial page.

29. In Allan Nevins, *The Evening Post, A Century of Journalism* (New York: Boni and Liveright, 1922), 288.

30. *New York World* (hereafter *NYWorld*), Sept. 2, 1862, editorial, "Are We Losing What We Are Defending?"

31. *New York Herald* (hereafter *NYHerald*), Sept. 23, 1862, "Important from Washington—The President's Proclamation," editorial page.

32. *NYWorld,* Sept. 24, 1862, editorial, "The Emancipation Proclamation."

33. *NYTribune,* Sept. 23, 1862, untitled section preceding full text of the proclamation, col. 2, editorial page.

34. *NYHerald,* Oct. 28, 1862, editorial, "The Two Great Revolutions Approaching."

35. *NYHerald,* Oct. 29, 1862, editorial, "Stand by the Union, the Constitution and the President."

36. *NYHerald,* Nov. 1, 1862, editorial, "The Nation and the People Against Traitors North and South."

37. Wood's defense of the *Times* building is from the website of *Harper's Weekly:* http://www.harpweek.com/09Cartoon/BrowseByDateCartoon.asp?Month=August&Date=31. William Finnegan, in the *New Yorker,* puts Henry J. Raymond behind a Gatling gun in a *Times* window (August 30, 2004, "Comment: G.O.P. City," 33).

38. *NYTribune,* July 14, 1863, editorial, "Martial Law."

39. *DNews,* July 15, 1863, editorial, "The Republican Party Responsible."

40. *DNews*, July 13, 1862, editorial, "The Conscription Unconstitutional."

41. *DNews*, July 7, 1863, editorial, "President Lincoln's Claim to Despotic Authority." In the editorial, Wood misquoted Lincoln's letter, inadvertently or deliberately, making it appear that Lincoln claimed more explicitly than was the case to decide which constitutional liberties might be suspended by presidential authority.

42. *New York Times*, July 7, 1863, "The Case of Vallandigham," 5, which includes the full text of Lincoln's letter.

43. At this time, Supreme Court justices heard cases in federal circuit courts when the Supreme Court was not in session. For Taney's opinion in this case, *Ex parte Merryman*, 1861, see: http://www.civil-liberties.com/pages/suspension.htm.

44. *DNews*, Nov. 10, 1864, editorial, "Mr. Lincoln's Opportunity."

45. For the majority opinion in the case, *Ex parte Milligan*, see http://www.constitution.org/ussc/071–002a.htm.

CHAPTER 4

1. *San Francisco Examiner* (hereafter *SFExaminer*), Feb. 9, 1898, "Spain's Minister Insults the American President," 1.

2. *New York Evening Post* (hereafter *NYEvePost*), Feb. 17, 1898 (semi-weekly edition; all citations are to this edition), "A Court of Inquiry," "Secretary Long Convinced that the Disaster Was Not Due to Design," 1, and editorial, "A Test of National Character." The advocates of a belligerent foreign policy became known as "jingoes" in the 1870s, when the phrase "by jingo" appeared in a popular chauvinistic song (Merriam-Webster's Collegiate Dictionary, 11th ed.).

3. *New York Journal* (hereafter *NYJournal*), Feb. 16, 1898, "Extra no. 9."

4. *NYJournal*, Feb. 16, 1898, "Extra No. 9," editorial, "The Maine."

5. *NYJournal*, Feb. 17, 1898, 1, facsimile in Roger Butterfield, *The American Past* (New York: Simon and Schuster, 1957), 279.

6. *NYJournal*, Feb.17, 1898, edition headline "WAR! SURE!" At this time, the word "torpedo" was often used interchangeably with "mine" in naval contexts, for any floating or anchored explosive device.

7. *SFExaminer*, Feb. 16, 1898, 1, and untitled item in editorial columns.

8. *NYJournal*, Feb. 17, 1898, editorial, "The Situation."

9. *NYJournal*, Feb. 18, 1898, editorial, "A Very Simple Situation." Hearst never allowed his papers to become Democratic organs, but early in his career he backed organized labor in its struggles with capital. David Nasaw's definitive biography, *The Chief: The Life of William Randolph Hearst* (Boston: Houghton Mifflin / Mariner, 2000) is an important source for much of the background on Hearst in this chapter.

10. In Allan Nevins, *The Evening Post* (New York: Boni and Liveright, 1922), 511; no date given, but taken in context, evidently published between the sinking of the *Maine* and the declarations of war. Nevins' work is the primary source for background on the *Evening Post* and its editors in chief, E. L. Godkin and Horace White, in this chapter.

11. *New York World* (hereafter *NYWorld*), Mar. 11, 1898.

12. *Wall Street Journal*, Mar. 19, 1898, "Early Morning Matter."

13. *NYEvePost*, Mar. 28, 1898, editorial, "The Situation at Washington."

14. *NYJournal*, Mar. 28, 1898, "Shameful Deal, Which Cubans Reject, for an Armistice," 1, and editorial, "A Shameful Backdown and Peace with Dishonor."

15. *NYEvePost*, Apr. 11, 1898, "The Message on Cuba," 1.

16. *SFExaminer*, Apr. 12, 1898, 1, and editorials, "Just Cause of War," and "It Sounds Like a Retreat."

17. *New York Times* (hereafter *NYTimes*), Apr. 26, 1898, editorial, "The Philippines."

18. All from editions of May 2, 1898.

19. *NYWorld*, May 2, 1898, editorial, "'Action' and Victory."

20. *NYEvePost,* May 5, 1898, editorial, "The War."

21. *NYEvePost,* May 30, 1898, editorial, "Aggrandizement or Honor."

22. East of the Philippines, now the Marianas.

23. *NYEvePost,* June 16, 1898, editorial, "A 'Dark Superstition.'"

24. *NYEvePost,* June 23, 1898, editorials, "Jingo Difficulties," "Forces Making for Annexation."

25. *NYTimes,* July 27, 1898, editorials, "The Terms of Peace," "Our Pupils in Politics."

26. *NYEvePost,* Apr. 11, 1898, editorial, "Just and Necessary War."

27. *NYJournal,* Aug. 13, 1898, editorial, "Welcome to Peace."

28. *NYWorld,* Aug. 16, 1898, editorial, "The Peace Commission."

29. Butterfield, *The American Past,* 236.

30. *NYEvePost,* Nov.21, 1898.

31. *NYTimes,* Nov. 22, 1898.

32. *NYEvePost,* Nov. 28, 1898, editorial, "The President's Power."

33. *SFExaminer,* Dec. 11, 1898, editorial re steamship line, and "Philippine Islands Are Not To Be Sold By Us to Any Nation," Arthur McEwen.

34. *NYJournal,* Dec. 17, 1898, in *SFExaminer,* Feb. 6, 1899, editorial, "Action! Action! Action!" Gold had been discovered in the Alaska's Klondike territory in 1897; in 1898 the rush was on.

35. *NYTimes,* Feb. 6, 1899, "Fight at Manila with Filipinos," 1.

36. *NYEvePost,* Feb. 6, 1899, editorial, "The Philippine Crisis."

37. *NYWorld,* Feb. 6, 1898, editorial, "Deplorable."

38. *NYEvePost,* Mar. 30, 1899, "No Heart in the War," 1.

39. In Nevins, *The Evening Post,* 496.

40. *NYEvePost,* June 15, 1899, untitled editorial page items.

41. Long excerpts at http://www.mtholyoke.edu/acad/intrel/ajb72.htm, which cites the Congressional Record, 56 Cong., I Sess., pp. 704–712. The *Boston Globe* (hereafter *BGlobe*) of Jan. 10, 1900, reported that Beveridge spoke for more than two hours.

42. *Hartford Courant,* Jan. 10, 1900, untitled item, 10; *Boston Globe,* Jan. 10, 1900, "Ours Forever; So Says Beveridge of Indiana in the U.S. Senate."

43. *NYEvePost,* Nov. 12, 1900, editorial, "Imperialism as a Condition."

44. *NYEvePost,* Nov. 12, 1900, "Philippine Campaigning."

45. Arthur MacArthur (1845–1912) was the father of Douglas MacArthur (1880–1964), the American Far East commander from early in World War II until he was relieved of command by President Truman in April 1951, during the Korean War.

46. In Jim Zwick, ed., *Mark Twain's Weapons of Satire: Anti-Imperialist Writings on the Philippine-American War,* (Syracuse: Syracuse University Press, 1992), 37–38.

47. *SFExaminer,* Mar. 5, 1901, editorial, "The Revolution Neatly Disguised."

48. *NYEvePost,* Mar. 28, 1901, editorial, "The Capture of Aguinaldo."

49. The Moros—Spanish for "Moors"—were Muslims, distinct from the Catholic Filipinos and long their enemies, who continued to resist the United States forces for another eleven years.

50. *NYTimes,* Apr. 9, 1902, "Major Waller Testifies."

51. *NYTribune,* Apr. 8, 1902, "The Waller Trial."

52. Zwick, *Mark Twain's Weapons of Satire,* 37.

53. *BGlobe,* Apr. 16, 1902, "Favor None, Shield None!" 2.

54. *NYEvePost,* Apr. 17, 1902, editorial, "The President's Demand for the Facts."

55. *Washington Post,* Apr. 25, 1902, editorial, "Another View of the Water Cure."

56. *NYTimes,* Apr. 29, 1902, editorial, "Congressman Sibley Attacks Gen. Smith."

57. *SFExaminer,* Apr. 19, 1902.

58. *BGlobe,* Apr. 23, 1902, editorial, "Is It 'Worth While'?"

59. *Atlanta Constitution,* Apr. 23, 1902, "'Jakie' is Jerked Before Roosevelt," Jos: Ohl.

60. *BGlobe,* Apr. 26, 1902, "Kill All Over 10," 1.

61. *NYTimes,* Apr. 27, 1902, editorial, "Gen. Smith's Orders."

62.   *NYTimes,* Apr. 29, 1902, "Congressman Sibley Attacks Gen. Smith." Press accounts at this time often identified senators and congressmen only by their last names, with no state or party affiliation. In determining the exact identities of many of these politicians, the website www.politicalgraveyard.com has been invaluable.

63.   *Washington Post,* June 12, 1902, editorial, "The Case of H. R. Jake." The editorial's title referred to Smith's nickname in the service, "Hell-Roaring Jake."

64.   The Philippines became a U.S. commonwealth in 1935 and achieved full independence in 1946.

CHAPTER 5

1.   Mark Sullivan, *Our Times,* vol. 5, *Over Here, 1914–1918* (New York: Chas. Scribner's Sons, 1933), 131.

2.   Nationally, Wilson won the popular vote by 600,000 votes, but he carried California, the last state to declare its results, only by a whisker—fewer than 4,000 votes. (Sullivan, *Our Times,* 5: 240–241).

3.   *San Francisco Examiner* (hereafter *SFExaminer*), Aug. 3, 1914, editorial, "Americans Should Be Thankful, Indeed."

4.   *SFExaminer,* May 8, 1915, editorial, "The Lesson of the Lusitania."

5.   David Nasaw, *The Chief: The Life of William Randolph Hearst* (Boston: Mariner / Houghton Mifflin, 2001), 226, 233–235. Nasaw's work informs the background on Hearst in this chapter, as it did in "Remember the *Maine.*"

6.   *SFExaminer,* October 11, 1916, 1.

7.   In *Boston Globe* (hereafter *BGlobe*), Feb. 18, 1917, "Declare Espionage Bill Too Sweeping." The *Globe* does not identify this account as an A.P. wire report, but other papers, including the *Los Angeles Times* and the *New York Times* contain identical text and attribute it to the A.P.

8.   *Los Angeles Times* (hereafter *LATimes*), Feb. 18, 1917, "Would Modify Espionage Bill." Source is "Senator Lee."

9.   *Washington Post* (hereafter *WPost*), Feb. 21, 1917, editorial, "The Espionage Bill." The *Post* had not yet fully gained the position of influence that it would achieve later in the century, but its influence was on the rise and the quality of its reporting and editorials already equaled that of any of its contemporaries.

10.   *SFExaminer,* Feb. 24, 1917, editorial, "The Espionage Bill Is Simply the Infamous Alien and Sedition Laws Under Another Name."

11.   *SFExaminer,* Mar. 2, 1917.

12.   The Congress that Wilson called into special session was the new Congress, elected the previous November. Following federal elections, the old Congress adjourned on March 4 the following year. The Twentieth Amendment, adopted in 1933, set January 20 as the expiration date for the terms of the president and vice president and January 3 for the Congress, greatly reducing the length of lame-duck sessions.

13.   In *SFExaminer,* Apr. 10, 1917, editorial, "Gentlemen of the Congress."

14.   *SFExaminer,* Apr. 3, 1917, editorial, "The Only Duty of Every American Now Is to Serve His Country With All His Heart and Mind."

15.   *SFExaminer,* Apr. 10, 1917, editorial, "Gentlemen of the Congress."

16.   *New York Times* (hereafter *NYTimes*), Apr. 13, 1917, editorial, "The Espionage Bill."

17.   Ibid.

18.   *NYTimes,* Apr. 19, 1917, editorial, "A Tyrannous Measure."

19.   *NYTimes,* Apr. 22, 1917, "Oppose Censorship As Now Proposed; Newspapers of the Country Generally Find Restrictions Unjustifiable." All quotations are from the April 21 issues of the newspapers, except the Philadelphia *Public Ledger,* which is from April 22.

20.   *SFExaminer,* Apr. 17, 1917; formal title of the Committee for Public Information from *Christian Science Monitor,* Apr. 18, 1917, editorial, "Common Sense in Censorship."

21. *SFExaminer,* Apr. 26, 1917, "Censorship of Cables To Be Fixed."

22. *SFExaminer,* Apr. 30, 1917, editorial, "This Espionage Bill Is a Violation of the Constitution of the United States and a Dangerous Assault Upon the Most Vital and Fundamental Liberties of the Land."

23. *SFExaminer,* May 9, 1917, editorial, "ALL Honest American Newspapers Are Fighting the Autocratic Espionage Bill as a Patriotic Duty, Declares Mr. Hearst."

24. *NYTimes,* May 3, 1917, editorial, "Otherwise All Right."

25. *BGlobe,* May 5, 1917, editorial, "Harm From Censorship Greater Than Benefit."

26. *WPost,* May 3, 1917, editorial, "Restriction of the Press."

27. *WPost,* May 4, 1917, editorial, "Let the People Know the Truth."

28. *WPost,* May 13, 1917, editorial, "Freedom of the Press."

29. *SFExaminer,* May 26, 1917, "New Gag Law Is Proposed for U.S. Press," 2.

30. *WPost,* May 26, 1917, editorial, "The Work of Congress."

31. *Atlanta Constitution* May 30, 1917, editorial, "Voluntary Censorship."

32. *WPost,* June 1, 1917, editorial, "Freedom of the Press Sustained."

33. *SFExaminer,* Apr. 6, 1918, 1. In its Apr. 11 edition, the *Examiner* reported that in accordance with his last wish, Robert Praeger, the man lynched by the Illinois mob, had been buried with an American flag.

34. *SFExaminer,* Apr. 6, 1918, "Gregory Demands Haste on Espionage Measure," 1–2.

35. *NYTimes,* Apr. 6, 1918, "Senators Favor Shooting Traitors."

36. *LATimes,* Apr. 25, 1918, editorial, "The President and Civil Rights."

37. *NYTimes,* Apr. 10, 1918, editorial, "The Sedition Bill."

38. *SFExaminer,* Apr. 12, 1918, editorial, "Let Us Preserve Democracy Here While Fighting for It Abroad."

39. *SFExaminer,* Apr. 25, 1918, "Johnson Defends Freedom of Speech."

40. *Christian Science Monitor,* May 6, 1918, "Senate Accepts Espionage Bill."

41. *SFExaminer,* May 8, 1918, "Sedition Bill Waits Signature of Wilson."

42. *Atlanta Constitution,* May 7, 1918, editorial, "Punishing Sedition."

43. *WPost,* May 14, 1918, editorial, "Help Scotch Sedition."

44. *SFExaminer,* May 8, 1918, "Sedition Bill Waits Signature of Wilson."

45. Nasaw, *The Chief,* 268–270.

46. *SFExaminer,* Nov. 12, 1918, editorial, "The World Has Been Saved for Democracy and Our Land Glorified."

47. Nasaw, *The Chief,* 271–272.

48. *NYTimes,* Aug. 28, 1921, "Harding Asks Light On War Law Status." In May 2006, the Associated Press reported that seventy-eight Montana residents who had been convicted of sedition "for criticizing the U.S. government or its war effort" during World War I were pardoned posthumously by Montana Governor Brian Schweitzer (*Boston Metro,* May 4, 2006).

CHAPTER 6

1. *New York Times* (hereafter *NYTimes*), Nov. 1, 1941, "Reuben James Hit," 1.

2. *NYTimes,* Nov. 1, 1941, "President Holds to Fixed Policies," 1.

3. *Chicago Tribune* (hereafter *ChiTrib*), Nov. 7, 1941, editorial, "The Americans Already Dead."

4. *NYTimes,* Nov. 1, 1941, editorial, "Open War in the Atlantic."

5. *ChiTrib,* Nov. 1, 1941, "Halts Attempt to Vote Repeal of Neutrality," 1.

6. *ChiTrib,* Nov. 7, 1941, editorial, "The Americans Already Dead."

7.   "The Colonel of the Plains," in Alistair Cooke, *Talk About America,* (New York: Knopf, 1968), 140–142.

8. *ChiTrib,* Sept. 2, 1939, editorial, "Not Our War."

9. *ChiTrib,* May 12, 1940.

10. *ChiTrib,* Sept. 10, 1940, 1.

11. *ChiTrib,* June 1, 1944, "New F.D.R. Plan Leaves Global Set Out on Limb,"

12. *ChiTrib,* June 7, 1944, editorials, "The Invasion," "The Cradle of Americanism."

13. *ChiTrib,* July 12, 1944, editorial, "The Man to Destroy the Republic."

14. *ChiTrib,* Nov. 6, 1944.

15. Roosevelt won by 442 to 99 electoral votes and by a margin of more than three-and-a-half million popular votes, his narrowest margins in four presidential elections.

16. *NYTimes,* Nov. 8, 1944, editorial, "Mr. Roosevelt Wins."

17. *ChiTrib,* Nov. 8, 1944, editorial, "War Time Election."

18. *ChiTrib,* Apr. 13, 1945, "Roosevelt's Health Failed Steadily Since Late in '43," 1.

19. *ChiTrib,* Apr. 13, 1945, "Truman Facing War, Peace and Domestic Tests," 1.

20. *ChiTrib,* Apr. 16, 1945.

21. The roster of participating nations increased in the course of the conference from the forty-five originally invited to fifty, the number that signed the United Nations Charter on June 26, 1945.

22. *ChiTrib,* Apr. 23, 1945, "U.S. Delegates Uphold Varying 'World' Views."

23. *ChiTrib,* Apr. 16, 1945, editorial, "Colonies and Security."

24. *ChiTrib,* Apr. 19, 1945, editorial, "Peace and the Rights of Man."

25. *ChiTrib,* June 27, 1945, editorial, "The Charter."

26. *NYTimes,* June 26, 1945, editorial, "Realism with Idealism."

27. Winston S. Churchill, *The Second World War,* vol. 6, *Triumph and Tragedy* (Boston: Houghton Mifflin, 1953), 354.

28. *ChiTrib,* June 4, 1944, editorial, "Peace in the Ruins."

29. Churchill, *Triumph and Tragedy,* 455.

CHAPTER 7

1. *Chicago Tribune* (hereafter *ChiTrib*), June 25, 1950, 1.

2. Truman Presidential Museum and Library, www.trumanlibrary.org. The Security Council resolution was made possible by the absence of the Soviet Union, which had walked out of the U.N. in January over the council's refusal to seat the new Chinese Communist government in place of the Nationalist Chinese delegation.

3. *New York Herald Tribune* (hereafter *HTrib*), June 26, 1950, 1. The *Herald Tribune* was formed in 1924 by the merger of the *New York Tribune* and the *New York Herald.*

4. *HTrib,* June 26, 1950, editorial, "Naked Aggression."

5. Truman Presidential Museum and Library, www.trumanlibrary.org

6. *HTrib,* June 27, 1950. Unless otherwise noted, all citations from Walter Lippmann appeared in his column "Today and Tomorrow."

7. *HTrib,* July 3, 1950, 1.

8. *HTrib,* July 3, 1950.

9. *HTrib,* July 4, 1950.

10. *New York Times* (hereafter *NYTimes*), July 24, 1950, "Tax Rise Effective at Once Is Urged by Taft, O'Mahoney," 1, continued as "2 Senators Urge Tax Rise at Once," 8.

11. *HTrib,* July 25, 1950.

12. *NYTimes,* Aug. 29, 1950, "Texts of MacArthur's Controversial Message and Truman's Formosa Statement."

13. *Washington Post* (hereafter *WPost*), Sept. 19, 1950. Because I could not locate *Herald Tribune* archives online, I conducted further research in the online archives of the *Post,* which carried Lippmann's syndicated column "Today and Tomorrow."

14. *WPost,* Sept. 19, 1950.

15. *WPost,* Oct. 25, 1950, "Most G.I.s May Leave Korea by Christmas."

16. *HTrib,* Nov. 10, 1950.

17.   *HTrib*, Nov. 11, 1950, "Allies Delaying Drive Into Areas Left by Chinese," 1.

18.   *HTrib*, Nov. 21, 1950, "G.I.'s Face Long Stay in Korea," 1, continued as "Winter in Korea," 40.

19.   *NYTimes*, Nov. 24, 1950, "The Korean War; United Nations," 2.

20.   *ChiTrib*, Nov. 24, 1950, "Face Equal Number of Communists in Northwest," 1.

21.   *HTrib*, Nov. 26, 1950, "G.I.s Occupy Chongju, Gain 2 More Miles," 1, continued as "Korea Fighting," 4.

22.   *NYTimes*, Nov. 29, 1950, "'Home by Christmas' Hope Disavowed by MacArthur."

23.   *HTrib*, Nov. 30, 1950, "Red Chinese Still Pouring Through Gap," 1; "How Allied Line Cracked Under Chinese Assault."

24.   *NYTimes*, Dec. 1, 1950, "Truman Says U.S. May Use Any Weapon," 1.

25.   *HTrib*, Dec. 2, 1950, "Billion Asked to Raise Atom Bomb Output," 1.

26.   *WPost*, Dec. 1, 1950, 1; "Voters Favor Use of A-Bomb in Event of All-Out China War," 1.

27.   *HTrib*, Dec. 3, 1950, "Enemy Force Put at 600,000 by MacArthur."

28.   *HTrib*, Dec. 6, 1950, "On the Battlefronts in Korea; Bigart Surveys Situation as 8th Army Continues Its 'Great Retreat'; Criticizes Strategic Decisions."

29.   *HTrib*, Dec. 6, 1950, editorial, "MacArthur's Disaster." *Time* and *Look* references from William Manchester, *American Caesar: Douglas MacArthur, 1880–1964* (Boston: Little, Brown & Co., 1978), 613. Manchester does not cite issue dates.

30.   *HTrib*, Dec. 7, 1950, "Dunkerque or a Bloodletting Called U.N. Korea Alternatives," 1.

31.   *HTrib*, Dec. 11, 1950.

32.   *HTrib*, Dec. 8, 1950, "Two Suspended in Montana," "Veterans Urge Bombing," "Light at Tunnel's End."

33.   In *NYTimes*, Dec. 2, 1950, "General Critical," 1.

34.   *HTrib*, Dec. 11, 1950.

35.   *HTrib*, Dec. 14, 1950.

36.   *HTrib*, Dec. 26, 1950, "Navy Labels Feat 'Inchon In Reverse," 1.

37.   *Look*, Jan. 30, 1951, 54–55, "Why We Got Licked."

38.   *WPost*, Jan. 31, 1951.

39.   *NYTimes*, Mar. 25, 1951, "Washington and MacArthur Clash Anew on Truce Offer," James Reston, 1; *NYTimes*, Mar. 27, 1951, "Joint Chiefs Tell MacArthur To Clear Future Statements," James Reston, 1; that the Joint Chiefs sent a copy of the proposed agreement to MacArthur is from Manchester, *American Caesar*, 634.

40.   *NYTimes*, Mar. 24, 1951, "M'Arthur Bids Foe Meet Him in Field to Discuss a Truce," 1; text of MacArthur statement, 2.

41.   *NYTimes*, Mar. 25, 1951, "Washington and MacArthur Clash Anew on Truce Offer," James Reston, 1; *NYTimes*, Mar. 27, 1951, "Joint Chiefs Tell MacArthur To Clear Future Statements," James Reston, 1.

      The text of the Joint Chiefs' letter read in full:

      "The President has directed that your attention be called to his order as transmitted 6 December 1950. In view of the information given you 20 March 1951 any further statements by you must be coordinated as prescribed in the order of 6 December.

      "The President has also directed that in the event Communist military leaders request an armistice in the field, you immediately report that fact to the JCS for instructions." (www.trumanlibrary.org)

42.   Truman Museum and Library, Independence, Mo. (www.trumanlibrary.org).

43.   *ChiTrib*, Apr. 8, 1951, editorial, "The War Without An End."

44.   *NYTimes*, Apr. 7, 1951, editorial, "Storm Around M'Arthur."

45.   *WPost*, Apr. 9, 1951.

46.   *WPost*, Apr. 10, 1951.

47.   *WPost*, Apr. 10, 1951, editorial, "The MacArthur Problem."

48.   *NYTimes*, Apr. 12, 1951, "President on Radio," 1.

49.   *ChiTrib*, Apr. 12, 1951.

50.   In *NYTimes*, Apr. 12, 1951, "U.S. Press Comment on the Removal of MacArthur."

51. *HTrib,* Apr. 12, 1951.

52. *WPost,* Feb. 15, 1951.

53. At the time of the armistice, the preliminary figure estimated by the Pentagon and reported in the press was about 25,000 U.S. dead, but the final official figures for the Korean War number more than 33,000 dead among more than 140,000 total American casualties. Of the other major combatants, China suffered almost a million battle casualties, North Korea more than half a million, South Korea about 280,000. An estimated three to four million Korean civilians, the majority north of the 38th parallel, died from battle and other causes resulting directly from the war, including disease and starvation.

54. *HTrib,* Jan. 15, 1951.

CHAPTER 8

1. *New York Times* (hereafter *NYTimes*), July 25, 1962, "Vietnam Victory Remote Despite U.S. Aid to Diem," 1.

2. *NYTimes,* Jan. 3, 1963, "Vietcong Downs Five U.S. Copters, Hits Nine Others," 1.

3. *NYTimes,* Jan. 4, 1963, "Vietnamese Reds Win Major Clash."

4. *Washington Post* (hereafter *WPost*), Sept. 3, 1963, "Text of Cronkite Interview with President on Television." *NYTimes,* same date, "Kennedy Warns Buddhist Dispute Imperils Vietnam," E.W. Kenworthy, 1, reported that JFK agreed to do the interview for Cronkite's first 30-minute *Evening News* broadcast "to demonstrate his interest in more extensive news coverage by television," and that Kennedy would be interviewed on September 9 by David Brinkley and Chet Huntley for the first 30-minute broadcast of their NBC evening news program.

5. *WPost,* Sept. 5, 1963. Unless otherwise noted, all citations from Walter Lippmann appeared in his column "Today and Tomorrow."

6. *Newsday,* Nov. 16, 1963, "Viet Chief Says Mme. Nhu Has Fortune."

7. In *Chicago Tribune* (hereafter *ChiTrib*), Nov. 5, 1963, "Guest Editorials; the Coup in Vietnam."

8. *ChiTrib,* Nov. 3, 1963, editorial, "Who Pulled the Rug?"

9. In *ChiTrib,* Nov. 5, 1963, "Guest Editorials; the Coup in Vietnam."

10. *NYTimes,* Nov. 10, 1963, editorial, "A Policy for Vietnam."

11. *NYTimes,* Nov. 10, 1963, "Two Focal Points of U.S. Foreign Policy: Saigon and Berlin."

12. *NYTimes,* Nov. 24, 1963, "Vietnam's New Leaders Face a Tough Challenge."

13. *Newsday,* Nov. 22, 1963, "Does Uncle Sam Always Know Best?" Higgins' column now has a regular format, headed simply "By Marguerite Higgins," and including her photo. The column does not yet have a name, but each column has a title.

14. *Newsday,* Dec. 27, 1963, "I told You So."

15. *Newsday,* Mar. 4, 1964, "New Hope in Vietnam."

16. *San Francisco Chronicle* (hereafter *SFChron*), Aug. 6, 1964, editorial, "Measured Reply to North Viets."

17. *NYTimes,* Aug. 8, 1964, "Resolution Wins," 1.

18. *Newsday,* August 7, 1964, "No More Red Sanctuaries"; August 10, 1964, "Taylor Would A-Bomb Chinese." Beginning with her column of March 27, 1964, Higgins' *Newsday* column was called "On the Spot." Unless otherwise noted, all Higgins citations hereafter are from this column.

19. *NYTimes,* Aug. 9, 1964, James Reston, "Washington; The Illuminating Flash in Southeast Asia." Reston's regular column in the *Times* was simply headed "Washington," with a subhead indicating the subject. Hereafter, I will give only the subheads when citing Reston's work in his column.

20. Neither columns that ran on the editorial page nor the page itself were yet known by the abbreviated term "op-ed."

21. *WPost,* Aug. 6, 1964.

22.   *NYTimes,* Mar. 2, 1965, editorial, "The Wider War."

23.   *Newsday,* Mar. 30, 1964, "Memories of MacArthur."

24.   *WPost,* Sept. 5, 1963.

25.   *NYTimes,* Nov. 24, 1963, "Vietnam's New Leaders Face a Tough Challenge."

26.   *The Fog of War: Eleven Lessons From the Life of Robert S. McNamara,* dir. Errol Morris, Sony Pictures Classics, 2003.

27.   *NYTimes,* Mar. 10, 1965, "America and Its Allies."

28.   *NYTimes,* Mar. 2, 1965, editorial, "The Wider War."

29.   *WPost,* Mar. 18, 1965.

30.   *WPost,* Mar. 30, 1965.

31.   *WPost,* Apr. 29, 1965.

32.   *WPost,* July 27, 1965.

33.   *Newsday,* Oct. 4, 1965, "Light at the Tunnel's End." Higgins died in Walter Reed Army Hospital on January 3, 1966, at the age of forty-five, of leishmaniasis, a rare tropical disease she may have contracted in Vietnam. She had spent a month and a half in South Vietnam in the fall of 1965 and was ill when she returned to the United States.

34.   *Saturday Evening Post,* Dec. 3, 1966, "Come home with that coonskin," 104. The administration's inability to share the view of those in the press, including the *Saturday Evening Post* and Walter Lippmann, who saw the strife in Vietnam as a civil war, is confirmed in *The Fog of War* by the film's subject, former Secretary of Defense Robert S. McNamara, who says, "We saw Vietnam as an element of the Cold War, *not* what they saw it as, a *civil* war."

35.   *NYTimes,* May 25, 1967, "Green Berets Called Tolerant of Brutality by South Vietnam."

36.   *LATimes,* May 28, 1967, "The Nation" column, D4, section headed "Total Victory Means WW III?"

37.   *NYTimes,* June 4, 1967, "Military Justice," E4.

38.   *WPost,* May 23, 1967.

39.   *NYTimes,* May 26, 1967, "Walter Lippmann Goes Home."

40.   *SFChron,* Mar. 1, 1968.

41.   *Boston Globe,* Feb. 27, 1968, editorial, "The forest and the trees." The *Globe's* "if it did occur" referred to an ongoing controversy about the government's accounts of the Tonkin Gulf incidents in August 1964. Secretary of Defense Robert S. McNamara stated long after the war that the August 2 attacks were real, while the August 4 attacks almost certainly were not (*The Fog of War*).

42.   "Which Side Are You On?" episode two of *Reporting America at War,* dir. Stephen Ives, Insignia Films, Inc., and WETA, Washington, D.C., 2003.

43.   *WPost,* Mar. 8, 1968, in Laurence Laurent's column "Radio and Television."

44.   "Which Side Are You On," *Reporting America at War.*

45.   *NYTimes,* Mar. 10, 1968, "Gallup Poll Reports 49% Believe Involvement In Vietnam an Error"; *Los Angeles Times,* Mar. 13, 1968, "The Gallup Poll; Vietnam Phase-Out Favored."

46.   *NYTimes,* Mar. 11, 1968, editorial, "Suicidal Escalation."

47.   *NYTimes,* Mar. 12, 1968, "The Big Peace Battle."

48.   In *SFChron,* Mar. 12, 1968, editorial, "The Inquest on Secretary Rusk."

49.   *SFChron,* Mar. 19, 1968, editorial, "Double Punch in Vietnam Debate."

50.   *Newsweek,* Mar. 18, 1968, "More of the Same Won't Do," 25.

51.   *NYTimes,* April 3, 1971, "Text of Calley Prosecutor's Letter to the President."

52.   *NYTimes,* April 8, 1971, editorial, "The Calley Issues."

53.   *NYTimes,* Oct. 17, 2004, Frank Rich column.

54.   *NYTimes,* June 16, 1971, "The Endless Tragedy."

55.   Quotation and background on the legal proceedings from Edwin E. Moise, "The Pentagon Papers," *Historic U.S. Court Cases: an Encyclopedia,* ed. John W. Johnson (New York: Routledge, 2001), viewed online at ProQuest History Study Center (not available to the public).

56.   Justice Black's opinion at http://supct.law.cornell.edu/supct/html/historics/USSC_CR_04 03_0713_ZC.html.

57. *WPost,* July 1, 1971, editorial, "The Pentagon Papers: Free At Last."
58. *NYTimes,* July 1, 1971, Tom Wicker, ""Preventive Government."
59. *WPost,* July 1, 1971, "U.S. Supported Coup Against Diem," Don Oberdorfer, A1.
60. *NYTimes,* Apr. 30, 1975, editorial, "The Americans Depart."
61. *NYTimes,* May 4, 1975, editorial, "After Vietnam."

CHAPTER 9

1. *New York Times* (hereafter *NYTimes*) Aug. 3, 1990, editorial, "Iraq's Naked Aggression."
2. Centcom was established in 1983 under the operational control of the secretary of defense. Its area of authority includes East Africa and Central Asia as well as the Middle East.
3. Author interview with Joseph Albright, April 7, 2006. Albright was a correspondent in the Gulf War for Cox Newspapers, of which the *Atlanta Journal and Constitution* was the flagship paper.
4. Author interview with Marcia Kunstel, August 14, 2006; Kunstel was a correspondent for Cox Newspapers in the Gulf War; author interview with Joseph Albright; *NYTimes,* March 3, 1991, Malcolm Browne, "The Military vs. the Press," 227.
5. *NYTimes,* Jan. 10, 1991, editorial, "The Larger Patriotism."
6. *Boston Globe* (hereafter *BGlobe*), Jan. 12, 1991, editorial, "Congress at a crossroads."
7. Also among those who opposed the resolution was John Kerry of Massachusetts.
8. *BGlobe,* Jan. 13, 1991, editorial, "The US goes to the brink of war."
9. *NYTimes,* Jan. 14, 1991. Here, and hereafter, references to Lewis are to his writing in his column "Abroad at Home" unless otherwise noted.
10. "Which Side Are You On?" episode two of *Reporting America at War,* dir. Stephen Ives, Insignia Films, Inc., and WETA, Washington, D.C., 2003.
11. CNN's reports from Baghdad were censored by the Iraqi government, which was evidently glad to pass video of the bombing. (Author conversation with Marcia Kunstel, following up on our August 14, 2006, interview.)
12. "Which Side Are You On?" *Reporting America at War.*
13. *BGlobe,* Jan. 20, 1991, editorial, "Packaging the war."
14. *NYTimes,* Jan. 19, 1991, editorial, "A Picture of the War."
15. *Atlanta Journal and Constitution* (hereafter *AtlantaJC*), Jan. 20, 1991, editorial, "Public needs to know more about the war."
16. Author interview with Marcia Kunstel.
17. *Boston Phoenix* (hereafter *BPhoenix*), Feb. 15, 1991, Mark Jurkowitz, "Don't Quote Me; War of the words," 3.
18. The alternative press challenged the Gulf War much less temperately than the mainstream press; it also helped to publicize upcoming protest rallies and marches, and offered a viewpoint not available in the major media by reporting the activities of the war protesters and the counterculture from the perspective of *us* rather than *them,* as it had done in the Vietnam War.
19. *Village Voice* (hereafter *VVoice*), Jan. 29, 1991, "The Mobilization the Media Won't Let You See," 33.
20. *VVoice,* Feb. 5, 1991, "Send Neil Bush!; Huge Antiwar Protest Given Scant Coverage by the Media," 27.
21. *VVoice,* Jan. 29, 1991, "The Mobilization the Media Won't Let You See," 33.
22. *VVoice,* Feb. 5, 1991, "Send Neil Bush!" 27.
23. *BGlobe,* Jan. 18, 1991, editorial, "Respecting the right to dissent."
24. *NYTimes,* Jan. 10, 1991, editorial, "The Larger Patriotism."
25. *AtlantaJC,* Jan. 16, 1991, editorial, "Perched on the precipice of war."
26. *AtlantaJC,* Jan. 20, 1991, editorial, "Preparing for Iraqi war aftermath."
27. *NYTimes,* Jan. 18, 1991.
28. *NYTimes,* Jan. 25, 1991.
29. *AtlantaJC,* Jan. 20, 1991, editorial, "Preparing for Iraqi war aftermath."

30.   *The New Yorker* (hereafter *NYer*), Jan. 28, 1991, "Islam and the West," 83–88.

31.   *BPhoenix,* Jan. 18, 1991, "New World, New Reality," 9.

32.   *NYTimes,* Feb. 12, 1991, R. W. Apple, "The Press; Correspondents Protest Pool System."

33.   *BPhoenix,* Feb. 15, 1991, "Don't Quote Me; War of the words," 3.

34.   *BGlobe,* Feb. 21, 1991, "Media; 3 Reporters complain about press curbs"; *Newsweek,* Feb. 25, 1991, Walter Cronkite, "What Is There to Hide?" 43. Quotations from Cronkite's testimony given in several newspapers correspond exactly with the text of Cronkite's opinion piece in the February 25 issue of *Newsweek.* It seems certain that the text Cronkite read before the committee was identical to the text of the article subsequently published under his byline in *Newsweek.*

35.   *VVoice,* Feb. 5, 1991, Curtis J. Lang, "It's Oil In the Family." 32–33.

36.   *NYTimes,* Feb. 17, 1991, editorial, "An Administration Still Hooked on Oil."

37.   Allentown (Pa.) *Morning Call,* Feb. 24, 1991, editorial, "No Vision In Bush's Energy Plan."

38.   *Seattle Times,* Feb. 21, 1991, editorial, "National Energy Policy—Conservation Must Be Key In Blueprint."

39.   *NYTimes,* Feb. 23, 1991. Here, and hereafter, citations to Wicker are from his column "In the Nation," unless otherwise noted.

40.   *BGlobe,* Feb. 23, 1991, editorial, "Riding the gulf-war roller coaster."

41.   *Atlantic,* Dec. 2005, James Fallows, "Why Iraq Has No Army," 68, 70.

42.   *BGlobe,* Feb. 24, 1991, editorial, "The 'final phase' of the war begins."

43.   *NYTimes,* Feb. 24, 1991, editorial, "More War—and Less."

44.   *BPhoenix,* Mar. 1, 1991, Leslie Kaufman, "The Pentagon's other victory; How the generals controlled the press," 16.

45.   Author interviews with Joseph Albright and Marcia Kunstel.

46.   *USA Today,* Feb. 27, 1991, Matt Roush, "Live From Kuwait City; CBS Regains Some Glory," D1; *TV Guide,* May 3, 2003, reported that the "cumbersome" satellite uplink equipment of the first Gulf War "took hours to set up," compared with the 10-pound satellite videophones available for 2003 war.

47.   *BGlobe,* Feb. 25, 1991, editorial, "The political battle to come."

48.   Author interview with Marcia Kunstel.

49.   *AtlantaJC,* Feb. 27, 1991, "What they want," (sidebar header).

50.   *NYTimes,* Feb. 27, 1991, editorial, "Beyond Fury, Cool Calculation."

51.   *NYTimes,* Feb. 28, 1991, "The White House; Transcript of President's Address on the Gulf War."

52.   *NYTimes,* Mar. 1, 1991, editorial, "'This Aggression Will Not Stand.'"

53.   *NYTimes,* Mar. 24, 1991, editorial, "The Damage Was Not Collateral." Iraqi casualty figures are still controversial. These web pages give a good introduction to the range of opinions: http://www.cnn.com/SPECIALS/2001/gulf.war/facts/gulfwar/; http://www.businessweek.com/bwdaily/dnflash/feb2003/nf2003026_0167_db052.htm; http://en.wikipedia.org/wiki/Gulf_War.

54.   *BGlobe,* Mar. 1, 1991, editorial, "Victory in the gulf."

55.   *NYTimes,* Feb. 28, 1991.

56.   *BPhoenix,* Mar. 1, 1991, "The Pentagon's other victory; How the generals controlled the press," 16, 18.

57.   "Which Side Are You On?" *Reporting America at War.* Amanpour later became convinced that the "sanitized" view of the Gulf War imposed by the U.S. military's press policies influenced not only the public perception, but also the military itself, making it more cautious, less willing to enter a conflict where American dead and wounded would result. The military's heightened concern about "image," as Amanpour saw it, had "a very negative bearing on policy and military strategy." (*The News Hour with Jim Lehrer,* PBS, April 20, 2000, from transcript at www.pbs.org.)

58.   *WPost,* March 5, 1991, editorial, "After Saddam Hussein."

59.   *AtlantaJC,* Feb. 28, 1991, "Saddam retains power, can claim wide Arab support."

60. *Washington Post,* Mar. 5, 1991, editorial, "After Saddam Hussein."
61. *BPhoenix,* Mar. 8, 1991, "Publisher's Notebook; The Middle East: thinking ahead," 3.
62. *NYTimes,* Mar. 29, 1991, editorial, "The General vs. the President."
63. *NYer,* Apr. 15, 1991, 29–30. At this time, "Talk of the Town" pieces were unsigned, but attributions, where the authors are known, are included in *The Complete New Yorker* (New York: The New Yorker, 2005, DVDs or external hard drive.)
64. *NYTimes,* Feb. 8, 1998, "Editorial Observer; The Battle of Baghdad That Might Have Been," WK14 (14 in News of the Week in Review).
65. Author interview with Joseph Albright.

CHAPTER 10

1. *New York Times* (hereafter *NYTimes*), Sept. 12, 2001, "A Somber President Says Terrorism Cannot Prevail," A1.
2. *NYTimes,* Sept. 21, 2001, "President Bush's Address on Terrorism Before a Joint Meeting of Congress," (transcript).
3. *Atlanta Journal-Constitution* (hereafter *AtlantaJC*), Sept. 23, 2001, editorial, "President sounded all the right notes."
4. *Washington Post* (hereafter *WPost*), Sept. 21, 2001, editorial, "A Call to War."
5. *WPost,* Sept. 23, 2001, editorial, "Rules of Engagement."
6. *NYTimes,* Sept. 22, 2001, editorial, "Calibrating the Use of Force."
7. *Boston Globe* (hereafter *BGlobe*), Sept. 22, 2001, editorial, "Disparate Allies."
8. *BGlobe,* Sept. 26, 2001, editorial, "Beyond the Taliban."
9. *NYTimes,* Oct. 8, 2001, editorial, "The American Offensive Begins."
10. *Boston Phoenix* (hereafter *BPhoenix*), Sept. 14, 2001, "Reflections," 11.
11. *NYTimes,* Sept. 17, 2001, "Lawmakers Hear Ashcroft Outline Antiterror Plans."
12. Cheney's much-quoted *Meet the Press* remarks are given in different forms in different publications and transcripts. This quotation combines elements from the *Boston Globe* of Sept. 17, 2001, "Expanded Authority is Sought in Tracking Activity," and PBS's *Frontline,* June 20, 2006, "The Dark Side," from transcript at http://www.pbs.org/wgbh/pages/frontline/darkside/.
13. *NYTimes,* Sept. 23, 2001, editorial, "Security and Liberty."
14. *BPhoenix,* Sept. 28, 2001, "Life During Wartime; How the terrorist crisis threatens our personal liberties," 1.
15. *Village Voice* (hereafter *VVoice*), Oct. 2, 2001, Cotts, "Press Clips; The Return of Censorship"; Hentoff, "The War on the Bill of Rights," 30, 32.
16. *WPost,* Oct. 16, 2001, editorial, "Stampeded in the House."
17. *NYTimes,* Nov. 16, 2001, editorial, "A Travesty of Justice."
18. *BGlobe,* Nov. 16, 2001, editorial, "Suspect Justice."
19. *WPost,* Nov. 24, 2001, editorial, "Connecting the Dots."
20. *AtlantaJC,* Nov. 19, 2001, editorial, "Bush team compromises American justice system."
21. *Christian Science Monitor,* Nov. 16, 2001, editorial, "Drawing a Line for Liberties."
22. *Los Angeles Times* (hereafter *LATimes*), Dec. 2, 2001, editorial, "Questioning Secrecy."
23. *NYTimes,* Dec. 2, 2001, editorial, "War and the Constitution."
24. *WPost,* Dec. 7, 2001, editorial, "The Ashcroft Smear."
25. *NYTimes Magazine,* Sept. 11, 2005, Mary Anne Weaver, "Lost at Tora Bora," 54–58.
26. *Christian Science Monitor,* December 17, 2001, "Tora Bora falls, but no bin Laden," 1.
27. *NYTimes,* Dec. 18, 2001, editorial, "The Hunt for Osama bin Laden."
28. *BGlobe,* Dec. 22, 2001, editorial, "Rebuilding Afghanistan."
29. *WPost,* Dec. 6, 2001, op-ed, "The Case for Judicial Review."
30. *NYTimes,* Dec. 29, 2001, editorial, "How to Try a Terrorist."
31. *BGlobe,* Jan. 23, 2002, editorial, "Detainees' Rights."
32. *NYTimes,* Jan. 22, 2002, editorial, "The Prisoners at Guantánamo."
33. *WPost,* Feb. 10, 2002, editorial, "Bending the Geneva Rules."

34.   Jane Mayer related Lindh's experiences, and how the conditions of his detention and interrogations eroded the government's case against him, in the *New Yorker,* March 10, 2003, "Lost in the Jihad," 50–59.

35.   *BPhoenix,* June 21, 2002, "Justice Deferred; Dirty deed, dirty deal," 21; first published at www.bostonphoenix.com.

36.   *Chicago Tribune,* June 19, 2002, commentary, "First the punishment, and then the crime." (Since Robert McCormick's death, the *Tribune's* philosophy has broadened to embrace a wider range of views.)

37.   *Chicago Tribune,* June 23, 2002, "A final toll; Were rights also casualties of Sept. 11?" 1. Cassel was not the only journalist who cited the majority opinion in the 1866 case *Ex parte Milligan* in criticizing the Bush administration's actions in the war on terrorism. See the complete majority opinion at http://www.constitution.org/ussc/071–002a.htm.

38.   *NYTimes,* Aug. 8, 2002, editorial, "Unlimited Presidential Powers."

39.   *BGlobe,* Sept. 11, 2002, editorial, "One Year Later."

40.   *WPost,* Sept. 15, 2002, editorial, "A Year in the World."

41.   *BPhoenix,* Sept. 6, 2002, "Lonely on the outside."

42.   *VVoice,* Nov. 27, 2002, "Resistance Rising; True Patriots Networking," 29.

43.   *VVoice,* Jan. 1, 2003, "A Citizen Shorn of All Rights," 23.

44.   *VVoice,* Jan. 8, 2003, "George W. Bush's Constitution," 27.

45.   *NOW with Bill Moyers,* PBS, Feb. 28, 2003, from transcript at http://www.pbs.org/now/transcript/transcript_hentoff.html.

46.   *WPost,* Jan. 25, 2002, editorial, "The Guantanamo Story."

47.   *WPost,* Dec. 26, 2002, "U.S. Decries Abuse but Defends Interrogations," A1.

48.   Ibid.

49.   *WPost,* Dec. 27, 2002, editorial, "Torture Is Not an Option."

50.   *VVoice,* Feb. 27, 2003, "The American Way of Torture," 27.

51.   *WPost,* Dec. 20, 2005, editorial, "Going Too Far."

CHAPTER 11

1.   Director General Mohamed ElBaradei to the U.N. Security Council, January 27, 2003, from http://www.un.org/News/dh/iraq/elbaradei27jan03.htm.

2.   *Washington Post* (hereafter *WPost*), Mar. 2, 1999, Barton Gellman, "U.S. Spied On Iraqi Military Via U.N.," informs much of the background in this head note, together with stories by Gellman published in the *Post* on Jan. 6, 8, and 28, 1999.

3.   *WPost,* Sept. 15, 2001, editorial, "Afghanistan."

4.   *Atlanta Journal-Constitution* (hereafter *AtlantaJC*), Oct. 11, 2001, editorial, "Present proof before attacking Iraq."

5.   *USA Today,* Nov. 19, 2001, "Pentagon builds case on Iraq; Sept. 11 link not vital for action," A1.

6.   In *NYTimes,* Nov. 21, 2001, "After Afghanistan," A1.

7.   *AtlantaJC,* Nov. 25, 2001, editorial, "Quagmire awaits if Iraq is invaded."

8.   *AtlantaJC,* Dec. 9, 2001, editorial, "Fall of Kandahar doesn't end battle."

9.   *Wall Street Journal* (hereafter *WSJournal*), Dec.14, 2001, editorial, "The Saddam We Know."

10.   *NYTimes,* Nov. 26, 2001, editorial, "The Wrong Time to Fight Iraq."

11.   *NYTimes,* Jan. 9, 2002, editorial, "Terrorism's Other Battlefields."

12.   Full text available at http://www.whitehouse.gov/news/releases/2002/06/20020601–3.html.

13.   *NYTimes,* Oct. 4, 2002, "Excerpts of Speeches Made on Senate Floor Regarding Resolution on Iraq."

14.   *NYTimes,* Oct. 11, 2002, editorial, "The Hazardous Path Ahead."

15.   *Los Angeles Times,* Oct. 11, 2002, editorial, "The Wrong Resolution."

16.   *Village Voice* (hereafter *VVoice*), Oct. 30, 2002, "Neohawks," 53. In 1965, contemplating America's dilemma in Vietnam, Walter Lippmann described the innovation of American for-

eign policy in similar terms, but with an important difference: "We are being isolated in the sense that while we are enormously extended, we are being compelled to rely more and more upon military power and upon money rather than upon the influence of our example, which was once our greatest asset in human affairs." (*Boston Globe* [hereafter *BGlobe*], Oct. 14, 1965, "Today and Tomorrow.")

17. *WPost,* Jan. 28, 2003, editorial, "No More Last Chances."
18. Full statement at http://www.un.org/News/dh/iraq/elbaradei27jan03.htm.
19. *NYTimes,* Jan. 29, 2003, "President's State of the Union Message to Congress and the Nation."
20. *NYTimes,* Feb. 6, 2003, "Powell's Address, Presenting 'Deeply Troubling' Evidence on Iraq."
21. *USA Today,* Feb. 13, 2003, "Marshall-like plan will fail in post-Saddam Iraq."
22. *Los Angeles Times,* Feb. 15, 2003, "Showdown with Iraq; Inspection Report Firms Up Council's Opposition to War."
23. *NYTimes,* Feb. 25, 2003, editorial, "Facing Down Iraq."
24. *WPost,* Mar. 8, 2003, "Blix's Iraq Report Deepens U.N. Rift; Team's Assessment Cautiously Upbeat," A1.
25. *NYTimes,* Mar. 9, 2003, editorial, "Saying No to War."
26. *WPost,* Mar. 18, 2003, editorial, "A Question of Will."
27. *Boston Phoenix* (hereafter *BPhoenix*), Mar. 21, 2003, "Don't Quote Me; Into the darkness,"
28. *BPhoenix,* Mar. 28, 2003, "Rules of engagement," 16, is also the source of the Rumsfeld and Bush quotes.
29. *WPost,* Mar. 23, 2003, "'Unilaterals,' Crossing the Lines," Richard Leiby, F1; Leiby reported that an additional "1,445 reporters, by the latest count, obtained credentials as unilaterals," operating independently of U.S. military units.
30. *BPhoenix,* Mar. 28, 2003, "Don't Quote Me; Picture imperfect," 27.
31. Interviewed by Marvin Kalb at the National Press Club, Washington, D.C., Apr. 21, 2003; summary posted to the web site of George Washington University, Apr. 24, 2003, www.gwu.edu.; CSPAN broadcast Apr. 25, 2003, under "American Perspectives." May also have been broadcast live on the date of the interview.
32. In *NYer,* Jan. 19, 2004, Ken Auletta, "Fortress Bush," 62.
33. *NYTimes,* Apr. 12, 2003, editorial, "Anarchy In the Streets."
34. *BGlobe,* Apr. 15, 2003, editorial, "Crimes Against History."
35. *WPost,* Apr. 13, 2003, editorial, "Calling Allies."
36. David DeBatto, a Army counterintelligence officer, tells the story of his efforts to secure one such depot at http://dir.salon.com/story/news/feature/2004/10/29/anaconda/index.html
37. *NYer,* Apr. 7, 2003, "Offense and Defense," 43–45.
38. *NYer,* Mar. 31, 2003, "Who Lied to Whom?" 41–44.
39. *NYer,* May 12, 2003, "Selective Intelligence," 44–51.
40. *NYer,* June 16 & 23, 2003, "Might and Right," 69–70.
41. CNN, July 9, 2003.
42. *NYTimes,* July 17, 2003, Thom Shankar, "U.S. Commander in Iraq Says Yearlong Tours Are Option to Combat 'Guerrilla' War," A1.
43. Ibid.
44. *NTimes,* July 6, 2003, op-ed, "What I Didn't Find in Africa."
45. *NYTimes,* July 22, 2003, op-ed, "Who's Unpatriotic Now?"
46. *BPhoenix,* July 25, 2003, "Don't Quote Me; Cooking the books," 14, 16.
47. *WSJournal,* July 10, 2003, commentary, "The Fog of Deceit."
48. *WSJournal,* July 14, 2003, editorial, "Lack of Intelligence."
49. *NYer,* July 28, 2003, "Faith-Based Intelligence," 28–29.
50. *NYer,* Oct. 27, 2003, "The Stovepipe," 77–87. In November 2006, Hersh quoted a Pentagon consultant who said that "intelligence professionals are always aghast when Presidents ask for stuff in the raw. They see it as asking a second grader to read 'Ulysses.'" (*NYer,* Nov. 27, 2006, "The Next Act," 103.)

51. Transcript of Kay's opening statement, January 28, 2004, http://www.cnn.com/2004/US/01/28/kay.transcript/.

52. *NYer*, Feb. 9, 2004, "Blame Game," 21–22.

53. Clarke's testimony of March 24, 2004, before the commission, http://www.washington-post.com/wp-dyn/articles/A20349–2004Mar24.html. Clarke's opening statement before the commission, http://www.msnbc.msn.com/id/4595173/. For a review that includes testimony excerpts from fourteen key witnesses, http://www.msnbc.msn.com/id/4568982/. (The 9/11 Commission's formal name was National Commission on Terrorist Attacks Upon the United States.)

54. *NYTimes*, Mar. 26, 2004, editorial, "The Wrong Target."

55. *Chicago Tribune*, Mar. 26, 2004, editorial, "Rice Blusters and Blunders."

56. *The Guardian* (London), May 4, 2004, "CBS delayed report on Iraqi prison abuse after military chief's plea," http://www.guardian.co.uk/Iraq/Story/0,1209025,00.html.

57. *NYer*, May 10, 2004, "Torture at Abu Ghraib," 42–47. The article was posted on the *New Yorker*'s website on April 30, two days after the *60 Minutes II* report aired, and the issue hit the newsstands on May 3. (*New Yorker* issues go on sale in the week before the nominal publication date.) In the article, Hersh refers to the broadcast and describes several of the photos shown in it.

58. In *NYTimes Magazine*, May 23, 2004, Susan Sontag, "Regarding the Torture of Others," 25.

59. *NYer*, May 10, 2004, "Torture at Abu Ghraib," 42–47. In the June 25, 2007, *New Yorker* ("The General's Report," 58–69), Hersh related that as a consequence of his report, Taguba's military career was ended and he was forced to retire in January 2007. Hersh also reported that although there have been a dozen government investigations into the abuses at Abu Ghraib, "none followed through on the question of ultimate responsibility."

60. *NYTimes*, May 3, 2004, editorial, "The Nightmare at Abu Ghraib."

61. *NYTimes*, May 7, 2004, editorial, "Donald Rumsfeld Should Go."

62. *NYer*, May 17, 2004, "Chain of Command," 38–43; May 24, 2004, "The Gray Zone," 38–44.

63. *NYTimes*, May 20, 2004, "Dogged Reporter's Impact, From My Lai to Abu Ghraib."

64. *WPost*, Aug. 27, 2004, "How Torture Came Down From the Top."

65. *NYTimes*, Apr. 30, 2006, op-ed, "Bush of a Thousand Days."

66. *BPhoenix*, June 4, 2004, "Don't Quote Me; Miller's *Times*," 14.

67. *WPost*, Jan. 16, 2005, "Bush Says Election Ratified Iraq Policy," A1.

68. *NYTimes*, Nov. 9, 2006, editorial, "Rumsfeld's Departure."

69. *Charlie Rose*, PBS, Apr. 9, 2007.

70. On *Charlie Rose*, PBS, Mar. 20, 2007; also Barre (Vt.) *Times Argus*, Oct. 13, 2006, report from Rutland (Vt.) *Herald* on Odom Oct. 11 speech at Middlebury College in which he expressed similar opinions.

71. *New York Herald Tribune*, July 3, 1950, "Today and Tomorrow."

CHAPTER 12

1. Wright expressed these opinions in an appearance on PBS's *Charlie Rose*, April 5, 2007.

2. *Washington Post* (hereafter *WPost*), May 9, 2004, "Pentagon Approved Tougher Interrogations," A1; May 11, "Secret World of U.S. Interrogation," A1; May 13, "Rumsfeld Defends Rules for Prison."

3. *The New Yorker* (hereafter *NYer*), May 24, 2004, "The Gray Zone," 38–44.

4. *New York Times Magazine*, May 23, 2004, "Regarding the Torture of Others," 24–29, 42.

5. *Wall Street Journal* (hereafter *WSJournal*), June 7, 2004, "Pentagon Report Set Framework For Use of Torture," A1.

6. *WPost*, June 8, 2004, "Memo Offered Justification for Use of Torture."

7. *New York Times* (hereafter *NYTimes*) June 9, 2004, editorial, "The Roots of Abu Ghraib."

8. *WPost*, June 9, 2004, editorial, "Legalizing Torture."

9. *Los Angeles Times,* Sept. 22, 2006, op-ed, "Our Torturer-in-Chief."

10. *NYTimes,* June 29, 2004, "Access to Courts; Ruling Applies to Those Held Either in U.S. or at Guantánamo," A1.

11. *Atlanta Journal-Constitution,* June 29, 2004, editorial, "Justices duly uphold due process."

12. *Boston Globe* (hereafter *BGlobe*) June 29, 2004, editorial, "The rights of detainees."

13. *Christian Science Monitor,* June 30, 2004, editorial, "Prudent Check on Detentions."

14. *NYTimes,* Oct. 15, 2004. Prof. David R. Dow cited *Vance v. Terrazas.*

15. *WPost,* Oct. 12, 2004, "Hamdi Returned to Saudi Arabia."

16. *NYer,* Feb. 14 & 21, 2005, "Outsourcing Torture," 106–123.

17. Ibid.

18. *NYer,* July 11 & 18, 2005, "The Experiment," 60–71.

19. *WPost,* Nov. 2, 2005, "CIA Holds Terror Suspects in Secret Prisons," A1.

20. *WPost,* Nov. 3, 2005, editorial, "Rebellion Against Abuse."

21. *NYTimes,* Nov. 3, 2005, editorial, "The Prison Puzzle."

22. *NYTimes,* Nov. 10, 2005, editorial, "Blaming the Messenger."

23. *NYTimes,* Dec. 16, 2005, "Bush Lets U.S. Spy on Callers Without Courts," A1.

24. *Los Angeles Times,* Dec. 18, 2005, editorial, "Bigger brother."

25. *WPost,* Dec. 18, 2005, editorial, "Spying on Americans."

26. *BGlobe,* Dec. 20, 2005, editorial, "Taking liberties."

27. *USA Today,* Dec. 19, 2005.

28. *WSJournal,* Dec. 20, 2005.

29. *Denver Post,* Dec. 17, 2005, editorial, "Domestic liberties require protection."

30. *WPost,* Dec. 20, 2005, editorial, "Going Too Far."

31. *NYTimes,* Dec. 23, 2005.

32. *BGlobe,* Jan. 31, 2006, "National Perspectives; In a values debate, Bush again paints his critics into corner."

33. *Harper's Magazine,* Mar. 2006, Lewis Lapham, "The Case for Impeachment: Why We Can No Longer Afford George W. Bush," 27.

34. I saw this interview and noted the points Conyers made in response to the question. My paper note, however, disappeared before I could transcribe the date and network into my computer files for *Reporting the War.*

35. *The Nation,* Jan. 30, 2006, "The Impeachment of George W. Bush." Holtzman's article was posted to *The Nation's* web site on Jan. 11, 2006.

36. *Harper's Magazine,* Mar. 2006, "The Case for Impeachment," 34.

37. See http://www.pulitzer.org/year/2006/beat-reporting/.

38. See http://www.pulitzer.org/year/2006/national-reporting/.

39. *WPost,* Apr. 18, 2006, "Post Wins 4 Pulitzer Prizes," A1.

40. *BGlobe,* Apr. 25, 2006, editorial, "Leaks: not who but what."

41. *BGlobe,* Apr. 30, 2006, "Bush challenges hundreds of laws," A1.

42. *NYTimes,* May 5, 2006, editorial, "Veto? Who Needs a Veto?"

43. *BGlobe,* May 2, 2006, op-ed, "Our monarch, above the law."

44. *USA Today,* May 11, 2006, "NSA has massive database of Americans' phone calls," 1A.

45. *USA Today,* May 12, 2006, editorial, "NSA has your phone records; 'trust us' isn't good enough."

46. *NYTimes,* May 12, 2006, editorial, "An Ever-Expanding Secret."

47. *NYTimes,* June 23, 2006, "Bank Data Sifted in Secret by U.S. to Block Terror," A1.

48. *USA Today,* June 26, 2006, editorial, "Oversight missing, again."

49. *NYTimes,* July 2, 2006, op-ed, "Can't Win the War? Bomb the Press!"

50. *New York Times Magazine,* Jan. 8, 2006, Jonathan Mahler, "The Bush Administration vs. Salim Hamdan," 44.

51. *WPost,* June 30, 2006, "High Court Rejects Detainee Tribunals," A1.

52. *NYTimes,* June 30, 2006, editorial, "A Victory for the Rule of Law."

53. *BGlobe,* June 30, 2006, editorial, "No blank check for Bush."

54. *NYer,* July 3, 2006, "The Hidden Power," 44–55.

55. On July 13, 2007, Fein and John Nichols, who writes for *The Nation,* argued on *Bill Moyers' Journal* (PBS) that both President Bush and Vice President Cheney should be impeached for unconstitutional 'overreaching' by the executive branch in the war on terrorism.

56. Ibid.

57. Ibid.

58. *NYTimes,* Aug. 18, 2006, Adam Liptak and Eric Lichtblau, "Judge Finds Wiretap Actions Violate the Law," A1.

59. *NYTimes,* Sept. 30, 2006, Scott Shane and Adam Liptak, "Shifting Power To a President," A1.

60. *WPost,* Sept. 29, 2006, "Many Rights in U.S. Legal System Absent in New Bill."

61. *WPost,* Nov. 19, 2006, editorial, "Reform on Detentions."

62. *NYTimes,* September 30, 2006, Scott Shane and Adam Liptak, "Shifting Power To a President," A1.

63. *NYTimes,* June 28, 2006, editorial, "Patriotism and the Press."

64. *CBS Evening News,* November 29, 1977.

INDEX